New York Baseball in 1951

ALSO BY RUDY MARZANO

*The Last Years of the Brooklyn Dodgers:
A History, 1950–1957* (McFarland, 2008)

*The Brooklyn Dodgers in the 1940s: How Robinson, MacPhail,
Reiser and Rickey Changed Baseball* (McFarland, 2005)

New York Baseball in 1951

The Dodgers, the Giants, the Yankees and the Telescope

RUDY MARZANO

McFarland & Company, Inc., Publishers
Jefferson, North Carolina, and London

All photographs courtesy National Baseball Hall of Fame Library, Cooperstown, New York.

LIBRARY OF CONGRESS CATALOGUING-IN-PUBLICATION DATA

Marzano, Rudy, 1927–
   New York baseball in 1951 : the Dodgers, the Giants, the Yankees and the Telescope / Rudy Marzano.
        p.   cm.
   Includes bibliographical references and index.

   ISBN 978-0-7864-4830-2
   softcover : 50# alkaline paper

   1. Brooklyn Dodgers (Baseball team)—History. 2. New York Giants (Baseball team)—History. 3. World Series (Baseball) (1951) 4. Baseball—United States—History. I. Title. II. Title: Fifty-one. III. Title: 1951. IV. Title: Nineteen fifty one.
   GV875.B7M338   2011
   796.357'640974723—dc22   2010045826

BRITISH LIBRARY CATALOGUING DATA ARE AVAILABLE

© 2011 Rudy Marzano. All rights reserved

No part of this book may be reproduced or transmitted in any form or by any means, electronic or mechanical, including photocopying or recording, or by any information storage and retrieval system, without permission in writing from the publisher.

Front cover: Bobby Thomson of the New York Giants has just hit a home run at the Polo Grounds against the Brooklyn Dodgers in the playoff game October 3, 1951; Ralph Branca is the Dodger pitcher who delivered the home run ball (AP Photo). Telescope © 2011 Shutterstock.

Manufactured in the United States of America

McFarland & Company, Inc., Publishers
  Box 611, Jefferson, North Carolina 28640
    www.mcfarlandpub.com

Contents

Introduction	1
One: January	5
Two: February	22
Three: March	40
Four: April	62
Five: May	82
Six: June	94
Seven: July	106
Eight: August	129
Nine: September	152
Ten: October	175
Appendix: The Telescope Scheme	187
Chapter Notes	193
Bibliography	197
Index	199

Introduction

It is 1951 in New York City. We have reached the middle of the twentieth century and baseball in the Big Apple is proceeding as usual. The Yankees, led by the best three-man rotation in baseball history — Vic Raschi, Allie Reynolds and Ed Lopat — are fighting for first place, the Dodgers are running away from the rest of the National League with what seemed to be a pennant-winning lead by midseason, and the Giants appear to have settled for second place, despite the histrionics of Leo Durocher, one of the best, most ruthless and nastiest managers who ever lived.

But in mid–August something happened. The Giants came alive and day by day started chipping away at that 13-game lead the Dodgers and the rest of the league had thought insurmountable. When it was all over and the Giants had won there was an air of joyful disbelief in Manhattan. Its team had done the seemingly impossible, finishing the season at 37 and 7, the hottest closing streak in the history of the game.

It started on that August day when the devious mind of Leo Durocher approved of a teammate's suggestion that became the most successful long-running cheating scheme in the annals of sports. We learned just a few years ago that for the last seven weeks of the season Durocher had a telescope placed in one of the Giants clubhouse windows that enabled its user to steal the opposing catcher's signs and then have the batter tipped off as to what type pitch to expect.

The resultant cheating, kept relatively quiet (or in many cases ignored) for an amazing 50 years, startled the country when reporter Joshua Prager of the *Wall Street Journal* broke the story on January, 31, 2001, accusing the Giants of, in effect, stealing the pennant from the Dodgers by illegal means.

This would have been impossible in the smaller ballparks, but the size of the Polo Grounds gave them the distance needed. The Giants clubhouse was some 30 feet high and about 500 feet from home plate. A man with a telescope peeking from a window that far out was impossible to spot with the naked eye.

The most remarkable aspect of the scheme was the many years it remained in the background. The "secret" had been written about in at least two books but was ignored by the public. But in the world of baseball when an entire team is in on a secret, it should not have remained a secret for long. There was, I am sure, a conspiracy of silence that prevailed for more than half a century in both leagues; otherwise, the scheme would have surfaced many years ago. The story no doubt was spread throughout the leagues, with many ballplayers enjoying the fact that the Dodgers—hated by many for their success—were finally done in, no matter how it was achieved.

Since it was revealed in a major newspaper, there have been questions concerning the effect the cheating scheme had on the final result, even given the 37–7 Giants streak. Did Dressen's oversized ego and stubbornness come into play in the Dodgers' losses? For the players Ralph Branca had an answer, although it was ignored during all the hoopla after the Giants won. Said Branca, "Dressen lost the pennant for us, not just that (playoff) game. He wore our pitching staff out." As an old Dodgers fan who remembers being amazed at Dressen's treatment of Labine and the rest of the staff, I agree in the main.

All the baseball experts I have read through the years aside, Ralph Branca is right: the telescope scheme did not solely decide the pennant. Charlie Dressen's stubbornness in handling Clem Labine and his startlingly stupid decisions in the last inning of the deciding game helped cost the Dodgers the pennant, not just Durocher's devious scheming. This is made very clear in the section covering the Dodgers-Giants playoff series.

Over in the American League the Yankees were grinding it out as usual, even as the old guard was passing. On other teams that expression would mean a number of men bowing out, but in New York it meant that Joe DiMaggio was nearing the end and Tommy Henrich had retired. With Mickey Mantle and future Red Sox star Jackie Jensen in the wings, Joe was having his most dismal season, batting .263 with 12 home runs.

To most Yankees and their fans the race was predictable, even in the last days of the season, as New York and Cleveland were tied for first place. They knew they had Raschi, Reynolds and Lopat, that historic threesome that would surely lead them to their third World Series in a row.

The 1951 campaign should be remembered as the only year in baseball history that all three New York teams were in the hunt during the last days of the season, the Yankees winning their pennant in the final week of the race and the Giants in the playoff against the Dodgers on the very last day. It also was the only time three teams were in first place on the last day of the season. Of course, the year will always be remembered for that second playoff in National League history, with the Dodgers losing both, but 1951 stands out in other ways.

As DiMaggio's career was ending, Mantle and Willie Mays were arriving. Warren Giles replaced Ford Frick as president of the National League, as Frick was elected commissioner of baseball, replacing Albert (Happy) Chandler. Walter O'Malley finally (and tragically) gained control of the Dodgers after getting rid of Branch Rickey. And Charlie Dressen, he of the supreme ego, took over the Dodgers, while over at the Polo Grounds Leo Durocher supervised the placing of a telescope in a window of the Giants clubhouse, some 500 feet from home plate.

Chapter One

January

As the year began Brooklyn's attention was centered on 215 Montague Street, the offices of the Brooklyn Dodgers Baseball Club. Burt Shotton was gone as manager and in his place came Charlie Dressen. The big question among the Dodgers faithful was how this new man would run the team.

It turned out to be a terrible move by Walter O'Malley but at the time nobody realized it. In Burt Shotton's place was the 5'5" Dressen, probably the worst manager in the team's history, a man who ruined pitchers and whose ego and carelessness cost the Dodgers a pennant they appeared to have sewed up in midseason.

Shotton had been fired, but not for the usual reasons. His mental lapse in keeping Eddie Miksis, one of the fastest men in the game, on the bench when Cal Abrams, one of the slowest, was thrown out at the plate in that pennant-deciding game in Philadelphia the previous September played no part. Nor did the fact that he wore business clothes and therefore could never charge onto the field to defend his men. His problem was that he was a Rickey man, and O'Malley was cleansing the team of any possible Rickey taint. The lone exception was Clyde Sukeforth, a pre-war ex–Dodgers catcher who was eventually fired after the 1951 World Series. Clyde was a scapegoat fired by O'Malley supposedly because he recommended Branca pitch to Thomson.

Sukeforth can be second-guessed forever but he probably made the right move. Labine had pitched a shutout the day before, and Erskine hit the dirt with a curveball at the wrong time. So it had to be Branca, whose fastball was humming and his curveball breaking. How was any coach to know that Thomson knew what pitch was coming?

Shotton, a friend of Rickey's for years, was an ex-major leaguer and experienced manager, the starting center fielder for the St. Louis Browns from 1911 to 1917, fast and sure-handed. He was hired by Rickey in 1919, and spent the last five years of his career as a reserve outfielder and coach with Rickey's St. Louis Cardinals.

Their friendship began in 1923 when Shotton was the only man on the team who stepped in to stop a fight between Rickey and the much younger and taller Rogers Hornsby in the Polo Grounds clubhouse when Rickey was managing the Cardinals. Ordinarily a number of players would step in and separate combatants, but Hornsby had a reputation for nastiness and an intimidating manner. The fight broke out after constant disagreements between the two over Rickey's managerial style and Hornsby's tendencies to be late and often absent on game days.[1]

Baseball people in general came down on Rickey's side because of Hornsby's personality flaws — a nasty, rude and mean man who on many occasions insulted teammates and owners. No wonder those in the know sided with Rickey. Shotton's loyalty, however, cost him.

"I wasn't fired because of my record," Shotton told the Dodgers beat reporters. "I was fired because of my long friendship with Branch Rickey. Everyone knew O'Malley hated him, and after me he got rid of all Rickey men one by one." But there was more to it than that. A number of players, Eddie Miksis in particular, resented what they considered his old-fashioned ideas and fixed habits

Also, it was common knowledge among the Dodgers beat reporters that many of the Brooklyn players were delighted that Shotton was replaced. Former Dodgers pitcher Harry Taylor said after he was traded to the Red Sox that "coach Clyde Sukeforth went around day after day patching damaged feelings under Shotton."[2]

Their delight melted away soon enough once they realized their new manager could be a laughingstock around the league unless he curbed his ego and stopped pacing the dugout, saying things like, "Hold 'em fellas. I'll think of something," when his team fell behind. There was even a code among the players: if one pointed to his eye, that meant Dressen.

Once in Milwaukee a homemade book, entitled *How to Manage in the Big Leagues*, was placed in Dressen's locker, by a fellow Dodger no doubt. Each page of the book was blank except for one word consisting of a large "I" printed in the middle. Charlie did not take the hint.[3]

In all justice, if athletics is your only yardstick, Charlie had reason for some sense of pride. Here was a man who at 5'5" and 146 pounds had played quarterback for two years in the early days of the National Football League and for eight years was a National League infielder. But his ego was such that he thought he knew more baseball than anyone else and considered himself a master sign stealer, even after he almost ended the careers of Joe Medwick and Joe DiMaggio.

The man in his extreme self-confidence was dangerous. He never learned that the supposed art of sign stealing from the third base coaching box was dubious at best yet persisted, ignoring his near-fatal mistakes. One instance occurred in 1940 after Dodgers president Larry MacPhail bought Medwick and pitcher Curt Davis for $125,000 and four second-line players from St. Louis. That was a lot of money in those days, but Medwick was a Triple Crown winner and one of the game's greatest hitters. Because of Dressen, barely a week after Medwick joined the Dodgers his days as a premier ballplayer ended.

Batting against his former teammates, Joe was hit in the head by a fastball from Cardinals right-hander Bob Bowman. He dropped to the ground, unconscious and suffering from a concussion, thought at first to be severe. There was an immediate hullabaloo in the press about threats and Joe being deliberately targeted.

The New York *Herald-Tribune* claimed the trouble started in the elevator where the players were staying, with Leo Durocher involved, naturally. The newspaper quoted Leo as saying he wouldn't be playing that day. Bowman, like most ballplayers not a fan of Durocher, supposedly said derisively, "Of course you're not going to play; you know I'm going to pitch." That remark, it was said, caused the combative Durocher to play, raising the usual tension at game time.[4]

In researching this story I could find no trace of an elevator argument in any other publication, including the *New York Times*. It appears to be *Tribune*-hyped nonsense. Medwick was hit by a fastball he wasn't expecting because Dressen had signaled curveball from his coaching box. The puzzling part is that Medwick, with the reflexes of a major league athlete, didn't pull back as DiMaggio did under the same circumstances. But the good that resulted from this beaning was incalculable as far as the future of baseball was concerned, for out of it came the batting helmet.

DiMaggio almost suffered the same fate as Medwick as he was batting against Fred Hutchinson when Dressen was a coach for the Yankees. Joe was expecting a curveball, as flashed to him by Dressen. But unlike Medwick, DiMaggio reacted instantly, pulling his head back as a fastball whizzed by. "No more signals," he told Dressen. "I want to stay alive."[5]

The Dodger rage quieted after Medwick insisted from his hospital bed that there was no bad blood involved, that the beaning "was just one of those things," and that he and Bowman had been friends on the Cardinals. Bowman stated that it appeared to him that "Medwick was looking for a curve ball, expecting the ball to break, as he made no attempt to get out of the way."[6]

As a result of Medwick's beaning and the genius of Larry MacPhail baseball would soon never be the same again. The batting helmet, MacPhail's great contribution to the game, was on the horizon, making the batter's box a safer place by protecting the hitter's head and later the cheek that faces the pitcher.

As Medwick lay in the hospital, MacPhail decided that some kind of protective headgear had to be developed. Pee Wee Reese had been hit twice earlier in the season and was still out of action. Medwick, his star outfielder, was now hospitalized and, as things turned out, he had no one to blame. That for Larry was important, for he loved a fight. His pacing in front of the St. Louis dugout challenging any and all Cardinals after Medwick was beaned wasn't grandstanding. He had to be dragged away, shouting, "Not one of you bastards will come out of there." With MacPhail, drink often played a part.

But his anger as his star hitter was hospitalized is understandable. Larry was of an age when any time a player was hit that seriously, the haunting image of Ray Chapman sprawled at the plate sometimes appeared in the press, reminding readers that Chapman was killed by a pitched ball, the only such fatality in major league history. Ray was the Cleveland shortstop when on August 16, 1920, he was struck in the head by a fastball thrown by Carl Mays, a submariner and spitballer, during a game against the Yankees at the Polo Grounds a few years before Yankee Stadium was completed.

Fred Lieb of the *New York Sun*, one of the best sportswriters of his time, saw Mays' submarine pitch rise on a straight line towards Chapman's head. "The ball," he said, "hit Chapman at the right temple and when he got up after a few seconds he fell again and never regained consciousness." After Ray died the next morning, Tris Speaker came to Mays' defense when the popular sentiment was to ban him from baseball, such was his reputation as a "duster" for his frequent near-miss pitches. "I don't think Mays deliberately threw at him," Speaker told the press. "The pitch was high and inside and for some reason Ray froze." Chapman was only 29 years old.[7]

Most baseball people today agree with Speaker, that Mays was sincere in his claim that he didn't intentionally throw at Chapman. But Mays always lived on the edge, that inside corner or even closer to the batter. In fact, he led the league in hit batsmen in 1917 and ranked second in 1918 and 1919. Ray Chapman "froze" as Speaker said and was tragically hit. His death was so shocking that it resulted in changes that made the game safer for the hitter, particularly important at a time Babe Ruth was leading baseball out of the Dead Ball Era.

Soon after his funeral the Rules Committee made it mandatory that the ball be changed when it got dirty so the batter could see it more clearly when it left the pitcher's hand. Until then it was customary to use a ball until it was no longer playable, blackened and even out of shape. That was the condition of the Chapman ball, raising the possibility that he never saw the fatal pitch as it left Mays' hand.

Hall of Famer Sam Crawford told Lawrence Ritter for his book, *The Glory of Their Times*, that the ball was used until it got lost somewhere out of the park. "In those days the ball was often lopsided, making it tougher to throw out a man at home than it is today," he said. "We'd play a whole game with one ball if it stayed in the park."[8]

The committee then banned the spitball even though it was not involved, such was the hatred for it almost to a man in both leagues. It was grandfathered, however, so that pitchers then depending on it could throw it until they retired. Looking back, it seems strange that some kind of protection wasn't developed after Chapman's death, that it took two decades for a Larry MacPhail to make helmets part of his team's equipment.

The origins of their development are so obscure that most people, including those in baseball, have no idea how helmets came about. Clem Labine, one of the most articulate of the 1950s Brooklyn Dodgers, thought Rickey was the father of the helmet. "We were all young," he said, "and because of Mr. Rickey's accomplishments we just assumed the idea was his."[9] This is understandable since in the early 1950s Rickey, by then general manager with Pittsburgh, modified the helmet by enlarging it so that more of the head, including the ear, was protected.

Even Roger Kahn, one of the best sportswriters of my generation and a closet Brooklyn fan, wrote in his book, *Men of October*, that helmets were first used in 1955, which is 14 years after the entire Dodgers team were ordered by MacPhail to wear them. If an insider like Kahn doesn't know the facts, all credit to MacPhail is lost.

The truth behind the helmets goes back a long way, to 1906, when Roger Bresnahan, catcher for John McGraw's New York Giants, designed one for his use after he was beaned. The idea never caught on, probably because players of that day, as well as some in the '50s and '60s, considered their use unmanly. Bresnahan's other idea, a brilliant one that caught on, was shinguards for catchers, one of the reasons he was elected to the Baseball Hall of Fame in 1945.

But none of the indifference to head protection fazed MacPhail. As Reese was still out with head injuries and Medwick in the hospital, he was determined to create some kind of protective headgear. He took up the matter with National League officials and then went on his own, discussing the idea with two members of the medical staff at Johns Hopkins in Baltimore.

The result was a cap with slots designed to fit plastic protective strips. As primitive as it was, for the first time in the game's history the hitter would have some protection against most pitches at his head, deliberate or not. This soon changed the batter's frame of mind as he faced even the fastest and trickiest pitchers in the game.

Bobby Bragan, catcher and shortstop for the Phillies and Dodgers in the 1940s, told me something that had never occurred to me about the batting helmet. "It not only protects the hitter but gives the pitcher a certain sense of security," he said. "With the batting helmet he knows that if a tight inside pitch gets away he won't kill or main the batter. That's important when throwing a 95-mile-an-hour fastball."[10]

Within a year the new plastic helmets paid off for the Dodgers in saving Pete Reiser, briefly one of the best center fielders ever. On April 30, 1941 Pete was hit on the side of the head by a fastball thrown by Phillies lefty Ike Pearson. The crack of the ball against the plastic could be heard throughout Ebbets Field as Pete slumped to the ground. It appeared he was seriously injured, carried off the field on a stretcher on the way to Brooklyn's Caledonian Hospital.[11]

In today's accounts, Pete was unconcerned about his injury, rejoining the team the very next day after promising his doctor that he would not play until given medical clearance. Pete told nationally known sportswriter W.J. Heinz that he left the hospital the next morning and went to Ebbets Field to watch the Dodgers play the Phillies again. According to Heinz's story, Durocher persuaded him to suit up for morale purposes.

Then, according to Heinz's account, Durocher told Pete to pinch-hit in the late innings and Pete responded with a home run with the bases loaded off Ike Pearson, the pitcher who beaned him the day before. That story has been believed through the years and was part of every obituary written about Pete after his death, including *New York Times* columnist Red Smith, guaranteeing that it would be copied by papers all over the country.

Unbelievably, Heinz didn't check out Pete's story, nor did Red Smith years later. All anyone had to do was check the box scores of the time, as I did, to find that Pete, suffering from aging possibly, made the whole thing up. True, he was beaned by Pearson but didn't face again him until a month later, when Pete indeed hit a grand slam off him.

Although Pete appeared seriously injured because of the sound when the ball hit the plastic strips, X-rays showed no injury. But the close call prompted teammates Bobby Bragan and Pete Coscarart to press for wider use of the protective caps. They did all they could to push the helmet, with Durocher's blessing, but because of the "unmanly" nonsense the concept was somewhat slow to catch on. As late as 1953 Don Zimmer was in a coma for 13 days after he was struck in the head while batting without a batting helmet at St. Paul. After a number of similar injuries in both leagues, and at least two deaths in the minors, wearing the helmet became mandatory in 1971. This, remember, was a step that changed baseball forever by taking much of the fear out of facing a Bob Feller or Bob Gibson. And to all baseball historians a reminder: It happened at Ebbets Field, the idea of its genius leader Larry MacPhail.

Reese's injury made the 1940 pennant race a runaway for Cincinnati, winners by 12 games over the Dodgers. Pee Wee played in only 85 games, batting just 312 times for a .268 average. Cincinnati would have won in any event but a healthy Reese would have made it closer. In the next year's race, Brooklyn won by 2½ games over an excellent Cardinals team led by Johnny Mize, Enos Slaughter and Terry Moore. Pee Wee missed only two games that season and even though he hit but .229 — 40 points below his lifetime average — he held the Brooklyn infield together as he was developing into one of the best shortstops in baseball.

Reese was the captain in more ways than one, setting an example in both baseball and racial matters. Although a Southerner from Kentucky, he refused to sign the petition urging that Robinson not be allowed to play for the Dodgers, causing a reaction that eventually ended the Dodgers careers of Kirby Higbe and Dixie Walker. After a 16-year career, Pee Wee was elected to the Baseball Hall of Fame in 1969.

Pee Wee, named because he won a marbles tournament, was born in Ekron, Kentucky, and raised in Louisville where his family moved when he was eight years old. The name stuck throughout his career even though he was 5'10" and weighed 160 pounds. He was also known as "the Little Colonel" because of his Kentucky background.

Being a Southerner never affected Reese's dealing with black players as they entered the league. He admits that on the troopship while returning from his naval service in the Pacific he was a bit concerned when told the Dodgers had signed the first black player in baseball history.

"I was in the Third Marine Division on a ship coming home from Guam when somebody told me the Dodgers had signed a black ballplayer," Reese told Peter Golenbock for *Bums*, his misnamed book about the Dodgers. "Then the guy came back and said that not only was he black, but he's a shortstop." Pee Wee admitted being worried for quite a while but finally convinced himself that if Robinson was man enough to take his job, he deserved it.

Thus, that first year, when Dixie Walker and others circulated a petition among the Dodgers protesting the signing of Robinson, Reese refused to sign it.[12] In fact, Robinson credited Reese with helping him withstand the torment he experienced in his first years.

"I was helped over (a number of) crises by the courage and decency" of Pee Wee Reese, Jackie wrote in his autobiography, *I Never Had It Made*. He cites a day in Boston when the fans were riding him hard and then began to heckle Reese for playing beside a black man. "Pee Wee didn't answer them," Robinson wrote. "He left his position and walked over to me. He put his hand on my shoulder and began talking to me. His words weren't important. It was the gesture of comradeship and support that counted."[13] That friendliness continued throughout Robinson's career.

Leo Durocher, in his book, *Nice Guys Finish Last*, writes that the Dodgers were able to buy Reese from the Red Sox because Boston shortstop Joe Cronin, a future Hall of Famer, was afraid of losing his job to him. Durocher said Cronin was 34 when Red Sox owner Tom Yawkey ordered him to scout Reese as he was playing for Louisville in the 1938 American Association playoffs. Durocher quoted Cronin as telling Yawkey that "the kid will never make it."[14]

Hearing that, Yawkey sold Reese to the Dodgers for $75,000 — $35,000 plus four no-name players valued by Larry MacPhail at $10,000 each. This turned out to be one of the worst deals in Red Sox history, although it has never stirred up Sox fans the way the Ruth deal to the Yankees does to this day. But all those proper Bostonians fail to remember that at least some good came out of the Ruth trade. Then Red Sox owner, stage struck Harry Frazee, needed the $125,000 to finance the musical *No, No Nanette*, which has been charming people all over the world ever since. Thus, that $125,000 was well spent, no matter what they think in Boston.

Rickey's idea that changed the game, the padded walls and warning tracks installed at Ebbets Field, met with a different kind of resistance, this time from the owners because of the cost. Some owners, however, took action after injuries to star players. The Red Sox padded Fenway after owner Tom Yawkey saw outfielder Fred Lynn carried off the field after hitting the wall breaking a shoulder. The last team to install padding was Cincinnati in 1992 after Phillies center fielder Len Dykstra broke his collar bone while crashing into the concrete.

Rickey's padding Ebbets Field came a year too late to save Pete Reiser's career. He is mostly forgotten today, but in 1941 he was the fastest man in baseball. Reiser won the National League batting title with a .343 average, and at 22½ was the youngest to do so in National League history. Only American Leaguers Al Kaline and Ty Cobb were younger in baseball annals. Kaline at 21 hit .340 in 1955 and Cobb, one day older than Kaline, hit .350 in 1907.

Back in the early 1940s, years before padding was even thought of, the concrete walls did Pete in as far as future greatness was concerned. He was the most reckless outfielder in the game's history and constantly disregarded the walls as he went for fly balls. Even Cobb, as crazy as he was, never was injured running into an outfield wall. On July 19, 1942, Pete hit the wall in St. Louis at full speed while chasing an Enos Slaughter fly ball. He never fully recovered but played out a string of years, hitting far below his .343 norm in his title year or his .350 average at the time he hit that first wall. In that inning Reiser the batting champion and .350 hitter disappeared forever.

He was still highly regarded in 1946 when he came out of the army but the recklessness continued. He hit the wall at Ebbets Field in July of 1946 and was carried off the field on a stretcher en route to Brooklyn's Peck Memorial Hospital. Finally, on June 4, 1947, he hit the wall at Ebbets Field chasing a fly ball by Pittsburgh's Cully Rickard. The *Times'* Roscoe McGowen saw Pete fall to the grass unconscious as the ball "stayed in his glove for one of the most dramatic putouts in the game's history."[15]

Dodgers outfielder Gene Hermanski described the situation differently, debunking the great catch. Gene said Pete was out cold when he went over to check on him and that the ball was between his body and the wall. "As I was waving for a stretcher I slipped the ball into his glove with my right hand. The umpire sees the ball in Pete's glove and calls the guy out. They (Rickey) padded the walls the following year because of that incident."[16]

The baseball hero of my youth never learned. In the fall of 1947 Rickey wanted Reiser to take the 1948 season off, to stay home and heal *at full pay*. Pete refused, and his numbers plunged. In later life he said he was wrong, that he should have rested that year.[17]

All that talent, speed and power wasted against a few outfield walls. But looking back, were it not for Pete Reiser, baseball's walls might never have been padded. Leo Durocher unwittingly gave us Pete's epitaph. "Willie Mays was the best ballplayer I ever managed," Leo said, "but Pete Reiser could have been."[18]

Those words "could have been" should be on his tombstone as a reminder of how recklessness ruined the career of one of the most gifted center fielders who ever lived. Toward the end Red Smith wrote in his *Herald-Tribune* column on the 11 times Pete was carried out of Ebbets Field on a stretcher.

As Dressen was taking over, the Dodgers were under a death sentence, but only Walter O'Malley knew it. One of the events that doomed the team had taken place two months before. On October 27, 1950, Rickey left after having been bought out and then dismissed by O'Malley. Walter was now in complete control of the Dodgers, owner of 75 percent of its stock, his objective for years attained as Rickey walked out of the door at 215 Montague Street for the last time. O'Malley had at last gotten rid of the man with enough prestige in the baseball world to block any attempt to move the team. With Rickey gone, the Brooklyn Dodgers, a founding member of the National League, had just seven years to live.

With 75 percent of the team's stock O'Malley had no need for the other 25 percent, since the only other owner, Dearie Mulvey, went along with whatever O'Malley did. I don't know if a 25 percent stockholder could have blocked the move to Los Angeles, but surprisingly Mrs. Mulvey to all outward appearances never tried. You would think she would have, seeing that she was of old Brooklyn stock and, with her late husband, James, had owned their share of the Dodgers since 1938.

The hatred between O'Malley and Rickey had been festering for years, brought on mainly by O'Malley's jealousy. Walter was simply a wealthy lawyer with a baseball title whereas Rickey was known as the shrewdest executive in the game's history and a man of historic accomplishments: patron saint of Jackie Robinson and father of the farm system, padded walls and outfield tracks, among them.

But what bothered Walter as much as anything was that Rickey was a former major league catcher and therefore had a rapport with players and coaches that a mere lawyer could never approach. O'Malley, as related by Roger Kahn, resorted to making up stories about how he had been a second baseman for Penn until an injury ended his career.[19]

All that aside, there were fundamental differences in how each man was raised, and their attitudes toward, life, religion and particularly money. Looking back, the fate of the Brooklyn Dodgers hinged on these differences.

Wesley Branch Rickey was raised on an Ohio farm to a family so religious they named him after John Wesley, the founder of Methodism. All his life the Sabbath was sacrosanct, to the extent that as a young catcher he was released by the Cincinnati Reds because he would not play ball on Sundays. His detractors said he was a sanctimonious fraud in all this, but to him Sunday was never a workday.

Contrary to his popular image, money was not the end-all of his life. He certainly was high-salaried in his later years, but a man who graduates from Ohio Wesleyan and then teaches and coaches college ball is not aiming at millions. He earned a law degree but never practiced, choosing to go up the ranks as a baseball executive instead.

MacPhail had brought the Dodgers to prominence in the 1940s, and in 1942 when he joined the army, Rickey took up where Larry left off, making Brooklyn one of the elite teams in baseball for the rest of its time in the borough. Rickey, though he knew he would soon be gone, was loyal to the end. Even after his forced resignation he made one last try to stay with the team, telling O'Malley he would remain as general manager, a move his pride should have prevented. But then, Ebbets Field was a tough place to leave, with one notable exception.

O'Malley was almost a mirror opposite. He was a lawyer to his core, driven by money and power. He was born in 1903 in the Bronx where his well-to-do and politically connected father Edwin was at one time commissioner of public markets for New York City. This was in the freewheeling days of Mayor Jimmy Walker, and, oh, how the money rolled in.

Through his father's connections Walter was hired as the Dodgers' chief legal counsel. Using those same connections, he was eventually able to buy 25 percent of the team's stock.* At the same time Rickey bought 25 percent, setting up their years of rivalry and discord. Walter waited

---

*Contrary to many newspaper versions O'Malley did not replace Wendell Willkie as Dodgers counsel. Willkie never worked for the Dodgers.

years in the grass before he was able to forcibly buy Rickey out, albeit on Rickey's terms, notching the hatred up a bit more.

As Walter was preparing to buy Rickey out, Branch contacted New York real estate power broker William Zeckendorf. They agreed that Zeckendorf would be Rickey's stalking horse to get the price up from the $320,000 O'Malley was offering for Rickey's 25 percent of the team.

Zeckendorf publicly offered Rickey $1,050,000, a sum that a furious O'Malley was forced to accept in order to maintain his control of the team. Zeckendorf accepted the odd $50,000 as his fee for getting O'Malley to raise his offer by some $700,000, thus making Rickey a millionaire as he headed for Pittsburgh to take over the Pirates.

Toward the end of Rickey's tenure, when O'Malley controlled the board of directors, their animosity sometimes erupted in public, making it obvious that Rickey would soon be gone. Red Barber recalled an argument that escalated into a loud cursing match in the Dodgers box during a game. "I had to partially cover the mike so that I could broadcast through the shouted cursing," he said. "I thought they would come to blows."[20]

Another factor in Rickey's leaving was the campaign to oust him conducted by Dick Young of the *Daily News*. Young hung the name "El Cheapo" on Rickey, as if he was any different from Hank Greenberg, George Weiss, or any other tough general manager.

Young forgot the battle of the Studebakers fought between Rickey and O'Malley at the end of the 1946 season. Brooklyn had lost the first playoff in major league history to a Cardinals team with one of the great pitching staffs of that time, led by Howie Pollett, Harry Brecheen and Murray Dickson. To express the club's gratitude, Rickey announced that each team member would receive a new Studebaker, no small gift just a year after the war.

After each player's wife chose one of the cars on display at Ebbets Field, O'Malley did his best to try to persuade the board of directors to cancel the gifts, even though they had been announced publicly and chosen. Rickey fought and won. El Cheapo indeed. "We got our cars," first baseman Howie Schultz told me during a telephone interview. "It was too late for O'Malley to stop the deal." He tried hard, though, and even his friends could not understand why the gift of a few cars would disturb a man of O'Malley's wealth, especially when it was the ballclub's money, not his.

But O'Malley always had a lust for money that was almost insatiable. Only a lust for money would persuade a man to leave his native New York. But new millions were waiting for him in California, and when it came to money, Walter felt allegiance to nothing and noone.

As far as allegiance goes, there are O'Malley apologists who in books, one very recently, absolve Walter of all blame for moving the Dodgers from New York, his native city. All the blame is heaped on Robert Moses, who would not let O'Malley have acreage in the middle of Brooklyn, a site that was unacceptable to Moses and other government officials. For those pro–O'Malley authors: The land was scheduled for redevelopment under Title I of the Federal Housing Act, and worse, there were almost no parking facilities available. Dodgers games would therefore cause massive traffic jams and other problems that Moses, New York City's construction coordinator, sought to prevent. As a result, O'Malley had a smokescreen. He kept pushing for the midtown land because he knew he could never have it.

And to those same O'Malley apologists, the following from *The Sporting News:* Between 1945 and 1957 the Dodgers were the most profitable team in baseball, despite O'Malley's outright lies. In the 1950s specifically, the three most profitable baseball teams, before expenses, were Brooklyn, $1,860,744; the Yankees with their stadium that Ebbets Field could fit into, $1,444,369; and the Red Sox, $1,113,309. Even in 1955 and 1956, the years of the Dodgers' disgraceful games in Jersey City, the team cleared $427,195 and $487,462, respectively — clear profit after all expenses.[21]

With that kind of fan loyalty it took a greedy scoundrel of a man to move that team out of Brooklyn. In all my adult years as a Dodgers fan, I felt that there was a bond between fans and team that existed nowhere else in baseball. Recently I read in Roger Kahn's 2005 book *Beyond the Boys of Summer* that newspaper people, those supposedly paragons of objectivity, felt the same tug as I and thousands of other Dodgers fans.

Kahn was writing of how after two years covering the Dodgers, he was switched to the Polo Grounds to cover the Giants, a job he didn't want. His sports editor at the *Herald-Tribune*, the legendary Stanley Woodward, understood his problem, saying the same thing happened to everyone he assigned to work Ebbets Field.

"Baseball writers always develop a great attachment for the Brooklyn ballclub if long exposed to it," he said. "We found it advisable to shift Brooklyn writers frequently. If we hadn't, we would find that we had on our hands a member of the Brooklyn ball club rather than a newspaper reporter. You watch a Brooklyn writer for symptoms and before they become virulent you must shift him to the Yankees or to tennis or golf."[22]

In any event as negotiations went on Brooklyn could not match the colossal bribes Los Angeles were throwing at O'Malley, including 300 acres of prime downtown land *free*. Retired *Times* sports columnist Dave Anderson once told me that if Los Angeles had built a mile-high brick wall around itself, O'Malley would have broken it down to take the Dodgers to the West Coast.

Anderson was with the *Brooklyn Eagle* then and remembered all the meetings during which O'Malley dodged questions about his moves. He even turned down officials of Queens when, with Moses' backing, they offered to build a municipal stadium for the Dodgers at the site where the Mets have been successful for years. Such was O'Malley's yearning for Los Angeles and those future millions.

It's hard to explain how truly money mad O'Malley was, but another example may make it clear. The Dodgers were planning a tour of Japan in the fall of 1956. After road secretary Harold Parrott completed the arrangements and guest list, he told O'Malley that Mrs. Harry Hickey had called and asked if she and her husband could go along.

Hickey was a member of the team's board of directors and one of O'Malley's closest friends. But Harry had been ill and, though almost fully recovered, was not allowed to accompany the team. "Keep their names off the list," O'Malley ordered. "Have you stopped to think how much it would cost to send a body home from Japan? We just can't take the chance." Harold was speechless.[23]

So as 1951 began this was the man in charge of the Brooklyn franchise, the man who would eventually kill it, leaving a hole in the area that not even the Mets have been able to fill. In my opinion, and many agree with me, it was O'Malley's intention for years to move the Dodgers to California, and that getting rid of Rickey was his first overt move. It is strange from our perspective that a man from Ohio would have fought tenaciously to keep the team in Brooklyn while a native New Yorker, a multimillionaire, would sell out his native city for gold.

As to feelings on the team after Rickey left, only Duke Snider publicly said he was glad Rickey was gone. It figures. "A lot of us feel more secure now," he said. "We're not afraid of being sold." Duke, of course, had no idea what he, his teammates and the borough of Brooklyn were in for with O'Malley at the top and Dressen in the dugout.[24]

On the good news side of baseball, Jimmie Foxx and Mel Ott were voted into baseball's Hall of Fame on January 26, two sluggers who could not have been more dissimilar. Ott was a Polo Grounds pull hitter; Foxx was a home run threat anywhere.

Even as a teenager Jimmie was a long ball hitter. After he was signed to play in the Class D Eastern Shore league *at age 15*, he hit a home run in his first professional game and then went on to hit .296 for the regular season in 76 games, again, at age 15.

It could be argued that Foxx, six-feet tall and very strong, was right behind Ruth as the greatest slugger of all time, a right-handed hitter in a left-hander's league, a man whose 534 home runs were hit in some of the biggest parks in the game. For him there was no "launching pad" as there was in Atlanta, or other friendly National League parks like Ebbets Field, the Polo Grounds, Wrigley Field, Baker Bowl or Crosley Field.

Nor in his day were the stands at Yankee Stadium moved in 60 feet or so, allowing many of A-Rod's looping fly balls to left field to fall in for home runs instead of the routine outs they would have been in DiMaggio's or Foxx's heydays.

Before he was traded to the Red Sox and the friendly "Green Monster," Jimmie hit 299 homers while playing for the Athletics in Shibe Park, where the dimensions were 360, 515 and 360. Despite those distances, he hit 58 homers in 1932, one every 9.9 times at bat, leading the league in both categories. But "Double X" began to fade in 1941 when his years of heavy drinking finally slowed him down at age 34. The drink probably contributed to his tragic death at 59 when he choked on a bone while eating in Miami.

Ted Williams remembered how Jimmie loved Scotch whiskey. "He used to say he could drink 15 of those little bottles of Scotch, those miniatures, and not be affected," Ted recalled. "Of course nobody could do that and stay healthy, and it got to him later on." Ted was right. Jimmie was virtually finished at 32, able to hang on a year or two more on manager's hopes and his past accomplishments.

Ott was different. A smaller man than Foxx at 5'9" and 170 pounds, the Polo Grounds was tailor-made for him with its 258-foot right-field line. He was such a dead pull hitter that those inviting right field stands were ideal for his swing, eventually leading to his total of 511 homers. The world saw how close those stands were when Dusty Rhodes hit his home runs off that superb Cleveland pitching staff in the 1954 World Series.

Mel was one of the few who never played a day in the minors, even though when he first arrived at the Polo Grounds Casey Stengel tried to persuade John McGraw to release him to Toledo for some minor league experience. " He's 17 and he stays with me," McGraw answered. John obviously didn't want anyone tinkering with the boy's unorthodox batting style, right foot in the air, "in the bucket" as they used to call it.[25]

Mel also suffered a violent death, in a head-on crash November 21, 1958, near New Orleans. He was the supposed subject of the remark "Nice guys finish last," attributed to Leo Durocher but possibly the invention of some bored sportswriter, since Leo denied he ever said it.

From the dark side of American sports reports surfaced in mid–January of the worst fix scandal since the White Sox threw the World Series in 1919. New Yorkers in particular were stunned to learn that basketball players from four of its colleges were indicted, charged with throwing games and shaving points. New Yorkers were used to scandal through the years. They certainly remembered 1919 and a few even recalled the Cobb/Speaker fixed game a few years later, even though Judge Landis did his best to bury it. But this was different. This was our youth, college students 18 to 22 year old. This was part of our future.

As the investigation moved along it uncovered what became a national disgrace, with a total of seven colleges and 32 players involved. It started with a player who could not be corrupted, Junius Kellogg, 6'8" and the first African American to play for Manhattan, then a small Catholic college in the Bronx.

Kellogg was approached by a former teammate who offered $1,000 to see that Manhattan exceeded the point spread in its game with St. Francis College of Brooklyn. Kellogg refused the money and then reported the offer to his coach, who called in the police.

The schools involved included City College of New York, Manhattan College, New York University, Long Island University, Bradley University and the University of Toledo. Columbia University got off lightly, never being investigated for the activities of basketball thug Jack Molinas, a Columbia basketball player who was graduated in 1953. Just a year later he was banished for life for fixing games while playing pro ball with the Fort Wayne Pistons.

Molinas was later involved in another basketball fix scandal but no one ever looked into his activities at Columbia. It would be reasonable to assume that a pro fixer might have done so in college, but no law enforcement official got involved. Perhaps the Ivy League aura came into play. The aura didn't save Molinas, though. He was murdered gangland style some years later.

When the investigation ended, the final fix total was seven schools and 33 players involved in 49 games in 23 cities and 19 states. Only one player, Gene Melchiorre of Bradley, deserves to be named after all these years. It would be hard to top the brazenness of his hypocrisy.

"How could they disgrace their schools and the game of basketball?" he was quoted as saying. Later he too confessed his involvement, was indicted and banned from the game. Nevertheless in 1996 he was inducted into the Greater Peoria Hall of Fame.

A fixer in a hall of fame! Shoeless Joe, where are you?

Chapter One: January

As the month was ending, 14 members of the Baseball Hall of Fame were converging on New York City to help celebrate the 75th anniversary of the National League's founding in 1876. Their careers virtually spanned the league's history, from Cy Young and the Dead Ball Era to the slugging royalty of Jimmie Foxx.

They had a number of things in common: They were all white, most of them Anglo-Saxon, and none were named Bonds, McGwire, Sosa or Palmiero. In some ways they take us back to baseball's lost age of innocence, when booze was a baseball staple more than it is today and steroids were unheard of. Admittedly, drinking ruined many a ballplayer, greats like Grover Cleveland Alexander and Jimmie Fox, for example, but it didn't kill. Today's athletes should read, or watch again, Lyle Alzado's farewell to football.

CHAPTER TWO

February

They gathered for a group picture at New York City's Broadway Central Hotel, with Cy Young front and center. He was the oldest of the group at 84 but could have passed for 100. Missing at this reunion were two recently gone — Grover Cleveland Alexander, who died of a heart ailment just the year before, and Babe Ruth, who died three years earlier at age 53 of throat cancer.

Looking at them is to look at one's youth. There's Hubbell, sitting with his hands together, possibly trying to hide that twisted left arm, the screwball arm that made him immortal. Jimmie Foxx stands there, handsome at age 44, the man of broad shoulders, as Carl Sandburg would say. Ty Cobb is there, standing while Tris Speaker sits, both of them lucky to have survived a fix scandal that Judge Landis apparently was afraid to pursue.

They all played in another world. Even as the ball livened up and Ruth led baseball into the Golden Twenties, the home runs weren't flying into the stands every five seconds. Five hundred home runs was not long ago the ticket to Cooperstown. Today's papers noted that Ken Griffey, Jr., hit his 600th. How could this be? The man spent half his career on the injured list, or so it seemed.

It could be because most fans love home runs and are bored by scoreless pitching duels unless a no-hitter is in the works. Consequently, the new stadiums are smaller, as in Baltimore, the bat is thinner and has more "whip" than ever, with the result that in almost every game nowadays at least one bat is split on contact. And, most important, the ball has been livened yet again, as it has been periodically since the days of the Babe.

As Lee Mazzone, one of our greatest pitching coaches, told writer Roger Kahn for his book, *Head Game*, "The baseball is juiced. I know it's juiced. You know it's juiced, and I don't care who denies it. And look at today's parks. They're smaller than the ones they replaced. You know what's happened there."[1]

But for some of our 14 Hall of Famers, the dead ball reigned to the extent that it was used until no longer playable. The ball that killed Ray Chapman was so blackened that one theory is he never saw it as it came at his head. Today the ball is replaced if it hits the ground. As they sat for their group picture in the Broadway Central, most could look back on those dead ball days. They were:

Fred Clarke was a brash rookie with what today would be called an attitude. At 22, in his first day in the majors, he refused to suit up because he hadn't been given $100 he had been promised. When team owner and baseball mogul Barney Dreyfuss finally paid him before game time, Clarke changed into his uniform and opened the season five-for-five — four singles and a triple.

That attitude carried him through 21 seasons, 15 with the Pittsburgh Pirates, where for years he was a playing manager. His Hall of Fame figures included a .315 lifetime batting average; 2708 hits; 1015 runs batted in and 223 triples, sixth on the all-time list. He died at age 88 in Winfield, Kansas, in 1960.

Waves went through baseball when **Ty Cobb** and **Tris Speaker** were forced to resign as managers in 1926 after they were accused of fixing a ballgame. Further, Cobb (now a player only) was traded from Detroit, where he had been an outfielder for 22 years, to the Athletics, where he was joined by Speaker in 1928, the year both retired from baseball. Cobb had the highest average in baseball history at .367 while Speaker, at .344 lifetime, was called the greatest center fielder of all time.

The evidence against them seemed pretty convincing, but not enough to cause baseball Commissioner Landis to ban them for life, as he did the 1919 fixers. Speculation was Landis feared that banishing two of the game's greatest players just years after that 1919 fix would threaten baseball's very existence.

The story broke on December 22, 1926, when Landis named Cobb, Speaker and pitchers Smoky Joe Wood and Dutch Leonard in a conspiracy to fix a game between Detroit and Cleveland on September 25, 1919, at Cleveland.[2]

Evidence included testimony by Leonard and, most damaging, letters written by Cobb to Leonard that would have proved the case had Landis wanted to. But Landis did not call for an investigation or involve the district attorney's office. He simply let the matter die, and perhaps he was right. Had he pressed all the gambling evidence and rumors in those days, it might very well have been the end of major league baseball.

One aspect of Cobb's character that separated him from his fellow players was his often psychotic nature, on the field and off. This was seen as attributable, perhaps, to the tragedy of his mother shooting his father to death, thinking he was a burglar. His teammates and others thought he was just plain crazy, such was his extreme intensity.

Cobb died at 75 in 1961 in an Atlanta hospital. Speaker was 70 when he died of a heart attack in 1958 in his home territory, Lake Whitney, Texas.

Mickey Cochrane was a rarity in baseball — a catcher who was superb in handling pitchers and could hit for average, his lifetime .320 being the highest of any receiver in history. His nickname was "Black Mike" because of his temper, especially after losing a tough one when he sometimes smashed a clubhouse, home or away.

Cochrane was 34 when he was forced to quit playing in 1937 after he was hit by a Bump Hadley fastball. He suffered a triple concussion and was unconscious for 10 days. After his 13-year career he was forbidden to play again and tried being a player-manager but was unsuited for the job. The batting helmet that would have saved him was three years away. Cochrane died at age 59 in 1962.

Eddie Collins began his career as a second baseman with the Philadelphia Athletics after graduating from Columbia University. He went on to a 25-year career, mostly with the Chicago White Sox. He was the highest-paid member of the Sox, and there were reports at the time that jealousy over his salary triggered the 1919 fix scandal.

Since he was not involved in the fix, he continued in baseball as a manager and then as a Red Sox executive from 1932 until his death in 1951 at age 64. His lifetime batting average was .333, including .328 in six World Series. With that average he was one of the best hitters of his day but was always outshined by Ty Cobb. Eddie was elected to the Baseball Hall of Fame in 1939.

Jimmie Foxx was known as "Double X" and looking back we can see that he was one of the great sluggers of all time, maybe even the equal of Babe Ruth had alcoholism not eroded his talent and finally ended his career.

Charlie Gehringer spent his entire 19-year career with the Detroit Tigers, where he one of the best-hitting second basemen of all time at .320. His fielding was so good he was known as "The Mechanical Man," of whom teammate Doc Cramer once said, "You wind him up at the beginning of the season and forget about him." This combination of skills and temperament probably add up to Charlie being the best all-around second basemen ever.

On the way to his 2,839 career hits, he had seven seasons of more than 200 hits. In a 14-year span he fell under .300 just once, at .298. As a fielder he led the American League seven times. Fielding averages can be deceptive, since a high average may reflect an infielder who plays on a dime, as they say. But Gehringer's 7,068 assists, second highest in league history, attests to his wide range.

In 1942, as he realized he was slowing down, Charlie joined the navy and served for three years, played service ball, and like many celebrities rose in rank to lieutenant commander. As a member of the Old Timers' Committee he voted for years against Phil Rizzuto's election to the Baseball Hall of Fame, saying the Yankees shortstop didn't deserve admission despite the Yankees' constant drumbeat on Phil's behalf. Charlie died at age 89 in Bloomfield Hills, Michigan.

Rogers Hornsby was not only one of baseball's greatest hitters but was one of the most cantankerous men who ever played the game. Unlike Ty Cobb, Hornsby had no mental problems, but was described by newsmen and many of his contemporaries as nasty, mean and rude.

But he was a superb ballplayer, a hitter almost without parallel. Here are the three top hitters in baseball annals — Ty Cobb at .367, Hornsby at .358, and Joe Jackson at .356, the royalty of hitting. Hornsby's world was so hitting-oriented that one spring training he said with disdain, "Shake any tree in Florida and 12 glove men will fall out and not one hitter."

Rogers could get along with very few people. He had a dugout fistfight with Branch Rickey when Rickey was managing the Cardinals. He stayed with the Cardinals despite his surliness because of his bat: the .367 lifetime, two Triple Crowns, and his .424 single-season average is still the highest in history. And he wasn't a banjo hitter, as his 301 homers prove. He died in 1963 at age 67 in Chicago.

Carl Hubbell was known as "King Carl" and "The Meal Ticket" because of his value to the New York Giants. Over a 16-year career he won 253 games with a lifetime ERA of 2.97. His best pitch, which baffled hitters for years, was his screwball, which earned him two Most Valuable Player awards.

The pitch got him into the Baseball Hall of Fame but there were lifetime consequences for Hubbell. Because of its unnatural motion — clockwise for left-handers like Hubbell and counter-clockwise for right-handers — it took its toll on Hubbell's arm. Eventually his left arm turned clockwise permanently, and for the rest of his life the palm of his hand turned outward.

Hubbell shared one historic moment, still talked about today on occasion. He was pitching in the 1934 All-Star Game and gave up singles to Charlie Gehringer and Heinie Manush and then struck out in succession Babe Ruth, Lou Gehrig and Jimmie Foxx, three historic high-average sluggers.

After retiring Hubbell was for 33 years the farm director for the Giants. He died in 1988 at age 85 in Scottsdale, Arizona.

Charles (Kid) Nichols is one of those pitchers from the 1890s who always seemed to be winning 30 games every season. As a result, he left a 360–202 won-lost record with an excellent 2.94 ERA after just a 14-year career. That divides out into more than 40 decisions a year, a workhorse pace not unusual among the pitchers of his day. The ball was soft, the bats were cumbersome, and the bullpen was nonexistent. Nevertheless, 360 wins in just 14 years seems incredible.

Nichols was the winningest pitcher of the nineties, a control artist who threw with a minimal windup because he thought it wasted motion. He played most of his career with the National League's Boston Beaneaters. His first year with them, 1890, shows how different the game was in those days: 27–19, 2.23 ERA, 46 starts, 46 complete games, seven shutouts.

Very impressive figures from many of the old-timers. But think on this: If those pitchers of the early twentieth century and before had to pitch under modern conditions — small parks, whippy bats, juiced baseballs, etc.— the results would have been far different.

Nichols made the Baseball Hall of Fame in 1949, four years before he died at 83 in Kansas City, Missouri, where he had run a string of bowling alleys with the immortal Joe Tinker of Chicago Cubs fame.

George Sisler had the misfortune to play 12 years with the St. Louis Browns and four with the Boston Bees. With those teams, despite his superb .340 lifetime average, he never played in a post-season game. His teams never made the World Series, and the All-Star Game was after his time.

Sisler was signed by Branch Rickey, then with the St. Louis Browns, in 1915 after his graduation from the University of Michigan, where he had been a standout pitcher. He was, in fact, a part-time pitcher for the Browns when he first reached the major leagues, once beating the great Walter Johnson in a 2–1 pitching duel.

But his hitting was such that the Browns switched him to first base to get his bat in the lineup every day. By 1918, his fourth year in the majors, he was considered one of the best first basemen in the game. His 1920 season still ranks as one of the best in history: .407 with 257 hits, the most for years until Seattle outfielder Ichiro Suzuki set the current record of 262 in 2004. With the modern schedule, however, Suzuki played in eight more games, roughly 32 at-bats, which at Sisler's .407 pace would have given him roughly 12 more hits.

Pie Traynor hit .320 over a 17-year span with the Pittsburgh Pirates. He was known as one of the nicest man ever to play the game and was beloved in the Pittsburgh area as a player who was always willing to talk baseball with anyone who recognized him. The nickname? Pie was his favorite dessert.

During his 17-year career he was considered the greatest team player of his time, a description from seldom satisfied John McGraw. He also managed the Pirates from 1934 to 1939. In a salute to his skills, major league baseball named him its all-time third baseman during the 1976 centennial. Traynor was voted into the Baseball Hall of Fame in 1948. He died in 1972 in Pittsburgh at the age of 73.

Edward (Big Ed) Walsh is baseball's all-time ERA leader at 1.82 over a 14-year career, thirteen of them with the Chicago White Sox. His career record was 195–126, ordinarily not good enough for the Hall (unless you're a Yankee, like Lefty Gomez at 189–102), but that 1.82 ERA assured his entrance.

Big Ed never lacked confidence. A sportswriter once described him as "the only man I ever saw who could strut standing still." He holds the record for innings pitched with 464 during the 1908 season when he had one of the best years in baseball history: 40–15, 1.42 ERA, 66 appearances, 269 strikeouts and 11 shutouts.

Ed left the White Sox after the 1916 season but retired after just four appearances, his career obviously over. He died in Pompano Beach, Florida, in 1959 at age 78, 13 years after he was elected to the Baseball Hall of Fame.

Denton (Cy) Young has a record that is beyond imagination today. The only answer to his 511 wins has to be threefold: his fastball, his endurance, and the dead, dead ball. He is first in wins and also first in losses, 313, both of which add up to an amazing 842 appearances. Today's pitchers must either cringe or laugh at such figures, so impossible they would be today.

His 22 years prove his endurance, and he must have been a rare talent to win so many games. Today we can deal with his excellent ERA, 2.63. But 511 wins stuns the mind. One factor that modern players can identify with was Young's fastball. He got the nickname "Cy," which was short for Cyclone, because he was so fast.

Along with that fastball was his impeccable control, issuing only 1,217 walks, averaging just over 55 walks per season, creditable to even the best of control pitchers. Cy was 88 years old when he died in Peoli, Ohio, his home state, in 1955. He was elected to the Baseball Hall of Fame in 1937, the second year of balloting.

Why the mathematically best pitcher in baseball history wasn't on the first ballot is a mystery to me. Those first electees were Ty Cobb, Babe Ruth, Honus Wagner, Christy Mathewson and Walter Johnson, worthies all. Maybe there was a five-man limit per year for electees. If that had been the case I would have put Young on that first ballot and Wagner the year later.

That Hall of Fame weekend signed contracts started arriving at 215 Montague Street with three of the biggest names agreeing with the Dodgers terms. Gil Hodges and Carl Furillo at $20,000 seemed reasonable given the economics of the day, but Jackie Robinson signing for $35,000 surprised both fans and sportswriters.

Jackie earned $35,000 when the aging Joe DiMaggio was given $100,000 for what would be his last season and the temperamental no-field Ted Williams was baseball's highest-paid player at $125,000. It made no sense. DiMaggio was down to .301, a sure sign of his decline, and his arm was gone. Williams had an off year for him —.317, 28 homers and 97 RBIs — but he had broken his elbow the year before and batted only 334 times.

Robinson, in contrast, was not only the man who broke the color barrier but was one of the key members of the Brooklyn team. Plus, he had not been justly rewarded for his 1949 career year during which he led the National League in batting at .342 and was named its Most Valuable Player.

His play at the end of the 1950 season should have assured him a substantial contract for 1951 but it never happened. During the final series with the eventual pennant-winning Phillies, Jackie made a spectacular diving catch of Eddie Waitkus' drive up the middle to keep the game tied in the ninth and then hit the winning homer in the 14th. The next day Dick Sisler, George's son, hit that pennant-winning homer.

It is strange that Jackie, one of the most fiery players who ever lived, should be so acquiescent at salary time. At other times he was so eruptive after Rickey relieved him of his vow of silence that Red Smith finally tired of him and Clem Labine, one of baseball's best relievers, told me that around the league Jackie was considered a "strict pain in the ass."[3] This was a serious matter for the entire team. "When Jackie was in involved in his frequent flare-ups," Clem said, "it affected all of us, for the animosity Jackie aroused rubbed off on our whole team. We became the bad guys all the time." It was Jackie's salary attitude, however, that finally cost him. His best contract during his 10-year career for a future Hall of Famer was just $42,500.

He grew up on the West Coast in Pasadena, California, where he was a four-sport athlete at Pasadena Junior College. Later he became the first UCLA athlete to star in the same four sports — baseball, football, track and basketball. It was a tough road for him, though, for as he grew up his mother, Mallie, had to work as a domestic and also take in washing after his father deserted her for another woman when Jackie was a year old.

Jackie was born in 1919 in Cairo, Georgia, but not long after his father abandoned the family, his mother left Cairo with her five children for Pasadena. As he recalls it in his book, *I Never Had It Made*, things were rough for Mallie during the 1920s. The 1930s were even tougher as the Depression deepened. As a single mother with five children Mallie needed help from welfare even though she worked long hours with seldom a day off.

"Sometimes there were only two meals a day," Jackie remembered, "and some days we ate leftovers my mother was able to bring home from the job. She got up before daylight to go to work, and although she came home tired she always managed to give us the attention we needed."[4]

It turned out she had raised two great athletes. While Jackie was growing up he idolized his brother, Matthew "Mack" Robinson. Five years older than Jackie, Mack was a sprinter of some note on the West Coast, so good that he made the 1936 Olympic team where, while Hitler turned his back, he finished second to Jesse Owens in the 200-yard dash. Some years later he was killed in a motorcycle accident, still a relatively young man.

Jackie, as a four-sport letterman, was one of UCLA's greatest athletes when he dropped out of school, stubbornly insisting that no amount of education would lead to a decent job for a black man. Not even his fiancée, fellow class member and future wife Rachel Isum, could convince him otherwise.

Other publications differ on what happened after Jackie left UCLA. In his own words he wanted to play professional football and the only club to offer him a job was the Honolulu Bears, where as the war was coming on he played ball on Sundays and worked weekdays for a construction company.

Back from Hawaii, he was drafted into the army in May 1942 and was soon selected for Officers' Candidate School. It was at Fort Hood, Texas, that he got into trouble for standing up for his rights. On one trip back to the base he sat in the front of the bus. When the driver stopped to order Jackie, now a second lieutenant, to get out of the "white section" and take a seat in the rear, he refused to move.[5]

This set off a military chain reaction that resulted in a court martial during which Jackie was found innocent of a number of seemingly trumped up charges. The army then apparently decided that it had to get rid of this defiant second lieutenant. Against all logic, Jackie was honorably discharged in November of 1944.

He heard through the athletic grapevine that the Kansas City Monarchs were looking for players and Jackie was soon their shortstop at $400 a month. Meanwhile, in Brooklyn Branch Rickey decided it was time for a black man to play in the National League, and he was successful in persuading the Dodgers' board of directors that Ebbets Field should be the place to start.

In deepest secrecy Rickey and his people started looking around. In August of 1945 Dodgers coach Clyde Sukeforth recommended Robinson after seeing him play in a Negro League game at Comiskey Park in Chicago. Jackie talked with Sukeforth and then agreed to meet with Rickey in Brooklyn, expenses paid.

Rickey laid it all out, no subterfuge about Robinson being recruited for the Brown Bombers. "The truth is ... I've sent for you being I'm interested in you as a candidate for the Brooklyn National League club," he said. "I think you can play in the majors. How do you feel about it?" He told me I'd be alone, Jackie wrote, with virtually nobody on my side, and with most fans hostile.

"Have you got the guts to play the game no matter what happens," Rickey asked. "Mr. Rickey, are you looking for a Negro who is afraid to fight back," Robinson responded.

"Robinson," Rickey answered, "I'm looking for a ballplayer with guts enough not to fight back." That response and Rickey's subsequent actions opened the door, and Jack Roosevelt Robinson became the first acknowledged black man to play in the modern major leagues.[6]

He opened that 1946 season as the second baseman for the Montreal Royals. From the start Rickey knew he had made the right choice, selecting in Robinson a black man who could play the game and keep his mouth shut until he was established enough to fight back. And with Rickey's approval, fight back he did.

They were called the "tools of ignorance" by yesterday's sportswriters, but for Roy Campanella they were the tools he donned as a 16-year-old kid playing for the Baltimore Elite Giants in 1936, his first step toward the Brooklyn Dodgers and eventually the Baseball Hall of Fame in 1969. In 1958 his career ended when he was paralyzed from the shoulders down when his car overturned on an icy road.

His politics were always Republican, unlike most of his black friends. He also did not see eye to eye with Roy Campanella, Jackie being a firebrand for civil rights while Roy chose the easygoing approach. Time, Roy felt, would heal all racial strife. For Jackie, it was *now*. For Roy, it was *patience*.

Campy had it much rougher than Jack. There was no college life for him. He was the son of an interracial couple in Philadelphia, playing ball from his early youth until at 16 he was the first-string catcher for the Baltimore Elite Giants. *At 16.* Instead of attending UCLA, Roy was sleeping in rundown hotels, eating in greasy spoons, suffering overnight bus rides and often playing in pain.

"You didn't get hurt in the Negro leagues," he recalled. "You played no matter what happened to you because if you didn't, you didn't get paid." And the scheduling wasn't anywhere close to white baseball, not even as low as Class D. As an example Roy cited the day he caught four Elite Giants games, a doubleheader in Cincinnati in the afternoon and another in Youngstown that evening.

Roy had been secretly scouted by Charlie Dressen for some time when Rickey ordered him to set up a meeting in the Dodgers' offices in Brooklyn. Charlie first approached Roy in October of 1946 at Ruppert Stadium in Newark, where Campy was playing in a mixed-race all-star game. He met with Rickey the following morning.

After the generalities were over they talked about Campanella's weight, with Rickey surprised that Roy could play at 220 pounds. "All I know," Roy said, "is that I've been doing it every day for years and it's worked out fine." Rickey then questioned Campy's age. "I have your age, 25, noted in this book. You sure this is your right age? You look older."

"Mr. Rickey," Campy replied, "I've been playing ball a long time." Rickey signed him that morning, telling him to report to Nashua, New Hampshire, where Roy would soon be catching Don Newcombe, the two being the first acknowledged black batterymates in baseball history.[7] By 1948 Roy was with the Dodgers, backing up Bruce Edwards behind the plate.

With Jackie signing at $35,000, it is strange that Hodges and Furillo each settled for $20,000. If they had been New York Yankees they would have gotten at least twice that. As it was, the $20,000 never seemed right since both were among the premier players in the game and contributed as much as any player, including Robinson, to Brooklyn's continued success.

Gil was born in Princeton, Indiana, on April 4, 1924. He came up as a catcher, but since he would have been wasted as third-string behind Edwards and Campanella, he was switched to first base, soon becoming the best fielding first baseman of his day, perhaps any day. Shamefully, his widow Joan has had to see some much lesser lights elected to the Baseball Hall of Fame while Gil is ignored to the point where his chances of entry are fading with each passing year. In 1993 Hodges was almost elected by the Veterans Committee but missed out by one vote because his friend and teammate, Roy Campanella, was ill and unable to attend the vote session.

Gil's strength was legendary throughout the National League. Dodgers third baseman Don Hoak, a Marine years after Hodges, recalls hearing tales of Gil's service in the South Pacific where, on running out of ammunition on occasion, he would kill Japanese soldiers with his bare hands.

Gil's .273 average and 370 home runs over an 18-year career compare favorably with many in the Hall, especially the great number chosen by the Veterans Committee, which for years has been electing a number of old ballplayers based on cronyism and ethnicity rather than skills. How else can one explain Harry Hooper, Lefty Gomez and Orlando Cepeda, the dope dealer, among many others?

The Mets were the surprise world champions in 1969 largely because of Hodges' managerial skill and discipline. They were a young team and sometimes undisciplined before Gil took over. They learned better soon enough. Cleon Jones loafed once too often out in left field and then, before a national television audience, Hodges not only took him out of the game but went into the outfield to escort him to the bench.

Cleon went meekly, knowing that no one crossed the man known as the strongest in baseball. During a melee, Gil dragged Eddie Mathews of the Milwaukee Braves off the field while Eddie, 6'1", 190 pounds, kicked and yelled. This wasn't one of your typical baseball "fights." This was an all-out slugfest that started when Don Drysdale hit Johnny Logan in the back. After an exchange of remarks, Logan charged the mound and took a straight right to the jaw from Drysdale. By then players were grabbing and hitting one another when Mathews jumped Drysdale, got on top of him on the mound and started punching away. Hodges got one of Eddie's legs and dragged him off the field, suffering spike wounds as Mathews was yelling and kicking. Eddie did not retaliate.

Gil may be elected by the Veterans Committee some day but it should have been by the baseball writers, as he deserves. It is possible that both Hodges and Furillo may be victims of the numbers game — too many of their teammates elected within a fairly short span of time including Snider, Reese, Campanella and Robinson. The writers may have been getting gun-shy.

Furillo was born March 8, 1922, in Stony Creek Mills, former coal mining country near Reading, Pennsylvania. He was therefore known as "the Reading Rifle" since he had one of the best arms of his generation, possibly of any baseball generation. He had solid credentials but he seems to be the forgotten outfielder. Maybe it's as Clem Labine explained it: "Carl would not socialize because he felt that with his eighth-grade education, he didn't fit in."[8] That really shouldn't matter, but it surely does. As a rule, Carl got along with everybody, except Leo Durocher. And it was his feud with Leo that convinced me, and many others, that baseball "hatreds" were much exaggerated, most often the results of the sportswriters' penchant for the sensational.

For example, the supposed hatred between the Dodgers and Giants, Durocher and Ed Stanky aside, never really existed. Intense rivalry, yes, but not hatred. Furillo once seethed for two seasons after being hit by a pitch he was sure was ordered by Durocher. Finally he was hit again on September 6, 1953, after he heard Durocher shout to Ruben Gomez to "stick it in his ear."

After being hit Carl took first and then ran at the Giants dugout. Not one Giant touched him as he went through the entire team to get at Leo. Giants players intervened only when they saw that Furillo had Durocher on the ground and was throttling him to the point where it was getting dangerous. Monte Irvin and Jim Hearn got Carl up and he walked back through the entire Giants team, again untouched.

He said later he felt no danger from the Giants. When asked how he thought he could get through the entire Giants team, he said, "I wasn't worried about the players ganging up on me. They hate him too." That statement by Carl showed the true nature of the Dodgers-Giants relationship.[9]

Contrary to all the media hype, there was no real hatred between the teams. If all the press baloney was true, the Giants players would have jumped all over Furillo instead of practically escorting him back on the field after his attack on Durocher. All the bad feelings centered around Robinson, Furillo and Leo, who was hated throughout the league.

Consider: The two teams have been out on the West Coast for 52 years now, and, except for the disgraceful bat attack on John Roseboro by Juan Marichal, there's never been any great fuss. California just doesn't have the volatility that New York generates. Besides, the fans aren't as knowledgeable as were those in Brooklyn and the Bronx. Imagine Orlando Cepeda being the fan favorite over Willie Mays.

Carl didn't often erupt in anger. He kept things to himself usually and was not a mixer, a somewhat shy man most likely because of his lack of education. This shyness and his not socializing with the writers probably cost him a place in the Baseball Hall of Fame. And if anyone thinks that's not important, think of the aforementioned Lefty Gomez, a great man at a cocktail party with a clever quip.

A typical Gomez reaction, of the type that endeared him to sportswriters, was his comment after the *Life* article of September 1941 "proving" that there was no such thing as a curveball. "Here I am try-

Carl Furillo has been one of the most underrated outfielders in baseball history, probably the victim of too many Dodgers elected to the Baseball Hall of Fame in close proximity. He had a 15-year career, a .299 lifetime batting average, a batting championship in 1953, and one of the best arms in history. There are many lesser men inducted at Cooperstown.

ing to make a comeback and they tell me my best pitch is an optical illusion."

You had to like a guy like Gomez — affable, talented, clever. Likeable, yes, but worthy of the Baseball Hall of Fame? Not with only 189 wins with some of the most powerful teams in baseball history behind him. His election, however, showed the power of the New York press, just as it did years later when Phil Rizzuto was finally elected after years of drumbeating by George Steinbrenner and the New York media.

Furillo had no such drumbeating for him, even though he deserves election just as much as Rizzuto and a number others. Consider: Carl retired with a 15-year lifetime batting average of .299, a batting champi-

Phil at 5'5" was turned down by several managers as too small to play baseball. The Yankees finally took a chance on him, and after he came out of the navy in 1946 he was one of the premier shortstops for the next 11 seasons, retiring in 1956 after playing in nine World Series. He never really got along with Casey Stengel and always remembered Casey's telling him to "get a shoebox" when he tried out for the Dodgers in the mid–1930s at age 16. He was elected to the Baseball Hall of Fame in 1994.

onsip, 1,910 hits, 192 home runs and 1,058 RBIs. He was the best defensive right fielder of his time with an arm that ranks among the best in baseball history.

During his career he threw out seven men who unwisely rounded first base after singling. Even more remarkable, he threw out pitcher Mel Queen, who had lined what was ordinarily a single to right. You had to see the man throw to believe it. I once saw Furillo playing center for an injured Duke Snider. Johnny Sain was on second and figured to score on a hit to deep center. Instead, he was out by two steps; such was the arm of Furillo. A pivotal player in six Brooklyn World Series, Carl may be elected to the Hall some day by the Veterans Committee, which, besides friendship, has at times corrected past injustices.

Steinbrenner's drumbeating aside, in all fairness Rizzuto belongs in the Hall, especially compared to the number who are in but don't belong. Reese was already in and Phil and Pee Wee are almost as one in their stats and stature. Rizzuto was .273 lifetime and Reese .269, they were shortstops at the same time in the most unforgiving sports city in the country, and they both held great infields together through 15 pressure-packed, pennant-winning years. Pee Wee had more hits and power than Phil, but that can be attributed to the vast difference in size when comparing Yankee Stadium to Ebbets Field.

Rizzuto, the son of a New York City streetcar conductor, was almost done in by his size. He was listed at 5' 6" but after seeing him in the Yankees clubhouse I'd say more like 5' 4". Two New York managers refused to let him even try out for their teams: Bill Terry, Giants manager, and Casey Stengel when he managed the Dodgers. Stengel is reported to have told him to "get a shoebox."[10] Needless to say, for all the years he played for Stengel, there was no love lost.

When he returned in 1946 after three years in the navy, he was beaned by Nelson Potter of the Browns and suffered dizzy spells periodically for the rest of his career. Although he didn't have a great arm, no other shortstop of his time got the ball away quicker. He held that Yankees infield together for some 13 years, during which he was the best bunter in the big leagues, probably the best who ever played. A valuable art, now pretty much lost. His playing days ended Yankees style. He was released on Old Timer's Day in 1956, a day that only the cold-blooded Yankees front office would choose.[11]

Gene Hermanski signed up when he got out of the navy, a somewhat lesser light but one of Brooklyn's more dependable hitters. Gene's problem was his fielding, acceptable on most clubs but not on the Reese/Robinson

Dodgers. His hitting, though, was timely and often enough at .277 as a Dodger.

Gene was born in Pittsfield, Massachusetts, but learned his baseball as a boy in Newark, New Jersey, where he was an all-state outfielder for East Side High School. After attending Seton Hall University he was signed as a free agent by the Philadelphia Athletics in 1939, but his major league debut was with Brooklyn in 1943, after which he served in the navy until the war's end.

He was valuable to the team on the field and off, for he had a sense of humor that was infectious and at times eased tensions in a Brooklyn clubhouse constantly in the midst of tight pennant races. His humor was never offensive, a tribute to his Newark upbringing at a time when Newark was a stable and safe city.

On the same day Hermanski signed, the Red Sox continued their game of DiMaggio tag. Tom Yawkey with his moneybags again waited for Joe's $100,000 signing so he could one-up the Yankees by signing Ted Williams for $125,000, a figure he didn't deserve for 1951.

Williams' 1950 year included a .317 average, 28 homers and 97 RBIs. Ted was hampered by the elbow he broke the year before but no matter; contracts are based on results. Yawkey was such a fool with his money that, except for the media, hardly anyone else noticed.

On February 20th the basketball scandal finally zeroed in on the City College of New York, 1950 NCAA and NIT champions, resulting in four of the best players in the country admitting they had taken $18,500 in bribe money to fix seven games. Those arrests were especially hard for the collegiate world to accept since CCNY had become during the previous season the first team ever to win both post-season tournaments.

Looking back today it is shameful enough that the fix occurred, but what is unacceptable is that no lessons were learned. At least two fixes that we know of took place in later years. The schools involved originally suspended basketball operations, but in just a few years were back at it again, paving the way for the scandals of 1961 and beyond, playing again in gambler's heaven, Madison Square Garden.

That same February 20 the Dodgers' pitchers and catchers started spring workouts at Vero Beach with their new manager telling them that there would be "no doghouses" on the team as long as he is manager.

"They tell me this club should have won the pennant last year," Charley Dressen told his team. "If that's so, why didn't it? I don't know anything about doghouses, but I know I haven't got any."[12]

There's a strong hint there that Shotton lost the 1950 pennant out of pique at certain players — players who would have made a difference had Shotton been more tolerant. Maybe so, but as we shall see, the Dressen doghouse, which he "never had," cost the Dodgers the 1951 pennant, not just the sign-stealing telescope scam.

One of the most likely candidates for Shotton's displeasure had to be Eddie Miksis, never shy about being outspoken, a characteristic Shotton didn't like. It is at least some kind of answer to why he didn't substitute Eddie, one of the fastest men in the game, for Cal Abrams, one of the slowest, as a baserunner in the 1950 pennant-deciding game against the Phillies.

You would think a man of Shotton's experience and maturity would have better judgement with a pennant on the line, but you never know. Eddie, in his very outspoken way, later said Shotton was simply a "dumb son of a bitch." There's a strong hint there of why that 1950 pennant was lost.[13]

CHAPTER THREE

March

As March opened it was apparent that the Korean War was not having much effect on our national sports scene. The draft was not nearly as extensive as in World War II and few athletes — with the later notable exceptions of Ted Williams and Jerry Coleman — were being called up.

As the Yankees gathered for spring training, no one would have believed just a few seasons before that the glaring weak spot in their lineup would be Joe DiMaggio. Joe wasn't hitting consistently and his arm was gone to the point that he sometimes had trouble reaching second base with his throws. This put more pressure on Hank Bauer in right and Gene Woodling in left, but they were able to take up the slack.

They were probably the two best substitute outfielders in the game's history. Both were 29 years old and no doubt could have been starters on just about any other team in the majors. Both came out of the Midwest — Hank from East St. Louis, Illinois, and Gene from Akron, Ohio.

Hank spent 12 glorious years in New York, playing in nine World Series, a lifetime .277 hitter and .245 batter for his Series years. Gene spent six years as a Yankee, reaching the World Series in five of them. His averages were somewhat better than Hank's, .286 lifetime and .318 in the World Series. They may have been discontent platooning but they made more money as Yankees, World Series and all, than most players on other teams.

For years DiMaggio had been part of those Yankees teams that had swaggered through the American League, starting in the days of Babe Ruth and continuing through the 1930s. Throughout that time they were either in first or second place each year until the last part of the decade when they won four pennants in a row, 1936 through 1939, with Joe in center field.

History was repeating itself. The Yankees had won the 1949 and 1950 pennants and World Series and saw no reason why they shouldn't keep winning. As we know, they did, eventually setting the major league record of five World Series in a row.

But as 1951 began, others weren't so sure the team wasn't whistling in the dark, shoring up their courage in a situation that was not necessarily promising. The team, after all, was in a transition phase with DiMaggio nearing the end and Mickey Mantle a 19-year-old question mark. There were also worries about the team's aging with DiMaggio at 36, Reynolds 35, Page 34, and Rizzuto, Lopat and Raschi at 32. Page, the best reliever of his generation when he wasn't drinking, was coming off a disastrous year with a 5.07 ERA year and no one knew if he could be counted on.

Page had two sensational seasons, 1947 and 1949, years when he apparently was controlling his drinking. In other years he was uncontrollable. At one time Joe DiMaggio took him on as a roommate in an attempt to straighten

The finest part-time outfielder in history, Hank Bauer always resented being benched as part of Casey Stengel's platoon system. Nine World Series checks helped but sitting on the bench always galled Hank, a tough ex-Marine who survived the Battle of Okinawa. His triple with the bases loaded won the deciding game of the '51 Series.

him out but it didn't work. It got so that he was cut from the '51 team in spring training and soon drifted out of baseball, a hopeless drunk.

Mantle's first professional stop was Joplin, Missouri, where he hit for both power and average. He started as a shortstop but was so erratic that manager Harry Craft recommended he be trained for the outfield, where Craft thought he might be ready when DiMaggio, clearly near the end, retired. Harry was optimistic since Mantle was one of the best hitting youngsters he had ever seen, ending his year at Joplin at .385, a switch-hitter with 26 home runs. When he reported for spring training with the

Yankees in early March, the *Times* sportswriter James Dawson soon tabbed him as the top rookie in camp.

Dawson first saw Mantle in a game against Cleveland, after which he described Mickey's "flashing" speed and three straight hits against Early Wynn and followers. He also felt that Mickey had played center field in a "highly credible manner."

As a result he was promoted to Kansas City, where former Yankees star George Selkirk was so impressed by the young switch-hitter that he assured his Yankees bosses the kid would be ready to take over from DiMaggio when Joe decided to retire. There were a few bumps along the road, however, partly because Mickey was still a 19-year-old scared and inarticulate kid.

One was when Mickey, despondent in Kansas City during a batting slump, called his father, saying, "I'm not hitting, Dad. I just can't play anymore." In a touching father and son scene, "Mutt" drove to Kansas City to remind his son of what it is like working the mine, as he did all his life. As Mickey told it in his autobiography, *The Mick*, his father's eyes were blazing when he arrived at the Yankees' hotel to tell his son, "Shut up. I don't want to hear that whining. I thought I raised a man, not a coward." "Pack up," he added, "you can go back and work in the mines like me." Remembering the life in the mines, Mickey settled down in Kansas City.

The Yankees had a number of experienced outfielders in that spring training camp, and as one result future star Jackie Jensen was shunted into the background. Jackie had batted 70 times for the Yanks in 1950 and had shown great power in the spring. Dawson reported one game in Phoenix when Jensen had four hits, two homers, a double and a triple. But the team had DiMaggio, Bauer, Woodling, Cerv and Mapes as well as Mantle down in Kansas City. Jensen, inexplicably, was overlooked. He hit .286 during the coming season but it wasn't enough. He was traded to Washington in 1952 and then to the Red Sox and future stardom in 1954.

Perhaps it was that Grand Canyon of a left field at the Stadium that did Jensen in with the Yankees. The power alley in left-center was then a formidable 457 feet, a distance that often frustrated even Joe DiMaggio. After Joe retired, Yankees announcer Mel Allen estimated that the vast distances had cost Joe at least 200 homers.[1]

Boston was made for Jensen with its "Green Monster." Jackie hit 25 homers in his first Boston year and was a star until he retired in 1961. Meanwhile, he was voted American League Most Valuable Player in 1958 and led the league in RBIs with 112, along with 28 home runs. Jackie retired at 33, a fairly young age at the time, because he had problems dealing with flying.

He was all right during the early years of his career since teams traveled in those days by train. His real troubles began in 1958 when the leagues expanded to the West Coast, resulting in many long flights, often overnight. It then became a serious problem for Jensen and nothing seemed to help. Red Sox owner Tom Yawkey arranged for therapy treatments but they didn't work. Jackie therefore retired in 1961, probably the greatest mistake in the career of Yankees general manager George Weiss.

There was more to it than that, according to my friends in the sports department of the *Newark Evening News*. I knew them all well since I had worked as a copy boy at the paper on Saturdays and in the summers during my last two years at Rutgers, in 1950 and 1951.

Our chief sports columnist, Hy Goldberg, who later became one of my lifelong friends,* thought Weiss acted too hastily in trading Jensen; he was probably right. He felt that if given time Jackie may very well have adjusted to the Grand Canyon in left and become a star in New York as he later became in Boston. Jensen, after all, was a superb two-sport athlete at the University of California, an All-America halfback and an outstanding pitcher and strong-armed outfielder.

Weiss was looking for power and speed in the Yankees outfield and was counting on Mantle and Jensen, both rookies of great promise. (Jackie was technically a rookie, having had but 70 at-bats for the Yankees at the end of the 1950 season.) "Weiss was just like Yawkey in that he didn't want black players on his team," Hy said during a bull session with other writers. "He was sure Jensen and Mantle would help him keep the team white."

He wasn't saying anything the entire sports world didn't know. Here it was four years after Robinson and Doby were signed and the Yankees didn't even have a black in their farm system. Weiss finally relented and signed Elston Howard in 1955. Yawkey waited another four years before signing Pumpsie Green in 1959.

Howard, as we know, was a Yankee for 11 years as an outfielder and then the first-string catcher when Berra retired. Green spent an undistinguished five seasons with the Red Sox. When he was released in 1963, Green appealed to the NAACP for help in getting reinstated. Nothing ever came of it.

For Weiss the legendary Yankees luck held for him and the team

---

As I relate in my book The Last Years of the Brooklyn Dodgers, *Hy offered me a job writing sports (I was then a reporter with the Newark News) but after seeing how the Mantle-led Yankees treated sportswriters, I declined. I probably would have anyway because of all the night work, travel and having to cover soccer and hockey.*

remained white, even though Mantle was sent down to Kansas City in midseason and Jensen played in only 56 games. Only Stengel knows why, since Jackie hit eight homers and batted .298 in 168 at-bats. Casey, known for his quirkiness and prejudices, may have simply taken a dislike to the kid. How he managed to beat both powerhouses Cleveland and Boston with his regulars is a tribute to his baseball instincts — father of the platoon system, for example.

At the start of spring training DiMaggio signed another $100,000 contract, but all of baseball knew he was no longer worth that kind of money. Outfielders had discovered his arm was gone but it had been so incredibly strong that by many accounts it took almost an entire season before they came to realize he could no longer throw as a center fielder must.

In signing DiMaggio, George Weiss for once did not check his stat books, or maybe sentiment got in the way. Neverthelessw, Joe DiMaggio was no longer the $100,000 ballplayer he once seemed to be or the genuine superstar he was before the war. Joe came back from the war still a superior ballplayer but never again was the .381 and .352 hitter he was before he enlisted in the Air Force in 1943. The service was his undoing, especially the weeks he spent hospitalized in Hawaii, suffering from ulcers.

On the fist of March, as soon as he arrived in Phoenix, Joe announced that he would retire at the end of the season. Often injured late in his career and approaching his 37th birthday, Joe said his decision was not based on physical ailment or complaints, but because he "had withstood the baseball routine" long enough. No one contradicted him but all knew his injuries *were* the reason for his announcement.

"I don't know of any other 13-year men who have played in at least 132 games every year, do you?" he asked the writers. Of course there were, but none of them interrupted him to answer. Managing was not part of his plans, he said. "I have enough trouble taking care of myself without trying to manage 25 ballplayers." For the entire season there were doubts he could turn down another $100,000, but he stuck to his word. Joe D knew he was through as a star ballplayer and his pride wouldn't let him be anything else.[2]

No doubt a Dodgers scouting report was leaked to him in 1951, months before it was published, saying he could no longer stop quickly or throw hard, his running had slowed down, and he no longer had the reflexes to pull a fastball.[3] Joe knew it all and knew it was time to go, the $100,000 be damned.

There were many of us back then who never realized DiMaggio was in decline. It just never occurred to us that the man who hit in 56 straight games was mortal, subject to the same aging process as the rest of us. It may be hard for people who never saw him play to understand the DiMaggio mystique. But for my generation it was always there.

The man transcended race, religion, ethnicity, even baseball loyalties. He was THE ballplayer of our generation and was not until the *Times'* Arthur Daley, in a moving, thoughtful column pointed out that DiMaggio never brought his skills back from the war and by 1951 was nearing the end. It would be the end of 14 years as a Yankee, 17 or 18 if it had not been for World War II. His coming to New York in 1936 at age 22 was the result of Yankees brains and willingness to take a chance.

At age 20 while playing for the San Francisco Seals, Joe suffered a serious knee injury, some accounts say a broken knee, while getting out of a cab. Although he had several outstanding years with the Seals, including a 61-game hitting streak, the Yankees were the only team to make a decent offer for Joe. Other owners feared Joe's knee would not recover enough to enable him to play in the majors.

Yankees owner Jacob Ruppert took a shot, offering the Seals $25,000 and five players. Seals ownership accepted on one condition, that Joe play one more season in San Francisco. In his last summer on the West Coast Joe batted .398 and led the league in RBIs and outfield assists.[4] The Yankees, with their willingness to take a chance, had gotten one of the greatest bargains in the history of the game.

Now, playing out the last and most miserable season of his major league career, Joe had been benched briefly for not hitting when Daley wrote that the war years and the ulcers that wracked him had taken more out of him than most people realized. He wrote that Joe was no longer the Yankee Clipper, the superlative hitter and baserunner and graceful outfielder he had been back in 1942. And true to his word, when George Weiss offered him the same $100,000 for the 1952 season, he turned it down. A class guy, no matter what author Richard Ben Kramer wrote in his undocumented book about DiMaggio. One hundred thousand dollars was a ton of money in 1952.

Even though he had deemed it to be his last year, Joe was determined to give it his best and worked hard to get into shape. Baseball was in the DiMaggio blood, even though their Italian immigrant father had never seen a baseball game as his children grew up in San Francisco.

Three of his sons — Joe, Dominic and Vince — worked on the family fishing boat for a time, but baseball was their passion and they all turned professional. Vince first, then Joe, and finally Dom, who when he played for the Red Sox was probably the best outfielder who ever played for Boston. What's more he was a .298 hitter over 11 seasons.* Vince, the eldest, bounced around the National League for 10 years, a fast and sure-handed center fielder who hit .249 with 125 homers.

The DiMaggio family as a whole was bitter at our government for its treatment of their parents during the war. Like many Japanese and German Americans, they were interned, but Giuseppi DiMaggio was dealt with more harshly than most. He and his wife, Rosalia, were classified as "enemy aliens" and not allowed to travel more than five miles from their home without a permit. Further, Giuseppi Senior was barred from San Francisco Bay where he had fished for a living most of his life. If that weren't enough, his fishing boat was confiscated. This occurred while Joe was serving in the army and Dominic in the navy.

Another major leaguer came out of that small and tightly knit community of Italian fishermen. Dario Lodigiani had a six-year career interrupted by World War II. He was a close friend of the DiMaggios and played his first baseball at Lowell High School in San Francisco as a second baseman beside shortstop Joe DiMaggio. After the war he played ball out in California including years with Oakland and San Francisco of the Pacific Coast League.

It seems strange looking back now but in those days many players in the Pacific Coast League didn't want to go up to the majors. One major leaguer, whom I got to know quite well through interviews, told me his life was actually better after he was sold by Pittsburgh to the then–minor league San Diego Padres. Pete Coscarart had some good years at second base with the Dodgers and Pirates before he was sold to San Diego — blackballed from the majors, in fact, because in 1946 with Pittsburgh he was one of the those outspokenly in favor of joining the American Baseball Guild, a union movement that died quickly.

On a visit to Pete's home in Escondido, down near San Diego, he explained the advantages of playing in the PCL back in the '40s and '50s. "Most people don't know this but the money in the Pacific Coast League was just about as good as in the majors," he said. "Plus the weather's always good out here and the teams were all in California so the travel was not nearly as tough as in the majors.

"I know a number of guys who refused promotion because they didn't

---

There are a number of players in the Hall of Fame — Old Timers selection, mostly — who are not in Dom DiMaggio's class. I give you, for an egregious example, outfielder Harry Hooper with his .281 average and 75 home runs over a 17-year career. A gift from his old friends on the Veterans Committee.

want to leave here," he said, "especially since in most cases money wasn't the incentive that it is today. And in my case you can't beat playing where you live." Pete lived to be 89 and never received a cent of today's benefits that he fought for so many years ago.[5]

Pete's Pacific Coast League is now Triple-A (on a par with Newark and Jersey City up until the 1940s) and lacks the incentives of Pete's day — salaries, weather and closeness. It now has 16 teams, stretching from Washington State to Tennessee and is seen by all players as a stepping stone to the majors.

Like the Yankees, the Giants were also training in Phoenix, but unlike the Bombers they were a team in transition. Since Durocher had taken over the team in 1948, he had been changing it gradually from the slow sluggers of 1947 who hit a then-record 221 homers but finished in fourth place. In place of Johnny Mize, Willard Marshall, Sid Gordon and Walker Cooper, Leo now had Whitey Lockman, Don Mueller, Willie Mays and Monte Irvin, men who could move on the bases and in the field. Bobby Thomson, fast as ever, was an outfielder/third baseman, replaced by Mays in center field. In '47 he had to be fast and quick out there in center with Gordon on one side of him and Marshall on the other. Only a Willie Mays could move a man as good as Thomson out of center field. But it was a lucky move on Durocher's part since Thomson proved to be a great third baseman.

Walker Cooper was a problem that Durocher solved within months. Cooper was not a Durocher–type ballplayer. At times he seemed lackadaisical. During one Giants-Dodgers game I attended at the Polo Grounds in early 1948, he practically ignored a pop fly behind home plate. I remember him looking back over his shoulder but never getting out of his crouch as the ball landed at least 10 feet from the screen. Ott benched him immediately but there was no further disciplinary action. If anyone ever really said "Nice guys finish last," they may well have been thinking of Mel.

Durocher traded Cooper to Cincinnati early in 1949, replacing him with Wes Westrum, seven years younger and a great defensive catcher. Cooper hung on for another nine years because of his hitting —.285 over 18 years, excellent numbers for a catcher. Westrum was never much of a hitter (.217 lifetime) but was excellent on defense as well as a student of the game. He coached and managed for 17 years in the big leagues after he retired as a player, leaving the game with one of the great quotes on baseball: "It's like church," he said. "Many attend but few understand."[6]

By 1950 Westrum was handling a superb pitching staff assembled by Durocher. But here too Leo got lucky again. In '49 he had the nucleus of a fine pitching staff in Larry Jansen, Dave Koslo and Monte Kennedy. During spring training the following year up from Mexico came Sal Maglie, one of the jumpers who didn't like playing south of the border. Sal had played for Mel Ott in 1945 and was thus Giants property. He was only 4–5 that year and was a pariah on returning but Durocher made him one of his front four with startling results.

Maglie, just 23, became the star of the staff at 18–4 with a 2.71 ERA. From 1950 until he was traded to the Cleveland Indians, he was 81–33, one of the best stretches by any pitcher in baseball history. One of his best years was the year we're covering as he led the Giants to their improbable pennant, pacing the staff at 23–5 with a 2.71 ERA.

Thus as the '51 training camp opened, Durocher had molded the Giants into his type team. Gone were Johnny Mize, Willard Marshall and Sid Gordon, all fine ballplayers but slow, not the Durocher type. Those three were the big Giants hitters in 1947 when the team clubbed 221 homers and finished in fourth place. By 1951 they had been replaced by Bobby Thomson, Don Mueller and Willie Mays, good hitters and fast.

One more move, replacing .220-hitting first baseman Tookie Gilbert with Carroll (Whitey) Lockman, gave Durocher the team that proved to be this year's pennant winner, with a little help from Herman Franks, Sal Yvars and a telescope. Whitey was fast, sure-handed, and proved to be one of the best first basemen in the league. Out of Lowell, North Carolina, he was with the Giants from the plodding years in the mid–1940s for almost 11 seasons, including the pennant-winning 1951 and 1954 seasons. Without his key double in the ninth inning of the deciding game, the Giants would probably not have won the playoff.

To me Whitey was one of those Giants who had no shame for his team's cheating their way to the pennant. In fact he had the gall to be quoted in Bobby Thomson's book *The Giants Win the Pennant* as saying, "Over the long haul the records show that the Dodgers had the best team of the entire era. But from August 12th to the end of the season in 1951 we were better than they were."[7] Of course, Whitey, the telescope being your 10th man.

The Dodgers started spring training with one of the best, if not THE best infield in baseball history. Hodges at first, Robinson at second, Reese at short and Billy Cox, a converted shortstop who had been involved in what turned out to the best trade in Branch Rickey's career, at third.

On December 8, 1947, Rickey traded Dixie Walker, Hal Gregg and Vic Lombardi to Pittsburgh for Preacher Roe, Cox and Gene Mauch. The deal didn't cause much excitement since, with the possible exception of Cox, the players involved were not what they once were. Dixie was nearing retirement and Gregg and Lombardi were used as fifth or sixth starters.

On the Pittsburgh side Roe was a 34–47 left-hander of no particular distinction while Cox would have been acceptable on any team in the majors: a .274-hitting shortstop with one of the great arms in baseball.

As soon as he arrived in Brooklyn, Roe's career gradually started turning around. His first year he was 12–8 with a 2.63 ERA, a figure he had approached only once previously and that was in 1945 wartime ball. He didn't reveal until after he retired that in his Dodgers years he had mastered the spitball and had almost complete control of it.

The other Dodgers knew about the spitter since Roe would tip the team whenever it was coming. "When Preacher went to his cap with two pitching fingers together that was the signal," Carl Furillo revealed years later. "If he went to his cap with fingers spread he was faking."[8]

Preacher was born in 1915 in Ash Flat, Arkansas, and started his career with Pittsburgh, where he pitched from 1944 until the end of 1947 when the Dodgers bought him. Through the years he was one of Brooklyn's most dependable starters in the team's history, going 93–37, with ERAs usually hovering around 3.00 before he retired in 1954. That 93–37 record represents a winning percentage of .715, one of the highest ever.

Roe always played the hillbilly from the Ozarks, masking the fact that in the offseason he was a high school mathematics teacher, his father a doctor and his brother a school superintendent. As a pitcher he was a mystery — 6'2", skinny at 170 pounds, without a fastball to go with his decent curveball. The spitter may have been the answer.

But there was something else. Casey Stengel thought he was one of the smartest pitchers he ever managed against, expert at pitching to spots and weaknesses. And he was clever. Through the years no one but the Dodgers knew of his spitter. Once in a while the umpires would ask for the ball, but none of them ever caught him.

Billy Cox was a marvel, not only because of his play but because of the physical handicap he overcame to make the big leagues. Billy was in the army during World War II, serving mostly in the South Pacific where in his 18 months on Guadalcanal he caught a malarial germ that stayed with him for the rest of his life.

Once a robust 5'10", he was but 130 pounds at the end of the war and played during his entire career at about 150 pounds, a weight that sometimes forced him to the bench to rest for a few games. But when he played, he was magic at third base. Many times on television and at Ebbets

Once a hearty 180 pounds at 5'10", Billy Cox caught malaria during the battle of Guadalcanal and for the rest of his life was a scrawny 150 pounds, as shown. Nevertheless, for his seven years with the Dodgers he became one of the best third basemen in history, though limited by his recurring illness to an average of 106 games a year. When traded to Baltimore he retired at age 36 in 1955, a career .262 hitter.

Field I saw him field a hot grounder on the third base line and then *look the ball over* before rocketing it to Hodges at first base, such was the arm.

He has been compared to Brooks Robinson, Mike Schmidt and Aurelio Rodriguez as the premier third basemen of modern times. I guess the comparison is a just one, but all I know is that during Billy's years at third he had no peer. In Roger Kahn's *Boys of Summer*, Pee Wee Reese described Cox as "the greatest glove and the least likely looking major league infielder he'd ever known." Fine words from the Captain.

Cox was one of those who never left his hometown when his career was over. That was Newport, a small town in central Pennsylvania where for *Boys of Summer* Kahn interviewed him in the early seventies as Billy was tending bar there. Kahn ended his chapter on Billy by terming him "the most glorious glove on the most glorious team that ever played baseball in the sunlight of Brooklyn." A stern and balanced editor was needed here.

As spring training was ending and the teams barnstormed north, basketball was in trouble of its own making, but baseball, innocent of any wrongdoing, was even worse off, its minor leagues in desperate trouble. New Jersey baseball, both black and white, was particularly hard hit. For the first time within memory there was no team from the Garden State heading north to start the season.

The Jersey City Giants had folded the previous September, joining the Newark Bears and the black Newark Eagles, both having gone under the year before. These had been elite minor league clubs, with Jersey City the farm team of the New York Giants, Newark of the New York Yankees, and the Eagles one of the biggest draws in black baseball.

The spread of television had killed them all, white and black. The Jersey City figures tell what happened eventually to most minor league clubs. In 1947 the Giants' farm club drew 337,000 paid. Just three years later, as the Yankees, Dodgers and Giants began televising games almost daily, they were down to just 63,000. That was 1950, the year they closed down.

The invasion of television was especially tragic for black baseball, as it was virtually wiped out during the late '40s and through the '50s. Sportswriters called it "Shadow Ball," not for any color connotation but because even though it thrived in parts of the country, white America knew so little about it.

I remember growing up in Newark in the 1930s and being only vaguely aware that black baseball players were at Ruppert Stadium at times when the Newark Bears were out of town. They got some coverage in the *Newark Evening News* and the *Star-Eagle*, but I, like most other Newark

Bear fans, paid little attention and was therefore unaware that there was great baseball being played when the Kansas City Monarchs or the Homestead Grays were in town to play the Newark Eagles. I could have seen Josh Gibson and the other greats had I known, for Newark was a safe city then and I would have been welcome at a black ball game.

This game of black baseball was hidden Americana that went as far back as the 1860s when black amateurs were playing in Brooklyn, Washington, D.C., and parts of the Midwest and Northeast, even before the Emancipation Proclamation. The game soon became a way of life that lasted almost a century for all those men who for all those years were barred from the major leagues.

In the early days of professional baseball there was never an official racial ban in most parts of the country. From the 1870s until about 1900 there were various instances of colored men, as they were called then, playing on white teams. The Walker brothers, Fleet and Welday, played in the original American Association, then a major league, and they were not the only ones.

One of the first known bans in a major league involved John McGraw of future Giants fame. He saw Charles Grant playing second base on a black team and wanted him for his Baltimore Orioles. Grant had straight hair and high cheekbones so McGraw signed him, passing him off as a full-blooded Cherokee Indian.

Grant was therefore nicknamed "Charey Tokohama" and practiced with the Orioles all spring until Charles Comiskey, owner of the White Sox, found out about the deception and caused Grant's release. It was probably from then on that the ban, though unofficial, was recognized throughout white baseball.

All during his career McGraw was color blind as far as baseball was concerned but he couldn't do anything about it. After his death in 1934, his wife found among his papers a list of black players he wanted but was unable to sign. "Mugsy," as he was called, became a powerful figure in the game, but never that powerful. He not only could not hire black players, but was unsuccessful in trying to keep the Yankees out of New York.

Many blacks had hoped to be recruited after World War I, during which a number had served bravely, notably the 369th Infantry Regiment known as the "Harlem Hellfighters," honored with 11 citations while on loan to the French army. They would have had better luck if someone other than Kenesaw Mountain Landis had been appointed baseball commissioner after the 1919 World Series fix.

Landis never made his feelings official, of course, but every owner knew he was adamantly against blacks in organized baseball. Branch Rickey said a number of times that he waited until after Landis died before signing Jackie Robinson because he knew Landis would not permit it.

In a strange twist, it was Robinson's signing that was the killing blow to black teams and leagues by opening the majors to such black stars as Monte Irvin, Larry Doby and in 1948 Satchel Paige. Others soon followed, including some brief flashes like Sam Jethroe and Dan Bankhead, both past their prime but understandably falsified their ages for a chance at the majors.

Thus it was that the Eagles, Monarchs, Grays, Baltimore Elite Giants and their leagues went under, leaving hundreds of black players on the sidelines, their fans at home watching black stars on television. The saddest epitaph for those black players who never got a shot was a saying by Satchel Paige: "There were a lot of Josh Gibsons, there were a lot of Satchel Paiges."

Possibly so, but too many people, sportswriters included, feel that just about every black player of those days could have made the major leagues. That was the impression I got while watching Ken Burns' television documentaries on baseball. In truth, although there were undoubtedly many black players who had major league potential, black baseball was probably on a par with the Triple-A teams, such as the Newark Bears and Kansas City Blues, or maybe even Double-A. No one will ever know. Larry Doby comes to mind here, a genuine major league star who was hitting .414 in the Negro League but was a .283 lifetime hitter in the majors. There was and always had been a big difference, no matter what today's revisionists claim.

In the long run, however, it wouldn't have made any difference. Television became so strong that all the low minor leagues were killed, white and black. This is reflected in major league attendance over a mere five-year span. In 1948 almost 21 million seats were sold, a figure that dipped to 14.4 million in 1953, as people watched baseball at home on television.

Attendance began to rise again in 1954, possibly due to franchise shifts and television becoming commonplace. But I think after a few years fans went back to the game to see the players live again instead of always settling for the sterility of TV game after game. If you've ever walked up a baseball ramp, stepped out into the aisle and been pleasantly startled by the green of the grass, the immensity of the stadium and the sheer beauty of the whole scene, you'll know what I mean.

And it doesn't matter where the stadium is or the level of baseball played in it. The grass in Ruppert Stadium in Newark was just as green as it was in Ebbets Field, the dimensions of the diamond the same, the players young and old, as always. I can see them now, the heroes of my youth: Charlie Keller, Tommy Padden, Bob Seeds, Georgie Sharein, Buddy Blair, Leo Nonnenkamp, Hank Majeski, George Washburn, Johnny Lindell, Aaron Robinson and Alex Campouris among them.

To me they were stars, and I didn't realize that some were coming up and others going down in the baseball world. I didn't know, for instance, that Padden had caught for six years with the Pirates before he was sold to Newark or that Kampouris had been a second baseman for more than four seasons with Cincinnati and two with the Giants before being sent down.

Thinking of Kampouris brings to mind my worst experience as a baseball fan. I had just turned 13 as I waited outside the Newark Bears clubhouse entrance hoping for autographs. It all started well as I approached Montreal's Tommy Holmes as he was talking to his mother. I didn't interrupt, and as he looked in my direction and saw the autograph book, he beckoned and signed with a smile and graciously patted me on the shoulder.

After that I was golden for awhile. I then got Ed Levy, Mickey Witek, Scharein, Padden, Blair, Walt Judnich, Montreal catcher Joe Cratcher and, to top it all, manager Johnny Neun and the Bears' announcer, Earl Harper. Then Kampouris walked out of the clubhouse door. Alex was a power hitter and at the time was tied for the league lead in home runs, 36 as I recall. But that day he had struck out four times; maybe I should have known the mood he'd be in.

I approached him innocently and was about to ask for his autograph when he angrily waved me away saying, "Get the hell away from me kid" as he walked toward a taxi. This was one of my heroes, and for the moment I teared up and then got angry myself. As he was closing the cab door I said, "Yeah, you're the home run king but you're also the strikeout king." He leaned out of the window and shouted, "You little son of a bitch" and took a swing at me but missed as the cab started to move. It wasn't until years later that I realized the pressure players like Kampouris were under as they were trying to get back to the majors. But back then how was a 13-year-old kid to know about that?

Thinking back on those autographs, I only read recently that Ed Levy's real name was Edward Clarence Whitner out of Birmingham, Alabama. The Yankees persuaded him to change his name in the hopes of attracting more Jewish fans to the Stadium. It didn't work, Ed being with the Yanks for two wartime seasons. It was a shame that he couldn't hit (.215) because when he was with Newark he was a very nice man. I remember talking to him and looking up to his 6'6" inch height as he signed my autograph book.

As New York's teams were heading north, the Dodgers from Vero Beach, the Giants from St. Petersburg and the Yankees from Phoenix, they were traveling in what is now the old-fashioned way, by train to Grand Central Station, the crossroads as the saying went "of a million private lives." Sleepers, club cars, evening card games and just plain proximity resulted in a team camraderie unknown since the advent of the jet age, airplanes that ruined baseball as we used to know it. Teammates could no longer sit in the club car, have a few drinks, talk baseball and then head for a decent night's sleep.

It was the jets that opened the way to the West Coast, something prop planes were too slow to do at a time when Chicago was six hours from New York and Los Angeles 11 or 12, depending on weather conditions that the later jets could simply fly over.

California was now opened to baseball. Instead of forming a third major league as the West should have done, the owners allowed O'Malley to steal the Dodgers while the Giants went along. Stoneham, his Giants nearing bankruptcy, had intended to move to Minneapolis but saw the same gold on the West Coast that O'Malley did. They joined hands because the other owners made it clear that one club could not go west by itself, that there had to be at least two teams on the West Coast to make the travel economics feasible.

Thus, players now spend half their careers at 35,000 feet, strapped into seats, the leisurely camaraderie of train travel gone forever. Instead of just two teams going to the West Coast together, it would have been an ideal time for a Western League to open the entire area to baseball while mixing air and train time in civilized proportions.

But Walter O'Malley at the time was the most powerful man in baseball and he wanted Los Angeles for himself, not some geographically sensible third league. The makeup of that league could have been San Diego, Los Angeles, San Francisco, Seattle, Phoenix, Denver, Houston and Dallas, eight teams, just like the East. But the "Lords of Baseball," as Dick Young used to say, were led around by their noses by O'Malley when it came to expansion.

On March 11 the Lords of Baseball got their revenge when they told baseball commissioner Albert Chandler that his contract would not be renewed. Chandler was baseball's second commissioner, succeeding Judge Kenesaw Mountain Landis, who was appointed to the newly created post after the 1919 scandal in which the White Sox threw the World Series to the Cincinniti Reds. Chandler was one of the few in that job who sided with the players when he felt it necessary and those are the times that doomed him. For example, when he concurred in the signing of Jackie Robinson, a few of the Klan-type owners never forgave him and waited patiently to get him. That day had finally arrived.

Chandler, one-time governor and then senator from Kentucky, was nicknamed "Happy" in college because of his jovial attitude. This carried over into baseball where he was known as the "Player's Commissioner," which further riled the owners. Partly because of this, Chandler's reign was more tumultuous than any within memory. He was faced with the signing of Jackie Robinson, the Mexican jumpers — those ballplayers who believed Jorge Pasquel's promises of easy living and high salaries south of the border — and, most seriously, Danny Gardella's anti-trust suit that threatened baseball's reserve clause.

The Gardella case was historic and interesting not only because it was the first real challenge to the reserve clause, but because the owners, feeling safe behind Justice Oliver Wendell Holmes' 1922 decision defending it, brushed it off as an inconsequential action by a wartime ballplayer trying to hustle some money.

Justice Holmes had written the majority opinion in *Federal Baseball Club v. the National League*, ruling that baseball is an "amusement" rather than a business. This meant that a schedule of games between clubs operating in various states did not constitute "interstate commerce." Thus, under the umbrella of the court's decision, the reserve clause survived for a number of years to come.

From the owners' standpoint the clause was vital in that if players were free to offer their services in a competitive market, salaries would escalate dramatically, as they are rising today. The owners' worst fears have come to pass and those hurt the most have been the fans, now paying ridiculous prices for tickets.

Gardella, a wartime New York Giant, was one of the first of the "jumpers" to the Mexican League but found conditions down there unacceptable and decided to return to New York. He sued in late 1947 when he learned he was barred from organized baseball because of his defection to Mexico.

The Mexican war on American baseball was one of the saddest periods in the history of the game and was caused primarily by our reserve clause. Jorge and Bernardo Pasquel, rumored to be from one of Mexico's wealthiest families and the driving force behind the Mexican Baseball League, knew that many major leaguers were unhappy with being tied to one club forever and the salaries the owners dictated.

Their raids started in February 1946, when they offered Brooklyn's Mickey Owen and Luis Olmo "fabulous salaries and luxurious living conditions," as *Life Magazine* described the negotiations.[9] Then some future big names started going south: Vern Stevens of the Browns; Max Lanier of the Cardinals; Sal Maglie of the Giants; White Sox farmhand Alex Carrasquel; and journeyman Ace Adams, a wartime pitcher for the Giants. Eventually there were 18 players from the big leagues and a number of minor leaguers in Mexico. Efforts to lure the likes of Stan Musial failed and finally when the Pasquels offered Pete Reiser $100,00 for three years and tried to sign Phil Rizzuto, both the Dodgers and Yankees sued, asking for restraining orders to prevent their players from "unlawfully breaking their contracts."

They lost, but as things turned out it really didn't matter. The big promises by the Pasquels — the high salaries and luxurious living — proved to be just that, promises. Either the Pasquels didn't have their rumored $60 million fortune or they refused to spend it as advertised.

Stephens was one of the first to return, jumping his five-year contract and leaving Mexico without his bonus after just two days. He told the press that he found conditions unacceptable and that he was glad to go back to the St. Louis Browns. After his departure, several others started leaving until there were just a few diehards left, the most important being Max Lanier and Mickey Owen, who would soon leave for the States.

According to Owen it was somewhat scary as he was making his way to the border, traveling with his wife under an assumed name. He told a reporter for *The Sporting News* that under his own name his life would have been in danger when the Pasquels found out he had left.

"The natural route for us would have been through Laredo but I never would have made it there," he said. "One of the Pasquel brothers lived there and I didn't want to take the chance. Those Pasquel brothers are the real power in Mexico no matter what anyone else tells you."

During the interview Mickey said his reasons for leaving were the terrible playing conditions, broken promises and just plain homesickness. There was also a feeling of isolation, not knowing the language and, not least of all, the glamour of playing in the major leagues. Mickey held out down there for four months, second to Lanier, who stayed through 1947.[10]

As most of the Mexican jumpers were recrossing the border, Gardella's suit was dismissed, with the owners then confident that the reserve clause was unassailable, that once a player signed for a team he was signed for life. But at least some of the owners should have known the clause was vulnerable, for as respected as he was, Justice Holmes' reasoning was on very shaky ground. Calling baseball an amusement and not a business was ludicrous at a time when the baseball business would soon pay Babe Ruth $80,000 a season based on thousands upon thousands of fans paying their way into the ballparks.

It was bad enough calling baseball an amusement rather than a business, but ruling that a team from one state playing one from another state with ticket money involved does not constitute interstate commerce seems nonsensical. One could conclude that only Justice Holmes' tremendous prestige and worldwide reputation kept any number of ballplayers from attacking the reserve clause until Gardella came along some 25 years later.

Two years after the Gardella case was dismissed the U.S. Court of Appeals dropped a bombshell on the owners on February 9, 1949, by reinstating Gardella's case, with Judge Learned Hand's written opinion that if baseball is declared a monopoly, the reserve clause must go. The owners, now in a panic, took a desperate but successful step: they bribed Gardella into dropping his suit. The sum, it was revealed later, was $300,000, money that didn't do anything for them except buy them some time.[11]

The reserve clause died a lingering death. Gardella's suit was withdrawn on February 8, 1949, leaving the owners untroubled until the arrival of Marvin Miller some 20 years later as head of the Major League Baseball Players Association with offices on Park Avenue in New York.

Miller was a brilliant labor negotiator, having started his career at the National Labor Relations Board, and it was his skill and brains that ended the reserve clause. In 1974 he persuaded pitchers Andy Messersmith of the Los Angeles Dodgers and Dave McNally of the Baltimore Orioles to play for one year without a contract on the chance that they could then be declared free agents. It was a gamble that Miller won when arbitrator Peter Seitz in effect killed the reserve clause by declaring both ballplayers free agents, enabling them to sign with any ball club of their choice.

Looking back, Miller is one of the most important men in baseball history, the man who changed the financial structure of the game. After the Seitz ruling was upheld in the federal courts, player salaries started skyrocketing. One of the first beneficiaries was Reggie Jackson who in 1977 signed a contract with the New York Yankees for five years and $3 million.

For all the good Miller did for the players, he has twice been denied Hall of Fame honors, each time falling below the 75 percent of the votes needed. I'm not surprised at the ingratitude of the players since similar things have happened to a number of players who should be at Cooperstown. But overlooking Miller is unforgivable.

While the owners breathed easier after preserving their precious reserve clause by bribing Gardella, some were still seething over the Robinson signing. They were joined by the others when Commissioner Chandler sided with the players in their successful fight against the owners for a pension plan. The lords had had enough. After dumping Chandler by a nine-to-seven vote, they later hired National League president Ford Frick.

Chandler was not the perfect commissioner. His handling of the Durocher suspension was seen as siding with owner Larry MacPhail, but the desegregation of baseball and his efforts for the pension fund mark him as one of the best, one who was looking out for the improvement of the game rather than the sensibilities and pockets of the owners.

And in the Durocher case, whether Chandler mishandled it or not, he was right. Durocher should have been suspended, even barred for life, for past serious transgressions: constant gambling, hanging out with mobsters and, worst of all, once luring a heckling fan under the stands where he beat him with a blackjack so badly he had to be hospitalized.

Over the years since Chandler departed it has become evident that his leaving was a tragedy for the game, but one that could not be avoided. The owners wanted control through a commissioner who would comply with their wishes. They got him in Ford Frick, and in the ensuing years the commissioner's office has been degraded to the point where a former owner of the Milwaukee Brewers is now in the office.

Chandler was unfortunate to be appointed at a time the owners had had enough of the dictatorial Landis years. Baseball was in no trouble in 1945 and the owners wanted more say in all matters. He was fortunate, however in that he was a slick politician, having been governor and senator of Kentucky and was thus able to handle the owners for some six years while resentments built up. He was the players' commissioner for years and got away with it at the owners' expense until a majority of them had had enough.

Some of the Dixiecrat-type owners were alarmed early when Chandler approved the signing of Jackie Robinson. They could do nothing to prevent him from playing with Montreal in the International League. But in early 1947, when it became apparent that Rickey would promote him, the owners in a secret ballot voted 15 to 1 to bar him from the majors.[12] Chandler's role in this was deeply resented. What further made his end inevitable was his approval of the Players Association's pension increases and his awarding them part of baseball's broadcasting revenues.

This deep-seated bitterness among the owners towards Chandler was revealed in an off-handed remark by Cincinnati Reds president Warren

Giles, who represented the other owners in a June 20 press conference on a possible new commissioner. Chandler, he said, would be paid until his contract expires "and not a cent more."[13]

The Dodgers ended March by sending five rookies, three of them names, down to their Montreal and Fort Worth farm teams. The baseball names were George Shuba and Ray Moore. The other, Bill Sharman, later became the all-star guard for the great Boston Celtic basketball teams of the Bill Russell years — late 1950s and through the 1960s. Moore had a decent 11-year career as a reliever starting with a 10–10 season on woeful 57–97 Baltimore team, which was in only its second year in the majors. Playing for mostly second-division teams, he ended with a 63–59 record and a career 4.06 ERA.

Shuba is the perfect example of how a ballplayer lived under the old reserve system where a player was signed for life, playing for the one club or not playing at all. In his case the situation was worse than others since the Dodgers in his day were loaded with talent. As Carl Erskine once said about why he hid his shoulder injury for his entire career, "The Dodgers had a bunch of pitchers, hard-throwing guys in the minors who could take my place in a day. When you faltered, you were gone."[14] A bit of exaggeration but not that far off the mark.

George told Roger Kahn that in 1947 he hit 21 homers and drove in 100 runs playing for Mobile. "Next spring at Vero Beach Rickey says he's sending me back, that I have great power but not enough average. It's 1948. I bat .389. He sends me down to Mobile again. Nice batting, he says, but your power fell off."[15] By the time he was brought up for good, the knee that dogged him for years came up with him.

George, well liked around the league, would have been paid several million a year in today's baseball market since his knee would have had much better treatment. As it was, he hit .259 lifetime and was .266 as a pinch-hitter.

As March ended so did the career of famous lefty Johnny Vander Meer. The only man ever to pitch back-to-back no-hitters loafed at the wrong time for the wrong manager. Johnny was with the Cubs for spring training when Frankie Frisch found him sunbathing after Frisch had told him to do several laps to strengthen his legs. His release was immediate and unconditional. "I don't want any lackadaisical players on my club," Frisch said, after ordering Vander Meer to turn in his uniform. Frisch knew what he was doing, however. Johnny wasn't picked up by an other major league team because he had nothing left.

A factor in the dismissal and Vander Meer not being given a last shot by another team was that he wasn't well liked, particularly among his own teammates. When major league veteran Bill Werber joined the Reds in 1939, he was surprised at the resentment most of the Reds felt toward Vander Meer. Team morale sank when he pitched because his teammates didn't want him on the mound. Werber added that it could have been because he was considered cheap and a moocher.

Said Werber, "I was told he would take a cab ride or eat with teammates in a restaurant and have only a $50 bill on him. He'd promise to pay but seldom if ever did. He'd even borrow from rookies, who could ill afford it, and never pay them back."[16]

In his prime with Cincinnati, Johnny had become nationally famous for his twin no-hitters, acclaimed by that day's adoring sportswriters as the greatest feat in sports history. But was it? The first no-hitter was genuine, a day game in good weather between Cincinnati and the Braves at Crosley Field. But the second four days later on June 15, was the first night game ever played at Ebbets Field and was dubious in the minds of the losing Dodgers players, although they never announced their discontent publicly.

After years had passed, Dodgers second baseman Pete Coscarart spoke out in an interview with me, expressing his and his teammates feelings. Press accounts pointed out that Vander Meer had not been sharp that night, having been helped by a number of great fielding plays. With two outs in the ninth, for example, he walked three Dodgers but his no-hitter was saved when, with all runners going, Leo Durocher popped up, ending the game.

"I'm not taking anything away from Johnny," Coscarart said. "A no-hitter is a no-hitter. But it was the first night game ever at Ebbets and we weren't used to night ball, especially with lighting not nearly as good as today's. All of us on both teams had some trouble picking up the ball as it left the pitcher's hand."[17]

Although it was the first night game in Brooklyn, it was only the eighth in major league history. Larry MacPhail scheduled the first in Cincinnati in 1935 and then followed that with six more. From seeing newsreels I would say Coscarart was right. The lights, at least until after the war, weren't nearly up to today's standards.

Today a disciplinarian like Frankie Frisch, firing a legend out of hand, probably wouldn't last a week in the majors. One cross word with one of today's millionaire players and he would be long gone. In this respect the game has changed drastically, and not for the better.

CHAPTER FOUR

April

With the Dodgers barnstorming their way north from Florida, it was just five years since Jackie Robinson broke organized baseball's color line. At that time, in 1946, Robinson and the rest of the Montreal Royals arrived in Jacksonville for an exhibition against the Jersey City Giants. To prevent him from playing, city officials ordered that Robinson be locked out of their ballpark as townspeople looked on with approval, even after both teams decided to cancel the game.

By early April of 1951, the Southern baseball world had turned upside down. They couldn't get enough of Robinson. As the Atlanta fans were waiting to welcome him, he had played two nights before at Savannah's Grayson Stadium before a standing-room–only crowd. And he was cheered as he went 2-for-3, including a double.

On Sunday April 8 the Dodgers arrived in Atlanta and walked onto the field to play the Crackers before an overflow crowd of 17,522, a shocking number considering they couldn't play there previously because of Robinson's presence. Again, Jackie is packing them in down in the solid South.

An another shock was their opposing pitcher, Kirby Higbe, the former Dodgers great who along with Whit Wyatt pitched Brooklyn to the pennant in 1941, Kirby going 22–9 and Wyatt 22–10. On this day Kirby reached back to his youth and went the full nine innings to beat the Dodgers, 8–6. Higbe was 36 years old and had ended his career the year before with a 3.69 career ERA and 118 wins against 101 losses. While he lasted, he was one of the great pitchers in Brooklyn Dodgers history, posting a 70–38 record while helping pitch them to the pennant in '41 and the playoff in '46.

Higbe was one of the stars of the National League when he went into the army after the 1943 season, but he never received the star treatment many other athletes were given. He was trained as a rifleman and fought through Europe until Germany surrendered, then was shipped to the Philippines in preparation for the invasion of Japan. But Higbe said years later that he enjoyed the whole thing, adding, "I wouldn't take anything for my war experience."

Kirby had one great season left in him, his 17–8 role in 1946, the first playoff year. Then in 1947 he requested a trade, telling Rickey he would not play on a team with a black man. He landed in Pittsburgh, where he was joined later by Dixie Walker, another of the signers of the anti–Robinson petition. Dixie recanted, too late to save his Dodgers career, but Higbe was adamant.

"If I could have looked ahead and seen all the changes that were coming, I still would have done what I did," he said. "I was brought up a Southerner, and I was brought up to stand by what you said and believed in even if you were the last one standing there."[1]

As the team resumed its trip north, Dressen took over again after having spent most of March in the hospital with pneumonia and other respiratory ailments. Almost at once, and unnoticed by the beat writers, a situation had developed that would cause trouble ahead and emerge as a major factor in Brooklyn losing the pennant: The team had no pitching coach. Dressen didn't think he needed one.

The team had plenty of coaches, but none who knew anything about the finer points of pitching. The front office hired Ted Lyons, a 260-game winner and future Hall of Famer, but he didn't last long, saying after he left that Dressen rarely talked to him and never asked his advice. The Dodgers of those years weren't big on pitching coaches, which partly explains Dressen's ignoring Ted Lyons.

So, in the most complex area of the game, Dressen did not want expert advice, but depended on his eight years of experience as a major league second basemen to evaluate and advise his pitching staff. Charlie thought he knew enough to be his own pitching coach, with occasional help from his coaching staff of Cookie Lavagetto, Bobby Bragan, Clyde Sukeforth, Joe Becker, Jake Pitler, Billy Herman, and backup catcher Rube Walker. That list included four catchers and three infielders, not one qualified to advise or judge a major league pitcher.

The men he leaned on most were Bragan, Sukeforth and Joe Becker, all catchers. Again, catchers know few of the nuances of pitching. "The only thing a catcher can tell you is whether your stuff was good when he caught it," Carl Erskine said in a SABR *National Pastime* interview. "Ted Lyons left because Dressen would rarely talk to him. Dressen didn't want any advice about pitching so he didn't seek advice from Lyons, and that was typical (of Charlie)." In analyzing the problem, Erskine explained that catchers can't help if the trouble is in a pitcher's motion, striding or any other mechanical problem. This is especially true under game conditions when pitcher and catcher are more than 60 feet apart.

The most egregious example of depending on a catcher is Sukeforth, in that playoff-deciding ninth inning against the Giants, choosing Branca to relieve Newcombe. Thomson had hit a few long balls off Branca, but Erskine in warming up had thrown a curve in the dirt so Sukeforth recommended Ralph. A great and gutsy pitcher throws a ball in the dirt and is then overlooked — one curve in the dirt! Sukeforth was soon fired, the last survivor of the Rickey era. But Dressen made the final decision, even while knowing from years past that Branca wasn't always there at clutch time. Years later Carl was asked what pitch was the best he ever threw. "The curveball I bounced in the Polo Grounds bullpen," he replied.[2]

The Dodgers had now reached Greensboro, North Carolina, about halfway to Ebbets Field, when the front office finally gave up on Rex Barney, for whom the word "fireballer" was no cliché. Rex was put on the waiver list, thus ending his erratic and sad Dodgers career. He was only 26 years old and had given every indication, including a no-hitter against the Giants, that he would be one of the great fastball pitchers in baseball history.

But in 1950 he couldn't find the plate and no one knew why. Rickey even had him undergo psychiatric treatment, such was his potential. He was without doubt one of the fastest pitchers who ever lived, and the Dodgers held on until there was no doubt his case was hopeless. In his last start, on April 9 in Greensboro, he threw 54 pitches, nine strikes and 45 balls, walking 11. This was his last in a series of equally dismal outings.

"In all my years in baseball," Chuck Dressen said, "I never saw a pitcher with so much who went so completely to pieces so fast." Rex wound up with a nice career, however, as a sportscaster for the Baltimore Orioles.

The rest of the pitching staff seemed in reasonable shape as Erskine was beaten by Robin Roberts, 6–2, on Opening Day at Ebbets Field. Behind Erskine the primary starters were Branca, Hatten, Newcombe, Palica, and Roe. Clyde King was the number one reliever who, with Clem Labine, would be an innocent observer as the season was ending so sadly. Joe Hatten, a 59–39 starter for Brooklyn, was soon gone, and a number of pitchers made a brief passage though the dugout: Johnny Schmitz, Phil Haugstead, Earl Mossor, Bud Podbielan and Chris Van Cuyk among them.

The Ebbets Field pitching corps was not a tranquil one, however. There was the ill feeling between Dressen and Branca, who had despised one another in the past because, again, of Dressen's tactlessness. Leo Durocher aside, how many managers are stupid enough to criticize a pitcher on another team, even in another league? Most would feel the comments would be pointless.

It started in 1947, strangely enough, when Ralph, a local boy out of Mount Vernon, was 21 years old and the 21–12 star of the Brooklyn staff. After such a breakout year at that age, there is really no explaining Ralph Branca. As the Dodgers' big winner, he pitched the opening game of the 1947 World Series, went four perfect innings and then fell apart as the Yankees scored five runs to win, 5–3, behind Spec Shea and Joe Page.

For some reason, and no one has ever given a logical explanation for it, Branca was never the same. The magnificent young pitcher of 1947, with all the physical gifts bestowed on him by his ancestors—6'3" and 220 pounds—became a journeyman instead of a star. Among indifferent seasons he was 14–9 in 1948 and 13–5 the next year, recording 88 wins in his entire Dodgers career.

In his later years he gave a possible answer to his troubles. He felt that he never got any help in his Dodgers days because there was never a pitching coach to guide him. For example, in an interview with writer Rick Westcott, he revealed that he had never mastered his curveball, that he never learned to shorten and control it "because the team had no pitching coach in those days." So his breaking ball remained "an overhand downer," he told Westcott.[3]

After his World Series debacle, Dressen rubbed it in for no sensible reason. Charlie had been a Yankees coach in '47 before going over to the Yankees the following year. He told Dawson of the *Times* that he knew all about Branca from his days in Flatbush, when Branca "rattled so easily with a man on base." (He didn't explain how Branca, with that flaw, won 21 games that season.)

Soon after, Stan Baumgartner of *The Sporting News* and a former major league pitcher made matter worse by writing, "Did Charley Dressen prove to the baseball world that Branca can't take it; that he has rabbit ears; that when the chips are down he goes up?"[4]

That kind of cruel criticism from a former pitcher for the Philadelphia Phillies, a member of the fraternity, must have been hard to take, especially for a 21-year-old. Branca may have never gotten over it. One result: he often referred to Dressen, the man who senselessly started the whole thing, as "dreck," Yiddish for garbage, or worse. A few years later the criticism might have been justified, but in 1947 all concerned should have remembered that Ralph was only 21.

Carl Erskine was quite another matter. He was a star pitcher with a secret that only his closest friends on the team knew. Coaches, team executives, the press and the baseball world at large were unaware that he pitched for his entire career with a sore right shoulder. How he could pitch for 12 seasons and win 122 games, including two no-hitters, is remarkable, especially since no one in the team's hierarchy had any idea the man was hurting.

"Some days I couldn't get loose but I took my turn anyway," he said in a SABR interview. "The trainers, the front office people, the managers never had a clue as to what I was battling." He never mentioned it, he said, because the Dodgers had a bunch of hard throwing young pitchers in the minors ready to take anyone's place. "When you faltered you're gone, so I gutted it out."[5] After baseball Carl went back to his hometown, Anderson, Indiana, where he eventually became vice president of the local bank.

Erv Palica, one of the most promising pitchers in the Brooklyn organization, went through a stretch of bad pitching, and instead of trying to help him, Dressen cruelly went out of his way on several occasions to publicly humiliate the young right-hander. The mystery of it all was that Palica in the last half of 1950 put together one of the great stretches of clutch pitching within memory. He kept the team in contention from August on, beating the first-place Phils four times under intense pennant pressure, and finished that last part of the season 7–1.

But now in 1951 he had blood pressure problems, his wife was sick, and he was worried about being drafted into the army. He said there was something wrong with his pitching, especially his fastball, that he couldn't figure out. Of course he couldn't figure it. He had no pitching coach, no Ted Lyons to analyze his motion and point out what he was doing wrong.

Dressen's answer was to tell the writers the 23-year-old "was a gutless kid who didn't belong in the majors." Clem Labine tells how he did it again in the clubhouse. "Charley challenged his guts once in front of everybody and Erv lost his confidence entirely." Clem added that Palica "probably had the best stuff of any pitcher I've ever seen."[6] Erv hung on until 1954 with Baltimore but the early promise, the future that once seemed so bright, never came about. Another pitcher was gone because, in effect, the Dodgers' pitching coach was Charlie Dressen, who knew little about pitching.

This ignorance went back beyond his Dodgers managerial days. When he was a coach with the Yankees in the late 1940s, he was generally disliked by the team, especially by the pitching staff. "Dressen thought he knew everything about pitching, and he knew nothing," catcher Charley Silvera told writer Sol Gittleman. "He would stop and tell pitchers what they were doing wrong. He almost ruined Allie Reynolds." Allie agreed, making no secret of his disdain for Dressen. "He would make himself look good by making you look bad."[7]

As the 1951 season started Ebbets Field was 38 years old, a park old beyond its years, unsung and unappreciated as the birthplace of modern American baseball, a fact that every baseball historian I have read has ignored: the first televised major league game; the batting helmet; the padded walls and warning tracks; and the first team baseball statistician. Jackie Robinson breaking the color barrier was, of course, recognized worldwide. Not much research required.

Part of Brooklyn's problem was that the New York press was in love with Yankee Stadium, "The House That Ruth Built," and all that nonsense. For one thing, it was much easier to reach than Ebbets Field. And, of course, there was all that Yankees winning and the aura it created. Oftentimes Ebbets Field was simply ignored by the Red Smiths and other sportswriters of his day. Their excuse, not made public, of course, was that it was too hard to reach.

All the Dodgers were aware of this attitude and resented it. Duke Snider spoke for the team when he told writer Roger Kahn that New York's top sportswriters, Red Smith of the *Herald-Tribune* and John Drebinger of the *Times*, for examples, looked down at Ebbets Field as too tough a subway ride from Manhattan with all that change at DeKalb or whatever.

"They all loved Yankee Stadium and the Polo Grounds," he told Kahn, "but the only time they came to Ebbets Field was for the big games, and then some of them would tell us what we were doing wrong. You were there, you didn't see Smith and the rest."[8]

Worse yet, Ebbets Field became the butt of jokes and jibes that demeaned the team and the park for years, even to this day with the Dodgers gone and Ebbets Field the site of high-rise apartment buildings. The jibes were made up, mostly by bored sportswriters who had nothing better to write about a team that had been floundering for years under manager Wilbert Robinson, during whose reign the Robins (later Dodgers) of the 1920s became known as "the Daffiness Boys." The team was named after its manager, and in headlines for many years were called the "Flock," a name that puzzled me until just recently when I read of it being derived from the team being called the Robins, after Robinson, their manager. Such was the sportswriting of the day.

The derision started in the 1920s and really never stopped until the Dodgers left for the West Coast. Back then there were stories about three men on third base, Babe Herman getting hit in the head by a fly ball, the antics of Van Lingle Mungo and Hack Wilson, and the general aura of comedy that seemingly surrounded the team and its home field.

Two perfect examples are the great baseball writers John Lardner and Roger Kahn, with Lardner leading the mocking and Kahn, who should have known better, going along. In his book *Memories of Summer*, Kahn quotes from a magazine article by Lardner, the great Ring's son:

> Floyd Caves Herman, known as Babe, didn't always catch a fly ball on the top of his head, but he could do it in a pinch. He never tripled into a triple play, but he once doubled into a double play, which is the next best thing. For seven long years, from 1926 through 1932, he was the spirit of Brooklyn baseball. He spent the best part of his life upholding the mighty tradition that anything can happen at Ebbets Field, the mother temple of daffiness in the national game.[9]

Clever writing for sure, but unresearched and untrue writing, as if that made any difference to a sportswriter like Lardner. The laugh, that's the important thing. Kahn said the Lardner piece was "about as funny as I've (ever) read." Well, maybe funny to him, but there used to be millions of us who were called "the Dodger Faithful" who wouldn't find it funny at all, just another writer copying his predecessors and doing sloppy research, if any research at all. That Roger Kahn, the epitome of Brooklyn writers, would find merit here is beyond understanding.

The facts: Babe Herman never got hit in the head with a fly ball but was a good fielder with a great arm.* He was a right fielder all of his career, the position played by Ruth, Bauer, Furillo, Kaline — not a place for clowns. As for the three men on base fantasy, anyone who knows baseball would understand after reading the *Times'* August 16, 1926, account that the man at fault in that now legendary baserunning fiasco was pitcher Dazzy Vance, not Babe Herman.

Writer Richards Vidmer of the *New York Herald-Tribune* took his shots at Herman as usual, but he pointed out that the baserunning of Vance was abominable. The bases were loaded when Herman hit what would have been a triple off the right-field wall, clearing the bases had Vance scored from second as he should have. But when he was halfway home he decided to go back to third as Chick Fewster was properly approaching on his way from first. Thus there were two men on third as

---

*For the real *Babe Herman* see Brooklyn's Babe *by Tot Holmes (Holmes Publishing, 1990).*

Babe cruised in. Herman took all the blame, as not one word was written on why Vance turned back.

During one of the few times Herman defended himself, he put the blame on Vance. "When I got to third Fewster was already there which surprised me," he said. "And then here comes Vance into third from the *other side*. There we were all on third at once and Fewster and I were both declared out. If there was any justice Vance would have been called out since he was the one who caused the traffic jam in the first place. But down through history for some strange reason it's all blamed on me."[10]

But except for a few Dodgers, it wasn't comedy; it was incompetence. It wasn't daffiness; it was drunkenness, a word the sportswriters never used, since it was conduct off the field, the privacy of players of that day being almost inviolate until later when Dick Young changed all that, starting with aptly named column "Clubhouse Confidential."

The demeaning continued even through the years of excellence when the Dodgers were one of the premier teams in the National League. I went to Ebbets Field many, many times during the years I paid as well as the six years I used one of the *Newark Evening News*' press passes.

During all those games I never heard the Dodgers called Dem Bums, or Erskine called "Oisk," or Dixie Walker called "the People's Cherce," not once. No one ever called out "wait 'til next year" within my hearing, and I never heard a fan yell "trun (throw) it to him." Wyatt was Whit, not "Whitelaw" and the team was always called the Dodgers or the Brooks, never, never the Bums. Imagine calling an outfield of Furillo, Snider and Pafko bums.

It just never happened, except in all the New York City papers and in one book entitled *Bums* by a writer who probably rarely, if ever, saw a game at Ebbets Field. Only one paper in the New York area, the *Brooklyn Eagle*, never called the team Bums and never ran Willard Mullins' famous cartoon. Both were forbidden.

All of it, every joke about the team, every slur, was press box driven and made the team look like a bunch of clowns, and not even the arrival of Larry MacPhail in 1938 made any difference. And the press never really let up, not until the team left town.

The Polo Grounds was different, the historic home of the great John McGraw and Christy Mathewson, adored by Grantland Rice and other sportswriters of his day. It made no difference that it was probably the worst permanent park in major league history. There were no press box jokes about 257-foot home runs or 400-foot outs, commonplace in a park shaped like a bathtub.

There was no outcry from the media when the 1954 World Series was decided by several typical Polo Grounds home runs by a non-entity ballplayer named Dusty Rhodes, whose homers would have been easy outs in any other ballpark in the major leagues.

Among the players, Duke Snider was in a class with Willie Mays, but he tended to take it out on the fans when things were going bad. Duke was moody and not always popular with the press because they never knew how he would react.

Mays, on the other hand, became known, as the "Say Hey Kid," words attributed to him by Barney Kremenko of the *New York Journal-American*, a typical Manhattan sportswriter. Mays said in later years that he never said those words in his life. But Willie for all those years let it ride. "The writers said I did and that's okay," he told Roger Kahn.[11] Like Babe Herman before him he let them write what they wanted, knowing that to the press he could do no wrong. His 1954 World Series catch of the long drive by Cleveland's Vic Wertz was played up in the media as the greatest catch ever. It wasn't. As Joe DiMaggio once said, the great World Series catch was by an unknown Al Gionfriddo in 1947 off a long drive by Joe himself. As shown many times on television, all Mays had to do was catch up to the ball. He had no cement wall to worry about and hadn't even reached the warning track.

In making the DiMaggio catch, Gionfriddo had to keep an eye on the ball while worrying about crashing into the metal gates at the 415 mark. As he caught the ball, he did crash into the gates but held the ball for the third out. There were no such dangers in the Polo Grounds. Willie therefore did not have to worry about concrete walls. He had all the room he needed to catch that long drive. The great thing about Mays' catch was what he did after he caught the ball. His turn and throw to second was so hard and accurate that the men on first and second were unable to advance. A great catch certainly, but the throw ranks among the best, if not the best, in baseball history.

In his comment DiMaggio wasn't taking anything away from Mays. "That was a great one too," he said, "but Mays had plenty of room. Gionfriddo had to worry about the wall and those gates. He had to worry about running out of room and getting hurt. With all that I say he made the greater catch."[12]

The Dodgers opened the season on the April 17, beaten at home by Robin Roberts and his Phillies, 5–2, one of the runs a homer by Mike Goliat, a .225 career hitter who was Lou Gehrig against the Dodgers, especially Don Newcombe. Mike was around for only four years but during that time he tormented Newcombe — one of the best pitchers in the game against one of the worst hitters, who just about owned him.

Roberts, who often had trouble against Brooklyn, would have had a shutout except for a Robinson homer with one on the sixth. Erskine, relieved by Clyde King, took the loss. King, out of Goldsboro, North Carolina, was the bullpen's big right-hander, on his way to a spectacular 14–7 year, his only great season, thanks to a nervous Charlie Dressen. Another fine pitcher, like George Spencer, ruined by having to get loose on too many unnecessary occasions. But after retiring as a pitcher, Clyde did very well, 60 years in baseball as a coach, manager, general manager and for many years baseball advisor to George Steinbrenner.

The Dodgers won a thriller the next day, scoring two in the ninth to win, 4–3, off Jim Konstanty, who was heading into a dismal season after his 16–7 performance helped the Phils win the 1950 pennant just months before. Konstanty came into the game in the ninth inning to protect a one-run lead. Bruce Edwards, batting for Roe, walked with Miksis running for him. In the next seven pitches Don Thompson sacrificed, Snider hit a triple off the scoreboard, and Robinson, up with two out, singled him home for the winning run.

Then the sweetest of Dodgers victories, three against the Giants, as Newcombe, Chris Van Cuyk and Newcombe again, in relief, beat Sheldon Jones, Larry Jansen and Sal Maglie, two of the Giants' big three, to sweep their first series of the season. It was not just the sweep but the way it was done that made Brooklyn fans sure that a banner year was underway.

The opener against Jones was a fairly easy 7–3 win with Campanella driving in the winning run as early as the fifth inning. The next day they beat Jansen by the same 7–3 score. The third game was a Dodgers fan's dream: Maglie went all the way but was beaten in the 10th inning, 4–3, as Furillo homered for the win. By the 10th the lights were on and Maglie was ahead in the count 1–2 when Carl caught hold of a sidearm curve, often Sal's best pitch, and drove it into the left-field stands. For the Dodgers any win over Maglie, who constantly threw at them, was doubly sweet.

On the 20th as the season was just about underway, Jackie Robinson's constantly worsening relationship with the league's umpires continued when he got into a shouting match with Babe Pinelli after he was called out on strikes. Afterwards Robinson complained to the press. "I have no doubt that there are some umpires in the National League who are on me," he said, adding that when the matter came up before league president Ford Frick, he would tell him so.

He did not receive a cordial reception from Frick, who was already involved in a Robinson-Durocher feud over Sal Maglie's knockdown and brushback pitches. At one point Frick said he was getting tired of Robinson's constant pop-offs. "It's got to stop. I've warned the Brooklyn club that if they can't control him I will."

There was division here. Fans like me sided with Robinson, thinking he had a right to assert himself at any time because of the treatment he received and the things he had to bear during his first two years in the league. But the other side is understandable. Sportswriter Red Smith said privately that he was tired of Robinson's constant tirades and antics.

Surprisingly, a number of black players around the league were too. Monte Irvin said years later that there were many blacks who were not in favor of Jackie's outspoken views. "Most (black) players thought Jackie was interjecting himself into situations that he shouldn't have been," Irvin said. "He was not a spokesmen for anyone but he was assuming that role. Some players didn't want him speaking or thinking for them and telling them what to do. Many thought he was setting himself up as the spokesman for the entire Negro race."[13]

During my Clem Labine interview* he expressed the opinion of some of his teammates in

As the player who broke baseball's color ban, Jackie Robinson unintentionally became the spokesman for all black ballplayers, a situation many of them resented. He had the skills, however, that made him one of the best second basemen of all time. Despite coming up late at age 28, he made the Baseball Hall of Fame in 1962. His play in Philadelphia that tied the Giants for the '51 playoff will never be equaled.

---

*"I had a special relationship with Clem. His secretary, Mrs. Louis Leight Heroux, and I were great friends as classmates for eight years at South Eighth Street Grammar School in Newark, N.J.

feeling that Robinson was getting involved in things that were none of his business. "The man was a great player," Clem said, " a great clutch player. But after a few years of him constantly sounding off, he became a liability at times. I know there were times he'd get on an umpire and that umpire would take it out on the rest of us."[14]

Often Jackie was involved in serious confrontations that weren't his fault, especially against Durocher and his Giants. The hatred, mostly on Leo's part, was inexplicable. When Jackie broke the color barrier Leo was one of his staunchest supporters. When some of the Dodgers threatened to go on strike if Robinson joined the team, Durocher ordered them all out of bed for a meeting in the middle of the night.

"I hear you fellows don't want to play with Robinson and you have a petition drawn up," he said to his half-dressed and pajama-clad team. "Well, boys, you know what you can do with that petition. I'm the manager of this ball club and I'm only interested in one thing: winning. This man is a great ballplayer. He's going to put money in your pockets and mine."[15]

His subsequent hatred of Robinson was not racial; it was irrational. The man who said he was practically Willie Mays' father bristled just about every time he saw Jack in a Dodgers uniform. Soon it became mutual, with serious results for Giants second baseman Davey Williams as the 1951 season was underway.

It started with Robinson trying to get even with Maglie for constantly throwing too close and sometimes at him. During one game Robinson bunted to get Maglie to field the ball and then bumped him, the two broken up before blows were struck.

The second time Jackie bunted on Maglie, Sal wouldn't cover the bag. From his second base position, Williams, seeing first base open, moved over to cover. Robinson barreled into him full force, thinking he was Maglie, since Maglie should have been covering. Davy was disabled with a bad back for the rest of the season. He played until partway through 1955 and then had to retire, with a back that never really healed. He was only 28.

Robinson apologized as well as he could for the play. "I wasn't going after Williams," he said. "It was Maglie I was after, and running with my head down it was Maglie I thought I hit. It should have been; he should have been covering the bag."[16]

I had friends back in those days who disliked baseball, calling it childish, with grown men fighting like kids in a schoolyard. It might have seemed so but I always reminded myself that these men were egged on by the media, plus they were playing in the most competitive city in the

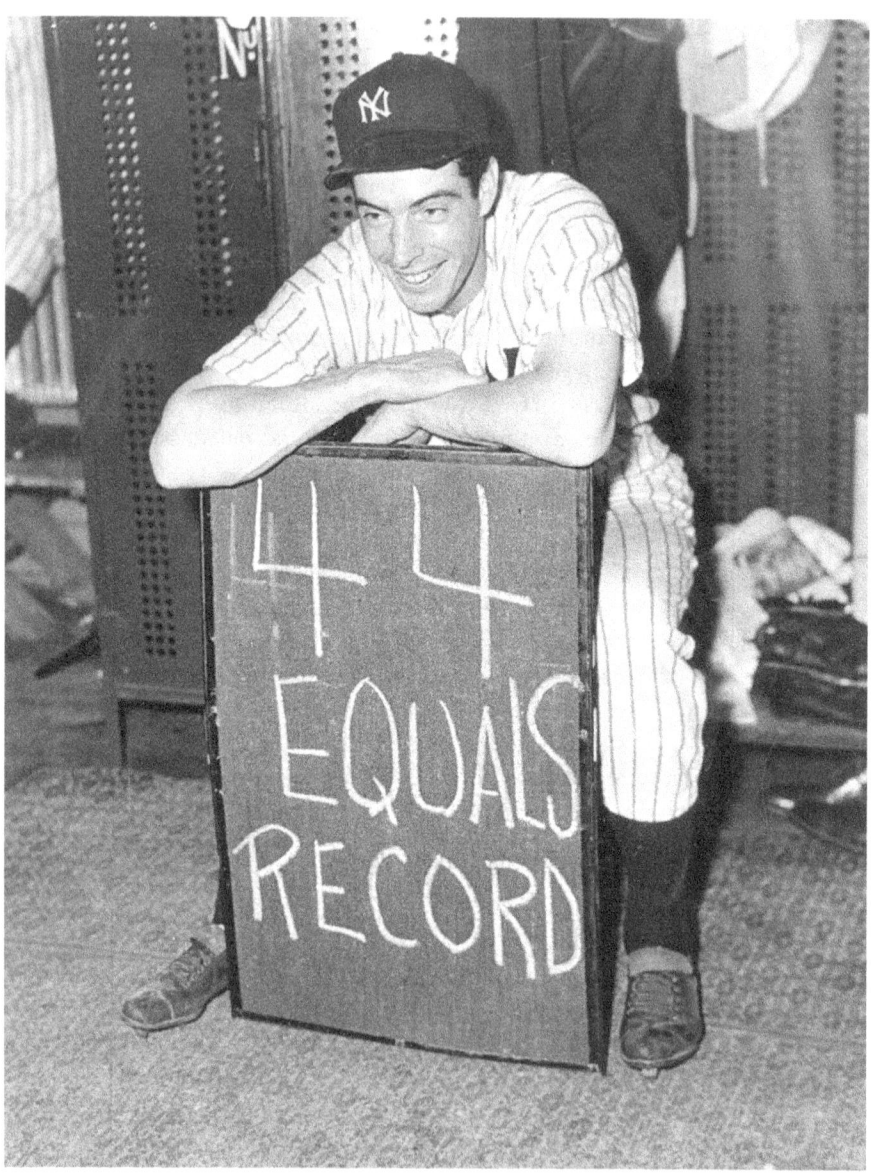

Joltin' Joe DiMaggio was in decline before anybody realized it, such were his skills before the war. When he came home after an ulcer-plagued three years in the army, he was no longer "The Yankee Clipper." But the magic never faded, though his .381 years were long gone. Even after that dismal 1951 he refused a $100,000 contract offer. This photo was taken after he hit in his 44th straight game, tying Willie Keeler's record.

world. Every incident was played up, hyped as we'd say today, by all eight newspapers in New York at the time and all the television stations. These were news professionals vying with each other for news items, with some of them not above making things up.

In April it looked like a banner season was beginning for the Dodgers. After the Phillies they were 5–2 while the Giants lost their first 11 in a row. One of the Dodgers wins shows how dramatically baseball has changed since the 1950s. The day of the nine-inning pitcher is probably over, though the process has been so gradual that many do not realize it.

The following is what we don't see anymore and will probably never will see again. On April 23 at Ebbets Field Warren Spahn went 16 innings in losing 2–1, as Furillo drove in Billy Cox with the winning run, unearned because of an error by third baseman Gene Mauch. God only knows what that pitch count was.

Spahn, one of the premier pitchers in baseball history, went two innings short of two complete games. Today his manager would start getting nervous around the 100th pitch and would have the bullpen up and working. Today that's what pitching is all about — the pitch count, something announcers never bothered with in years past. In all the years I listened to Red Barber and Mel Allen I never heard a pitch count mentioned, not once. It just wasn't part of baseball. Pitchers were expected to go nine innings or as close as possible. Now 116 pitches, and sometime even 100, gets the manager itchy. Not even a 266-game winner like Mike Mussina is immune to this today. The game becomes a countdown to the 100th pitch in too many instances.

Today's 20-game winners are especially watched over as the 100th pitch is delivered. Contrast that with great pitchers of the past and the not-too-distant past. In 1972, for example, three of the prime starters of the day were Steve Carlton, Steve Blass and Bob Gibson. Carleton was 27–10, Blass 19–8 and Gibson 19–11.

Along with such sterling percentages, Carlton pitched 30 complete games, Gibson 23 and Blass 11. As has been noted, that would be impossible today, since managers no longer leave their men in long enough to develop that kind of arm strength. That tendency might also result in the end of the 300-game winner, since relievers now benefit from late-inning rallies that a Spahn would be in there to win.

Blass is worth mentioning as one of the great mysteries of baseball — a latter-day Rex Barney. Steve had a much better career than Barney, but ended up the same way, leaving managers all over the league shaking their heads and asking what happened overnight to one of the top pitchers in the game.

No one has ever come up with an answer. Blass was at 110–67, coming off a wonderful 1972 when he was selected for the All-Star team and had a star World Series performance to top off his 19–8 year. He took the mound in 1973 and it had disappeared, all gone in his ninth season with the Pirates. He could not find the plate and never did again.

The Dodgers and Giants closed out April together at Ebbets Field where on the 29th Brooklyn beat New York, 6–3, for the Giants' 11th loss in the row, a dismal way to start a season that ended so gloriously for them. Leo got his first win the next day as Maglie won, 8–5.

The real season had now begun, one with the weirdest ending in National League history thanks to a telescope at the Polo Grounds and the ineptitude and stubbornness of Charlie Dressen. The Dodgers players, despite Dressen and their heart-breaking loss to the Phillies just months before, felt they had the best team in baseball. Their luck, they thought, would turn.

Over in the Bronx the Yankees weren't so sure. Everyone knew DiMaggio was in steep decline and Joe Page, at times the best reliever ever, had finally drank his way off the team and out of baseball. Mantle and Jensen were question marks, and there were doubts that the pitching could hold up, age being the issue.

The big three were getting on, Reynolds at 36, Lopat 33 and Raschi 32. Endurance was another worry. Lopat with his soft stuff could seemingly go on forever but Reynolds and Raschi were power pitchers whose arms could go at any time. The best threesome in history, they had already won two World Series after pennant races that went down to the last week of September. In '49 they beat Boston twice at season's end to win by one game. In '50 they clinched on September 30, ending up three games over Detroit.

The American League season opened strangely. For the first time in league history a season's opener was played at night, Washington versus Philadelphia at Shibe Park. Why in that day and age would anyone play night ball in April? Baseball was civilized then. No steroids, games lasting about two hours and home runs within reasonable limits, and no players making up to $26 million a year. As if to certify a new era, the game marked the end of 88-year-old Connie Mack's 56-year career as a major league manager, 50 of them in Philadelphia. He watched from a special box as Jimmy Dykes took over his Athletics.

April in Washington was true to its tradition as the Yankees-Senators opener was rained out, with President Truman on his way to Griffith Stadium to throw out the first ball. Disappointed about not seeing the president, the Yankees headed back to New York where they opened the season with a two-game sweep of the Boston Red Sox, continuing their domination over their East Coast rivals.

Raschi opened it with a 5–0 shutout, aided by a two-run homer and double by the seemingly unwanted Jackie Jensen, playing in place of injured Hank Bauer. Then it was Lopat's turn, a 6–1 two-hitter before some 15,000 chilled fans. For both pitchers it was win number one in what would be 21-win seasons for both.

With the season underway a current of discontent ran through the team, particularly in the outfield where Stengel's platoon system limited the playing time of everyone except DiMaggio. But their gripings, sometimes disguised in the press, made no difference to Stengel. How could anyone argue with success? Casey invented the platoon system and it served him well throughout his career, starting when he replaced Bucky Harris as Yankees manager in 1949. By 1951 he had won two pennants in a row platooning outfielders Hank Bauer, Gene Woodling, Cliff Mapes and later Bob Cerv. At third base it was Bobby Brown and Gil McDougald.

At first base he really had to juggle. Tommy Henrich was gone, Mize and his valuable long-ball bat was 37, and Joe Collins at 28 was then a .234 hitter. Mize was particularly valuable as pinch-hitter, his .283 average among the highest. Collins, happy to be a Yankee, never complained. He was in New York for 10 years and in my opinion was underrated. A fine fielder, he finished the decade at .256 but through the years so very often came up with the big hit at crucial times. When his career as a Yankee was over and they were going to trade him he retired, saying he would always be a Yankee and would not play for any other team. In Union, New Jersey, where he settled in when he made the majors, there is a park and children's playground named after him.

At third Gil McDougald was a better all-round player than Bobby Brown, but they batted from different sides of the plate. Brown was often useful, particularly as a pinch-hitter. They were both from the West Coast, Brown from Seattle and McDougald from San Francisco. Bobby left the Yankees after eight seasons to attend medical school but during those eight years he was a .245 pinch-hitter, and like Joe Collins, often came though with the big hit.

Gil was an unexpected asset for that Stengel team, and Casey was smart enough to realize it. He was a 23-year-old rookie, shuffled between second and third yet he hit .306 in 402 times at-bat. He retired in 1960 to found a successful janitorial service covering Hudson and Bergen counties in New Jersey.

The justified gripes were from Bauer and Woodling, who everyone knew would be regulars on just about any other team in baseball. Bauer over 14 years was a .277 hitter and a solid right fielder with a good arm. Woodling, six-plus years a Yankee, hit .284 lifetime while playing left field. The major complaint, behind the scenes, was sharing playing time with Cliff Mapes, who in his five-year career was .242 lifetime and in no way in a class with either Bauer or Woodling. With Woodling batting from the left side and Bauer the right many thought there was no excuse for them having to share playing time with a .242 hitter. But there were compensations. Bauer collected nine World Series checks and Woodling five. Gripes or not, Stengel made it work year after year. As Red Barber used to say, Stengel was the smartest baseball man he ever knew, a man who used his double talk only when he wanted to.

> On April 23 the army rejected the 19-year-old Mantle as physically unqualified for military service. Even though outwardly healthy and a major league ballplayer at that, there is little doubt today that Mantle's left leg, infected with osteomyelitis caused by a football injury, would never have held up under a military regimen. The infection, treated with penicillin, troubled him the rest of his life. During his later career, his legs — both of them — were so heavily taped that he was compared to a mummy from the hips down.

To the fans in his early years he was often taunted as a draft dodger, unfairly, of course, but he became such a nasty person that only his teammates could feel sorry for him. Nasty when sober, he was even worse when drunk, which was much too often, sometimes even on the field and at bat.

I crossed paths with Mantle three times. The third time, the only personal contact I had with him, was in 1966 when I was stationed by AT&T at New York's St. Regis Hotel as part of our national strike information team while the Bell companies were on strike. I entered the elevator one afternoon and there was Mantle. "Hello, Mr. Mantle," I said, and after he returned my greeting I added, "Are the Yankees going to leave town as O'Malley did with the Dodgers?"

He said no and we continued talking through the lobby and outside as he waited for a taxi. I was stunned at how nice he seemed. But then I looked into his eyes as he left and they, as my mother used to say, "mirror the soul." He had learned to be nice, finding that since he was no longer the star baseball player of New York it was more profitable to be nice than nasty.

I had observed the nasty Mantle twice before, when I was a reporter on the *Newark Evening News*. I was on sports overtime one Saturday afternoon writing my usual Essex County high school baseball roundup when sports columnist Hy Goldberg was inquiring around as to who was doing the Essex wrapup each week.

He came to my temporary desk and we talked baseball awhile before he asked me to come into the sports department to talk to Len Elliot, our sports editor, to see if I was interested in being a sportswriter since there were some retirements coming up. I had never planned on it because of the night hours and travel and the possibility of having to cover hockey and, worse, soccer, but I said I'd think it over. Hy countered by suggesting I go with him to two weekend games at Yankee Stadium before deciding.

After both games I went into the Yankees clubhouse with Hy, under instructions to keep quiet and not ask any questions. Both times I saw how Mantle, Martin and a number of other young players — all taking their cue from Mantle — treated the writers — with sneers, grimaces and constantly making fun of their questions.

I never saw young men treat older men — old enough to be their fathers and in some cases even their grandfathers — so shabbily. I felt sorry for every one of those writers, young and old. I noticed that some of the Yankees veterans, like Rizzuto, Bauer, Berra, Raschi and a few others, were looking on in silent disapproval. Even young Whitey Ford, Mantle's buddy, didn't seem to like what was going on.

As we were driving back to New Jersey after the second weekend game, I asked Hy if it was always like that. He said it was since they were the Yankees, young and arrogant, used to winning. "Rudy, it goes with New York," he said, "and I'm not going to kid you. I don't have to take it because I'm a columnist, not a beat writer. But if you take a job with us, you'll have to deal with that Yankee attitude whenever you're assigned to them." I declined and he understood. Hy and I became friends for the rest of his life.

I had second-guessed myself on this for years, especially since friends I respect thought I was crazy to turn down such an offer. Then a while back I read the following on the sportswriters life in *The Jocks* by Leonard Schecter, veteran sportswriter for the *Times* and the *New York Post*:

> Baseball writing used to be a position for gentlemen. A typical day on the road meant breakfast and then heading for the golf links and lunch at the ninth hole. One arrived at the ball park at 2:45, 15 minutes before game time. The game was usually over before five when the writer wrote his little review and was ready for cocktails or other diversions.
>
> The life of a baseball writer today is far different, the work harder,

the hours impossible. Whether one works for an afternoon or evening newspaper, night games, expansion and coast-to-coast jet scheduling have reduced the world of the writer to a nightmare.[18]

After reading that I felt vindicated in my youthful decision and happy that I have never had to cover a hockey or soccer game. I recall now that just a few years before Hy made the offer to me it was still mainly a sports world of train travel, two- or three-hour ball games and, until Dick Young's style of reporting caught on, not much snooping around the dugout or in the clubhouse. By the time things had changed for the very worst, with teams all over the Pacific coast and therefore jet travel a constant, Hy was working for ABC Sports and I was with AT&T. The paper he and I had grown up with and worked for, the *Newark Evening News,* was dead.

April ended with one of the biggest American League trades in years — seven players involving Cleveland, Philadelphia, Chicago and including Lou Brissie, one of the most remarkable pitchers in baseball history. Except for Minnie Minoso, then an unknown, the others were run of the mill, if that can be applied to major leaguers.

Gus Zernial, Paul Lehner, Sam Zoldak, Dave Philley and Ray Murray were the others traded by Cleveland, Philadelphia and Chicago. The trades were unremarkable for the most part except for Cleveland's move. They guessed wrong on Minoso who became a star with the White Sox, up in the majors for 17 years, a fast and sure-handed outfielder with a .298 lifetime batting average. There are a number of players in the Baseball Hall of Fame whose numbers cannot match those of Minoso.

Brissie, out of Anderson, South Carolina, went from the Athletics to the Indians in exchange for Zernial, a .265-hitting slugger who finished his 11-year career with 237 home runs. Lou was the headliner in the trades, a war hero corporal whose left leg was shattered by German artillery fire during the Italian campaign in the Appenines. He was 20 years old, 6'4" and 215 pounds, faced with his army doctors telling him his leg was too far gone and had to be amputated. He then begged them not to, telling them he was a professional baseball player.

As Lou is quoted in Ira Berkow's *The Corporal Was a Pitcher: The Courage of Lou Brissie,* the doctors told him repeatedly that the leg was shattered beyond repair but he insisted it not come off. "You can't take my leg off," he said. "I'm a ballplayer. I can't play on one leg." Years before, the White Sox' Monte Stratton, as depicted in the fine 1949 Jimmy Stewart movie *The Stratton Story,* tried but couldn't make it.

In Berkow's account Lou was lucky to even get to the hospital. Most of his squad was killed during the barrage and he at first was left for dead, found hours later unconscious on the bank of an icy creek. It was when they got him to a nearby base hospital that he persuaded the doctors to operate rather than amputate. He had one important factor in his favor that the doctors didn't realize: he threw left-handed, and it was his left leg that was shattered, not the right, a left-hander's push-off leg.

After a number of operations Lou was fitted with a knee-to-ankle steel and aluminum brace that allowed him to pitch major league ball in Philadelphia and then Cleveland for seven years, compiling a 44–48 record mostly for the second-division Athletics. In 1949, a 16–11 year for him in Philadelphia, he made the American League All-Star team. As much as I abhor calling baseball players heroes, I make an exception for Leland Victor (Lou) Brissie.

CHAPTER FIVE

May

As May opened a Dodgers clubhouse episode occurred that I had never heard or read of before. Charlie Dressen became enraged over a 75-cent side dish of creamed cauliflower.

The story is so incredible, so bizarre, and reveals so much about Dressen that I'll have Duke Snider tell it in his own words, his story of the cauliflower dispute. I quote from his book *The Duke of Flatbush*.

> Dressen had a team meeting to caution us against running up the tab for meals on the road. We had no specific allowance as long as we kept the amounts reasonable. Dressen was lecturing us while I was getting itchy to get out and warm up for the game. He kept droning on about our food checks and then started on Dick Williams about a side order of creamed cauliflower he had the night before with his dinner at the hotel. It cost seventy-five cents.
>
> Finally I couldn't take any more of it. "Christ Charlie," I said, "take it off my allowance last night. I didn't even eat at the hotel. I ate at a restaurant at my own expense. Deduct the damn seventy-five-cents from what you saved on me. Let's go out and warm up."
>
> Dressen exploded. It was like a scene in the movie *The Caine Mutiny* when Captain Queeg conducts an investigation to find out who ate the missing strawberries. "Who the hell do you think you're talking to Snider? I'm the manager here and don't you ever forget it. Don't *ever* try to tell me how to manage my ballclub."[1]
>
> All that over a dish of creamed cauliflower.

Captain Queeg of the Brooklyn Dodgers. Right there in that clubhouse was the first appearance of the mean-spiritedness and stubbornness that was one reason Brooklyn lost the pennant months later.

Snider was certainly one of the premier center fielders of his time but he was also one of baseball's all-time prima donnas as most Brooklyn fans knew from watching him on the field and reading the *Brooklyn Eagle*.

Nothing was ever his fault. It was the umpire, the fans, the press, whatever. Snider was 6' tall and 198 pounds but inside there was a little boy who sulked after a bad at-bat and sometimes dogged it.

As early as high school he was a terrific all-round athlete. Future National Football League commissioner Pete Roselle, then a Los Angeles sportswriter, scouted him and was so impressed that he wrote a letter that caused Branch Rickey to eventually sign him for Newport News, a Dodgers farm team where he played for Jake Pitler before going into the navy in 1944.

Duke was a Brooklyn Dodger for nine seasons before O'Malley went for the gold in California. During all that time he never appreciated the Dodgers fans, often blaming them for things that were his fault — batting slumps, for example. His most childish moment came on August 26, 1955, when he was in a 27-game slump during which his average dropped from .331 to .299. The fans were to blame he told the press after another hitless night. They had the nerve to boo him occasionally during that dreadful time.

A "pouter" as Labine once termed him, Duke Snider rarely made a mistake. It was always the other guy's fault. Although a superb outfielder and hitter, when he suffered through a batting slump it was because of the fans at Ebbets Field. His 407 home run total is a bit weak, but the writers, taking into consideration his five seasons at that misshapen Los Angeles Coliseum, voted him into the Baseball Hall of Fame in 1980.

"Brooklyn fans don't deserve a pennant," he ranted in the clubhouse. "They're the worst fans anywhere." The next day more of the same. "There are some good Brooklyn fans but maybe there are more bad ones."[2] That night he was cheered after three singles.

Although I never met the man it got personal between us after publication of my first book, *The Brooklyn Dodgers in the 1940s*, in which I described Snider as I have here. But even as I was researching that book, things didn't ring true with the man. I wrote him, among others, asking for information and some possible quotes about Pete Reiser, one of my subjects at the time.

He wrote back saying he didn't know Reiser well enough to comment. Well, he played on the same team with Pete for two years, and later when Pete was manager at Portland he hired Snider as a coach and then had Snider replace him when he had heart trouble. I wouldn't call anyone a liar in print, but I can think what I think.

During my research for my second book, I found that none of the Dodgers I had gotten friendly with — fellow Newarker Gene Hermanski, for example — would answer my letters or return phone calls. Then I received a letter returned from Snider unopened marked "Return to Sender" and the Snider address slashed a number of times in black crayon. I realized then I had been blackballed and by whom. Still childish in his late 70s.

The strangest part of this whole Snider episode is that a couple of years ago I was watching a television film about the "Boys of Summer," as that 1950s Dodgers team was known after Roger Kahn's book. Snider appeared and confessed to almost all the things I had written, calling himself "immature" and all the rest. Clem Labine got on and described Snider as a pouter. "That's the only word I can think of to describe him," Labine said. "He was a pouter."

On that same early May day the Giants won their first game, breaking an improbable 11-game losing streak to start the season. Improbable because the oddsmakers had the Giants favored to win the '51 pennant on the strength of their pitching staff, their big three being Jansen, Maglie and Jim Hearn. The Dodgers had Newcombe and Roe as their big starters, followed by Ralph Branca, who was almost through, and Bankhead, Podbielan, and Erskine, who had yet to blossom into the star he became.

It seemed particularly dark for Durocher's men since just the day before the Dodgers had beaten them for their 11th straight loss, routing their ace Jansen as New York stranded 11 men on the bases. The game went along peacefully until the Durocher-Robinson-Maglie feud took on a physical dimension that would continue until Robinson retired. At the time, though, it seemed like any other baseball blowup, one of those sudden on-field squalls gone the same night. But, as described in the previous chapter, this was the beginning of the physical confrontations that eventually ended the career of Giants second baseman Davey Williams at 28. An innocent caught between two large antagonists.

Chapter Five: May

That first confrontation started with Maglie, at his most aggressive in trying to break the Giants' losing streak, brushing back the Dodgers lineup until he came too close to Robinson once too often. Jackie laid down a bunt along the first baseline, and when Maglie fielded it in foul ground, Jackie gave him the shoulder, hard.

As Maglie went for Robinson, enough Giants had gathered to prevent a fight, and by that time Durocher had reached the mound shouting that Robinson had pulled one of his "bush league" tricks. As Jackie responded the next day saying Durocher had taught him numerous tricks, their feud was gathering momentum until it tragically and by accident eventually ended Davey Williams' career.[3]

I realized while watching that game on television that Durocher, for years one of my Dodgers heroes, was now the enemy. Strong words, but you must remember the blood runs high in one's early twenties. Once outraged when Leo was banned from baseball for a year, as I watched his antics I remembered Chandler's reasons: the blackjacking of a fan under the stands; the association with gamblers and gangsters through his friendship with George Raft (the most wooden actor in the history of Hollywood); and the reaction of the Catholic church to his flouting the law in the manner in which he married Laraine Day. Bad enough that Leo was named correspondent in Laraine's divorce, but then he married her in Juarez, Mexico, in defiance of California law that required Laraine to wait one year before marrying again. The Brooklyn Diocese, finally out of patience with Leo's cavalier actions, had threatened to boycott the Dodgers unless something was done about him.[4]

Nothing the diocese or the baseball commissioner could do would change the man since basically he had been an incorrigible for most of his life. I knew all about his trouble on the Yankees in the mid-1920s, Babe Ruth accusing him of stealing his watch (which he probably did) and of him shoving Babe into a locker and then running off.

But only recently did I find that this sort of thing started when he was a teenager growing up in West Springfield, Massachusetts, where he was expelled from high school for punching a mathematics teacher. This was the start of his aggressive approach to life. Years later Branch Rickey mistakenly thought he could control what he termed Leo's "delinquent behavior off the field." As it turned out nobody could control him, least of all himself.[5]

Years later I met an entirely different Leo Durocher in 1968 when he was managing the Chicago Cubs. By then I was with the Bell System writing for *Western Electric* magazine. With Western having more than 200,000 employees, I came up with the idea to do a series of features on families having sons playing major league sports. There were quite a few.

My first choice was spring training with the Chicago Cubs for a feature on rookie Garry Jestadt, a 21-year-old third baseman up for seasoning.* When I arrived at Scottsdale I looked for the team's publicity man to introduce me to Durocher. I couldn't find him so with my ex-reporter's nerve I introduced myself and, expecting coolness, got one of the shocks of my life.

After I introduced myself a beaming Durocher shook my hand saying, "Western Electric, that's part of AT&T. Your company helped me become a rich man." He then called one of his coaches, Harry Bright, and introduced us. "Harry will show you around," he said, "and you'll have the run of the camp. But, one rule. Around the ball field never turn your back on home plate. They hit hard around here."

This wasn't the Durocher of the Polo Grounds, or of Ebbets Field. This couldn't be the man who blackjacked a fan under the stands. But it was, and as I watched him I realized there were two Durochers, and that he could turn on either one at will. And the ladies, how they crowded around him adoringly when he went into the stands to meet the fans, spring training style, and to sign programs.

I couldn't figure the allure. He seemed to me just another middle-aged man, not handsome, of average height, trim for his age, but with nothing that would make him stand out among other men. But the women swarmed around him, seeing something there that I couldn't see. Anyway, who am I to question the judgment of Laraine Day?

Thus began one of the most exciting weeks of my life. I remembered Harry as a former Yankees outfielder as he started showing me around. We ate together and became friends as he introduced me to various ballplayers, including Ron Santo, who, unlike the old days in baseball, was giving the rookie Jestadt tips on how to improve his fielding.

My highlight of the week resulted from a casual remark I made to Harry about how I wondered what it was like to face major league pitching. Instead of trying to explain it, he took me to a batting cage so that I could actually experience it. As a favor to Harry a tall left-hander stood on the mound. We were never introduced because this wasn't supposed to be happening, but I knew who he was. As I stepped into the batter's box, Harry told me not to swing since he wasn't wearing catcher's equipment.

---

*No one at that time could replace Ron Santo at third. Consequently, Garry was traded to Montreal.

Swing! I couldn't if I had wanted to. This was baseball on a terrifying level. Nothing I had ever done in sports on the Newark sandlots, at Newark's Central High School, in the navy or at Rutgers had in the slightest prepared me for anything like this. Even though curves were not at my head before dipping since I hit right-handed, I was bailing out half the time. And the fastballs! I could hear the ball buzz as it passed me. My friends never believed I could hear a fastball. But I later discovered a witness, the eminent baseball writer Roger Kahn.

He describes how he once stepped in against his friend Clem Labine, whose fastball was major league but not Feller-like. "The ball exploded past the plate with a sibilant whoosh, edged by a buzzing as of hornets," he wrote somewhat flamboyantly. Then he described another pitch "that made the noises of hornets and snakes." Kahn could sometimes get carried away, but his testimony silenced my doubting friends.[6]

When I left the batter's box Harry asked, "Now do you have any idea of what it's like up here?" I just nodded, overwhelmed at what I had experienced — baseball from another world. When I hear that a major league hitter has maybe one-tenth of a second to make up his mind, I believe it.

In May, the Dodgers team had not yet jelled into the one that would continue to dominate the National League for years before the move to Los Angeles. There were still a number of fringe players who would soon disappear: Belardi, Rojek, Haugstad, Bankhead and the like. Two fine ballplayers, Miksis and Hermanski, would go in the Pafko trade with the Cubs.*

The nucleus, however, was in place: Hodges, Robinson, Reese, Cox, Hermanski, Snider, Furillo and Campanella. The big four on the pitching staff were Roe (23–2), Newcombe (20–9), Erskine (16–12) and King (14–7). Branca was almost through at 13–12.

One problem at the time was the team being leery of Dressen, who was so different from his quiet predecessor, Burt Shotton. The players were wise enough to know that his bragging about stealing signs was an ability that has always been overrated. The Brooklyn organization still remembered Medwick and how Dressen almost ruined his career. And his Captain Queeg act over the creamed cauliflower was still on everyone's mind. A crazy episode like that doesn't soon go away.

These men were professionals who didn't take to Dressen's dressing down his players before the entire team and worse, as in the case of Erv

---

*The Pafko trade will be covered later, a strange chapter in Dodgers history that proved Walter O'Malley didn't have the baseball knowledge to run a Little League team.

Palica, denigrating them in the press. Palica down the stretch in 1950 was the best clutch pitcher in the game, whose wins kept Brooklyn in the race until the last day of the season. But to Dressen he was "gutless."

The players realized soon enough that Palica, like Branca, didn't have a pitching coach to break down his motion and analyze what the trouble was with his curve ball or any other pitch he threw. Imagine Ralph Branca with a sharp-breaking curveball under the tutelage of a coach like Johnny Sain. Dressen would never hear of it.

For the Yankees May started well as they beat the White Sox, 3–1, with Vic Raschi winning his third game of the young season. Mickey Mantle's first major league homer, a 420-yard blast into the upper-right-field stands at Comiskey Park, drove in the winning run. It was the first of Mantle's 536 career homers, not too impressive in this age of steroids but an outstanding number back then when the 500 mark meant certain entry into the Baseball Hall of Fame. Now thanks to steroid morons like Alex Rodriguez, Barry Bonds, Mark McGwire, Rafael Palmiero and a number of others, the 500 number is fading if not gone as a Hall standard.

The next day's game illustrated the genius of Casey Stengel. With DiMaggio, Berra and Mantle injured and out of the lineup he juggled a 17-man roster to win 6–4 with a key hit by Jackie Jensen and Joe Collins' game-winning triple in the ninth inning. I had completely forgotten that along with the majestic Big Three the Yankees had a pitcher named Joe Ostrowski on the staff. He was the winner that day and stayed with the club until the end of the 1952 season.

Out in St. Louis during this early May week, Bill Veeck was trying to set a precedent by owning the first team in the modern era to move a franchise. The Boston Braves were actually the first in their move to Milwaukee in 1953. But it was Veeck who started things off a year earlier when, on May 10 with co-owner Fred Saigh, he "denied" they were planning to move their St. Louis Browns to Milwaukee, but added that continued poor attendance might force their decision.[7]

Major Browns stockholders Bill and Charley DeWitt said the move, revealed in the *St. Louis Post-Dispatch*, "seems to be the one that could be worked out." At the time everyone associated with the club knew that something had to be done since the Browns' attendance had been dismal for years, mainly because the Cardinals were the big team in the area, with the Browns always trailing behind.

You can't blame the fans in St. Louis for favoring the Cardinals. Attendance was bad because the Browns of 1951 were one of the worst teams in baseball history at 52 wins against 104 losses. One early May series against the Yankees in St. Louis illustrates just how bad they were.

Total runs for the three-game series were 39 for the Yankees to 10 for the Browns. In the ninth inning of the first game, the Yankees scored 11 runs to win, 17–3. Game two was 5–1 Yankees. In the third game New York scored 10 runs in the third inning in winning 17–6.

As a result of such dismal play, their attendance, always poor, was 247,131 in 1950 and 293,790 in 1951. The Cardinals meanwhile drew 1,093,411 and 1,013,429 during those two seasons. It had been obvious for years that St. Louis could not support two teams. The Browns had tried a number of things over the years — vaudeville acts, stunts and the rest. Veeck and DeWitt struggled on but by the early '50s they gave up and decided to move. The stumbling block, however, was Bill Veeck.

Bill was disliked by the other American League owners for his flamboyant publicity stunts when he was the owner of the Cleveland Indians. As plans for the move were formed during the season, on August 18 in a game against Detroit, Veeck went too far, sending a midget, 3'7" Eddie Gaedel, to bat against Tigers pitcher Bob Cain, who walked him. As Gaedel came to bat, Tigers management protested. Cleveland manager Al Lopez then produced a valid contract with a date stamped.[8]

Will Harridge, American League president, voided the contract the next day "in the interests of baseball," but the damage to Veeck had been done. The other owners' dislike of Veeck turned to something more like hatred, and they got their revenge by blocking his move to anywhere.

The owners were aware that Veeck was a baseball maverick long before the midget episode. It wasn't obvious at first, probably because he was following in the footsteps of his father, Veeck Sr., who wrote himself into the presidency of the Chicago Cubs when he was a local sportswriter for the *Chicago American.*

The year was 1917, not long after we declared war on Germany, when Veeck Sr. was appointed president of the Chicago Cubs by team owner William Wrigley, Jr., of the chewing gum fortune. As a sportswriter Veeck had written a number of columns on the changes he would make if he owned the Cubs. Finally Wrigley called him on it, appointing him president to see what he could do.

The Cubs won the pennant that year. With his father as president, young Veeck left prep school to work for the team, starting at the bottom as a vender, then moving up to ticket seller and then junior landscaper before he was appointed club treasurer in 1937. One of his first acts at the time was ordering the ivy planted along the park's walls that is unique to Wrigley Field.

His first ownership was during the war when he and baseball legend Charley Grimm bought the Milwaukee Brewers of the American Association. In his biography one chapter is on gamesmanship and in it Bill describes how he would game by game change the distance along the park's short 268-foot right-field line. He did it by installing a screen on wheels to make it more difficult for an opposing team's left-handed pull hitters. He got away with this for several weeks since there was no rule against it until one day he went too far. He rolled the screen out for the opposing team and rolled it back when the Brewers came to bat.*

The league passed a rule against it the next day, but the memory lingered in baseball's executive offices across the land. They knew that the late illustrious Bill Veeck, Sr., had a son who didn't always play by the rules and would therefore need watching. Some owners may have been amused by Veeck's Milwaukee antics but years later the midget incident in Cleveland, among other stunts such as his hiring rubber-faced Max Patkin, the "Clown Prince of Baseball," as a coach, caused some of the owners to wait in the grass for revenge.

Their chance came in 1954 after the Braves moved to Milwaukee. Veeck then tried to switch the Browns to Baltimore, but the owners blocked him. Knowing he was beaten, Veeck sold his interest in the Browns and the move to Maryland was made. In their moves, however, the Braves and Browns had broken baseball's 50-year mold, thus clearing the way for teams to start hopping from city to city. In the case of the Philadelphia Athletics, it was a cross-country journey—Philadelphia to Kansas City to where they are now, in Oakland, California—where they still bear the name Athletics.'

The Braves and Browns were living on the edge of bankruptcy as the game's welfare cases. They had to move but it's unfortunate that in doing so they destroyed baseball's mindset against abandoning cities. It made the disgraceful decision of Walter O'Malley to leave Brooklyn easier for the rest of the owners to accept. Even today I don't think we've seen the last of carpetbaggers like O'Malley.

Veeck came back to baseball in later years unhindered by the owners. Most were new to the game at the time and there may have been some sympathy for him being in ill health as a result of the 36 operations he had to undergo for injuries suffered during World War II. Bill had been

---

*There has been some doubt about this account since the Society for American Baseball Research (SABR) investigated and found no evidence that the screen business actually happened. However, Veeck writes of it in his Veeck as in Wreck, and I can see no reason he should have made up such a story.

with a Marine unit for three years when in battle a recoiling artillery piece crushed his leg, requiring amputation first of the foot and later of the leg above the knee.

Aside from the ivy on the walls of Wrigley Field, Veeck's other lasting contribution to the game occurred to him while he was head of the White Sox in 1959, his third tour in Chicago. To enable the fans to better identify the players, he had their last names stitched onto the backs of their uniforms, an idea taken up by most teams today.

On May 11 the draft had what probably was a significant effect on the American League pennant race. The United Press sent a story over the wires saying that "the Army today all but killed off the Tigers' hopes of becoming a pennant contender." Ray Herbert, a 21-year-old, had already won four games in the young season when he was called up.

Detroit manager Red Rolfe had hoped that keeping Herbert would offset the earlier loss to the draft of Art Houtteman, one of the league's best pitchers who was drafted after having won 19 games during the previous season. Stats support the UP prediction. The previous year, 1950, the Tigers were in the race until the final week, losing to the Yankees by just three games. Without Houtteman and then Herbert, they finished in fifth place in 1951, 15 games behind the Yankees.

On May 20 in Cincinnati the FBI told Jackie Robinson they had received a threat to his life in letters signed by "the Three Travelers" saying that Robinson would be "shot from a window" during a Reds-Dodgers game. The park was soon swarming with local police and FBI men who thought the letters were from a crank but they were taking precautions nevertheless.

During a team meeting on the threats, Gene Hermanski came through again with his unfailing sense of humor and rocked the clubhouse when he suggested that all players wear the number 42 so the assassins wouldn't know which one was Robinson. "It was a Sunday afternoon and Dressen came into the clubhouse to tell us of the death threats," Hermanki told me in a telephone interview. "After he spoke there was a lull and I came up with the idea about Jackie's number. That broke up the room, relieved the tension, and we relaxed a bit."[9]

On May 23, *The Sporting News* did something surprising, at least to me. The newspaper ran a full-page spread on Kenny Raffensberger, one of the most unsung pitchers in major league history and one of my all-time favorites. One reason he should be better known is why he was traded from the Phillies to the Reds in 1947 for catcher Al Lakeman.

The official reason given for the trade was that his arm went dead but all of baseball knew the real reason was the wire service reports that he wouldn't obey manager Ben Chapman's orders to throw at Jackie Robinson. "I wouldn't do it," Raffensberger told the Associated Press. "I never believed in throwing at hitters."

Ken can be described best as the Eddie Lopat type — slow with pinpoint control. "To listen to the hitters I don't have anything," he told *Sports Illustrated* writer Joe King. "I take a lot of kidding that I don't have a fastball. All I have, I guess, is confidence in myself to get the ball over."

He did it so well that he ended up with a 119–154 record and a 3.60 ERA, mostly with bad teams. One of his proudest moments, he recalled in his later years, was when "Stan Musial said I was the toughest left-hander he ever faced." Ralph Kiner agreed.

On May 25 Willie Mays joined the New York Giants for a night game against the Phillies at Shibe Park. When he was called up Willie was batting .477 for his month or so at Minneapolis. In *Nice Guys Finish Last*, Durocher tells a highly suspect story of Willie going 24 times without a hit and then asking to be sent back to Minneapolis.

"Miss-a-Leo I can't get a hit," Leo quotes Willie as sounding like Stepin Fetchit. "I can't help you and I know you're gonna send me back to Minneapolis where I belong. I don't belong up here. I can't play up here." His voice, Leo writes, "went right up the scale and clear out of sight." Just like Mantan Morland of the Charlie Chan movies, if you can believe Durocher.

"I just patted him on the back," Leo went on. "I brought you up here to play center field. You're the best center fielder I ever saw. Go home and get a good night's sleep. Tomorrow is another day."[10] The next day Willie hit one off Warren Spahn and started his trip to Cooperstown. He ended the season batting a respectable .274 and was in the on-deck circle when Thomson hit that unforgettable homer.

Willie hit 660 homers in his career but many in baseball have always contended that had he stayed in New York instead of that wind-plagued Candlestick Park in San Francisco, he might well have been the man to break Babe Ruth's single-season and career home run records. Perhaps that is one reason why he turned into the grouchy, impolite man he became in his later years. I think it's *the* reason. If any man was robbed of immortality, of being the man who broke Babe Ruth's record, it was Willie Mays.

Hank Aaron was a great ballplayer, clean, honest, and for 23 years not a blemish on his record. But he was no Willie Mays. Except for those home runs, he could not compare to the man who might well have been the greatest outfielder who ever lived. Willie can thank Stoneham for taking him to San Francisco and costing him maybe 150 or more home runs.

Brooklyn ended the month beating Philadelphia, 4–3, in a game in which teammates prevented Robinson and Russ "Mad Monk" Meyer from fighting it out down one of the park's runways. Meyer exploded when he thought Jackie jostled the ball out of his hand during a rundown. After words the two headed down to fight but blows were prevented when men from both teams separated them.

What actually happened was a squeeze play called by Dressen with Hodges on second and Robinson leading off third. As Robinson went by Meyer, the ball hit the ground, triggering the pitcher's always-volatile temper. Russ later apologized after his teammates convinced him that Robinson made no contact with him and that he simply dropped the ball. "I was as much at fault as Monk was," Jackie said later.[11] As they went into June the win gave the first-place Dodgers a 24–15 record, a 2½-game lead over second-place St. Louis. The Giants, at .500 after their 0–11 start, were in fifth place at 21–21.

The Yankees ended May in second place two games behind the White Sox after losing a doubleheader to Boston, 11–10 in fifteen innings and 9–4. If only once in a while the Red Sox had played that way against New York in clutch situations, the Yankees stranglehold could have been broken any number of times.

Chapter Six

June

By mid-1951 the batting helmet, brainchild of Larry MacPhail, had been accepted by most ball clubs, but the wearing of it wasn't mandatory. Therefore, every once in a while a ballplayer would be killed, all in the minor leagues. The reasons they weren't being used universally centered on comfort and bravado. Some players simply didn't like them, while others thought the wearing of them to be unmanly. On June 9 that attitude cost the life of Otis Johnson, an outfielder for the Dethan Browns of the Class D Alabama-Florida League.

Johnson, a high school teacher in the offseason, suffered a fractured skull when hit by a fastball and was semi-conscious for a day before he died, leaving a wife and one child. Sadly, his death was just another of a series that no one seemed to be paying attention to. In 1953 Don Zimmer, for example, was in a coma for 13 days and had those titanium plugs placed in his head after he was hit while playing for St. Paul of the American Association. For years he joked about the four titanium-filled holes in his head, saying he doesn't have a hole in his head, he has four. Four that had to be drilled through his skull to save his life — nothing to laugh at unless you're a fool.

I always thought anyone who did not wear a helmet in those days was either crazy or very stupid. There have been no fatalities, or even severe injuries, since wearing the helmet was ruled mandatory in 1971. Fifty-one years after Ray Chapman's death some action was finally taken. It took all those years because many players felt wearing a helmet violated their manhood.

MacPhail was aware of this attitude when he went ahead with developing the helmets for his 1940 Brooklyn Dodgers. "The objections I heard from the other club owners was that the players would never wear them," he told Roscoe McGowen of the *Times*. "Well, my players are solid for this one, and they're all going to wear it."¹ Whether they liked the helmets or not was never known. What they did know was they had better wear the helmets, or else.

On their first western trip of the season, the Yankees suffered a shocker: Ed Lopat was beaten by the Cleveland Indians. No one knew if it was a record, but before the game started Eddie was 30–6 lifetime against the Indians, including eleven straight victories as he took to the mound. The hex so bothered Cleveland management that they went for a suggestion by a Cleveland writer that rabbit feet be distributed to the first 15,000 fans. It worked, if you believe in that sort of foolishness, as Eddie was driven from the game in the second inning and Cleveland won, 8–2, dropping the Yankees 3½ games out of first.

On arrival in Detroit they were shutout, 5–0, by Bob Cain, a Tigers left-hander, who lasted just six years in the majors but should always be remembered as part of baseball history, Bill Veeck-style, that will never be repeated. He will forever be known by those with very sharp memories as the pitcher who walked Veeck's midget, Eddie Gaedel, banished the next day from the major leagues "in the best interests of baseball."²

Things got worse in St. Louis as Stengel tried to get by with third-line pitching and lost to the Browns, 5–4. The loss, one of their few to the Browns, was stinging since the Yankees went into the ninth winning 4–2. Joe Ostrowski was relieved by Tom Ferrick, who took the loss after St. Louis scored three runs for the win. Things got back to normal the next night as the Yankees, down 5–4 in the ninth, scored three off Stubby Overmire to win, 7–5. Consecutive hits by Rizzuto and Bobby Brown and an intentional walk to DiMaggio set up Ralph Houk for the winning hit.

I remember covering Bergen County for the *Newark Evening News* in 1961, the year Houk had taken over as manager for Casey Stengel. A young reporter for one of the area papers had written something about the Yankees that "The Major," as Houk liked to be called, didn't like. He called the young man into his office where a commotion was soon heard. Players entering found both on the floor, with Houk on top choking the reporter.

After order was restored the young man refused to press charges. Later the word was that he didn't want to pursue the matter and risk losing his job covering the Yankees. It didn't matter. Houk being Houk, the young man was soon gone anyway. Ralph the big shot, the Major, played eight years as Yogi's backup and just *91 games played, 43 hits for 158 at-bats*. In eight seasons. As we used to say in my youth, big deal.

It was soon obvious that Casey was 10 times the manager Houk was,

Maybe the irascible wasn't so irascible, the gibberish an act. So says Red Barber, who claimed Casey Stengel was very intelligent and coherent, but not when he wanted to fend off fools and scoundrels. While with the Yankees he ranked among the best managers in history, the inventor of the platoon system. After 10 pennants in 12 years he was fired, saying, "I'll never make the mistake of being 70 again."

a much more civilized man with a keen sense of humor that sometimes rubbed his players the wrong way. When he wanted to play the fool, as Red Barber used to say, he'd come up with something like "Now take Ty Cobb, who is dead at the present time." But when the Yankees let him go, he wasn't in the mood for Stengelese. He knew he was being fired because of age in the fall of 1960, after the most successful 11-year run in the game's history. At his last Yankees press conference, he told the assembled newsmen, "I'll never make the mistake of being 70 again."[3]

In the Dodgers clubhouse that first week in June, Jackie Robinson's zest for playing in Brooklyn was turning to bitterness as O'Malley's attitude toward him became increasingly hostile. Jackie couldn't find any reason for this until he and his wife Rachel discussed the situation for several days and finally came up with a reasonable answer that proved to be the true one: the psychological term known as transference.

O'Malley's hatred of Rickey was based, as noted, on jealousy because of Rickey's historic accomplishments and, as a former major league catcher, his rapport with players. The hatred was obviously transferred to Robinson, Rickey's prima donna, as O'Malley called him.

Things never really got better between them. Months later the relationship turned ugly when during a meeting with the Robinsons O'Malley accused Jackie of faking injuries to avoid playing in exhibition games. He added that Jackie had no right to complain about separate hotel accommodations for blacks since "such accommodations had been good enough in 1947" so why not today? At this point Rachel, who had sat by fuming, exploded, especially about O'Malley calling Jackie a prima donna. "I've seen him play with sore legs, a sore back without anybody on the team knowing it," she said. "Doing it not for praise but because he was thinking of the team. Nobody worries more about this club than Jackie Robinson, and that includes the owners.

"You know, Mr. O'Malley, bringing Jack into organized baseball was not the greatest thing Mr. Rickey did for him. He never listened to the ugly little rumors like those you have mentioned today. He understood Jack and stuck by him to the very end. They had mutual respect for the abilities and feelings of each other."

Jackie then reminded O'Malley that baseball had changed since 1947, but not hotel accommodation for black players. "It doesn't strike me as fair to have people sitting in comfort in an air-conditioned hotel room lecture me about not complaining." O'Malley backed off for the time being, but the anti–Rickey slurs and Robinson slights continued through the years until Jackie retired in 1956. The change of managers made no difference when Walter Alston took over from Dressen. Walter was an O'Malley loyalist and proved over the years to dislike Robinson's strong personality and outspoken ways.[4]

While Jackie was nursing his grievances, the Dodgers made one of the most important trades in their long history. On June 15 Brooklyn traded for the left fielder the front office had been looking for since the end of the war. In a deal with the Cubs, the Dodgers got Andy Pafko, one of the league's premier outfielders, and pitcher Johnny Schmitz, known as "the Dodger Killer." Brooklyn also received second baseman Wayne Terwiliger and catcher Rube Walker in exchange for outfielder Gene Hermanski, catcher Bruce Edwards, infielder Eddie Miksis and pitcher Joe Hatten.[5]

In those days getting traded to the Dodgers was euphoria for those coming in but a sad day for those going out, knowing they were leaving a potential pennant winner. So it was with Pafko, who said, "It's like someone just gave me $5,000." When Hermanski, who lived in New Jersey and was one of the happiest of Dodgers, heard of the remark, he said, "Yeah, my $5,000."

That same day Hodges produced one of the hits of his life. Playing in St. Louis with the Cardinals just two games behind the Dodgers, Gil came to bat with two out in the ninth, Snider on base and the Brooks down, 1–0, to the pitching of a brilliant Cardinals rookie, Joe Presko. Gil hit one out for a spectacular win that put the team ahead three games in first place.

The day of the Pafko trade was one of the busiest in years, four trades in which 22 players were exchanged. Locally, the Yankees got pitcher Bob Kuzava for pitchers Bob Porterfield, Fred Sanford and Tom Ferrick. They also sent pitcher Tommy Byrne and $25,000 to the St. Louis Browns for pitcher Frank "Stubby" Overmire. Byrne to St. Louis was one of those typical Yankees deals of that era where they sent a player to the Browns or Kansas City with a return address. When Byrne learned control while pitching for the Browns, the Yanks dealt to get him back in 1954.[6]

When word of the Pafko trade got out, the other National League clubs went crazy, with front office executives from all over the league charging some sort of collusion between the Cubs and the Dodgers to hand the pennant to Brooklyn. This was nonsense, but the other clubs were that angry. From their point of view the only weakness on the Brooklyn club was solved to the extent that the Dodgers now had one of the strongest outfields in history: Furillo, Snider and Pafko. Ever since the war, left field had been played by a holdover from wartime ball, a list that included Luis

Andy Pafko was a great outfielder mishandled by an arrogant, ignorant owner. Bought from the Cubs in 1951, he solved Brooklyn's perennial left-field problem. But in 1953 it shocked all of Brooklyn when he was dealt to Milwaukee for almost nothing, with O'Malley never explaining the most stupid deal in Dodgers history. Andy will always be remembered as the outfielder who saw Thomson's homer sail over his head into the stands of the Polo Grounds, carrying with it the '51 pennant.

Olmo, Pete Reiser (a shell of what he had been before hitting all those walls), Marv Rackley, Cal Abrams and Gene Hermanski. None of them approached Pafko's caliber.

The reaction of the *Times* Arthur Daley was typical:

> There was a moaning and groaning all over the National League last week when the power-laden Brooklyn Dodgers pried the power-hitting Andy Pafko loose from the Chicago Cubs. The Brooks need help as much as Custer needed more Indians.

He added that "with Pafko it's no contest." This was Daley's mundane style, reflecting the anger of executives throughout the league.[7]

The Dodgers got another plus, they thought. In acquiring Johnny Schmitz, they seemed to be getting one of the league's top pitchers, a left-hander who had won 68 games in seven years for the mostly last-place Cubs. Of those 68 wins, 18 were against the Dodgers, thus Johnny Schmitz "the Dodger Killer."

Things started well for Johnny as he gave up just two hits in seven innings in losing to Cincinnati's Ken Raffensberger, 2–1. But it soon appeared he had nothing left and was sold to the Yankees and then to Washington, Cincinnati, Baltimore and Boston, all of them hoping the magic would return.

As things turned out, the Pafko trade proved to be one of the strangest in the history of the Dodgers, perhaps in all of baseball. On January 17, 1953, without a word of warning or explanation, Walter O'Malley sold Andy to the Milwaukee Braves for $50,000 and second baseman Roy Hartsfield, who was never heard of again.

The trade was such a bombshell that it made page one above the fold in the the *Times*. Pafko was as puzzled by the deal as anyone else. As he was leaving Brooklyn, his regret was obvious as he expressed his feelings to the writers. "I don't know what's going on here," he said. "Three teams in three years is something I don't understand. Mr. O'Malley said he'd explain it to me in a letter why the deal." He never did. How could he explain the most senseless sale in Dodgers or maybe even baseball history?[8]

Pafko was replaced by Sandy Amoros, a fast, fair-hitting outfielder famous for saving Johnny Podres' shutout in the '55 World Series. As for Pafko, he played only 1½ seasons in Brooklyn but he'll always be remembered for that dramatic picture of him back against the wall in the Polo Grounds watching Bobby Thomson's historic home run sail over his head and into the stands.

With the arrival of Amoros the Dodgers faced a situation commonplace today but a rarity back in the early 1950s. Amoros was from Havana

A brilliant strategist who managed the New York Mets to their first pennant and World Series in 1969, beating the highly favored Baltimore Orioles, Gil Hodges was the best first baseman of his generation and one of the most feared sluggers of the late 1940s and 1950s, skills that deserved election to the Baseball Hall of Fame years ago. The bats represent the game he hit four homers in a nine-inning game on August 31, 1950.

and didn't speak a word of English. With so many Hispanic ballplayers that is not a problem today since there are enough Spanish-speaking teammates to help those who don't learn English.

But this was a new experience for a Dodgers team — outfielders not being able to communicate verbally, plus all the social situations where a common language is necessary. Some of the players in later years resented Hispanic players who made no attempt to learn our language while earning their living here.

Amid all this turmoil stirred up by Pafko's leaving, Gil Hodges was having a hell of a spring. On June 14 against the Cardinals in Sportsman's Park, he came up in the top of the ninth and hit his 20th homer, scoring Snider ahead of him for a dramatic 2–1 victory. Erskine earned the win after Branca had pitched one-run ball for eight innings.

Then on the 24th he had one of the best days of his career, hitting three homers in a losing doubleheader against the Pirates in Forbes Field. Gil had many multiple-homer games, most notably his four-homer game at Ebbets Field on August 31, 1950. Only 17 other men have hit four in a game. And only one man in history has come close to hitting five. Joe Adcock, a first baseman for Milwaukee, hit four in a row at Ebbets Field on July 31, 1954. His fifth shot hit the top of the screen in right field for a double.

In 2009 Jim Rice was elected to the Baseball Hall of Fame. At .298 with 382 home runs — 208 in cozy Fenway Park — Rice's stats seem a bit weak, but that doesn't matter any more. As I've written before, once Orlando Cepeda was voted in, weak stats and all, anything goes.

With those two in, there is still a case here for Hodges, but it's fading year by year. It doesn't seem to matter that he was not only a great slugger but the best fielding first baseman of his generation, or possibly any generation He once lost out by one vote of the Old Timers Committee because Roy Campanella was too ill to attend. Gil's one weakness was the low outside curveball. But for that he would have been in the Hall years ago with certainly 500 homers or more.

On June 18 in Chicago Campanella came up in the ninth inning with Brooklyn behind, 2–1 and Hodges on base. He hit one off Omar "Turk" Lown, at the time one of the league's top relievers, to beat the Cubs, 3–2.

Two days later, June 20, was one of baseball's busiest days. The owners were getting rid of Albert "Happy" Chandler, who as the years have passed seems to have been the best baseball commissioner the game has known. That same day Bill Veeck decided to form a syndicate to buy the St. Louis Browns from his partners rather than sell it or try to move it.

Chapter Six: June

Chandler had been commissioner since 1945 when he replaced Kenesaw Mountain Landis, who died the year before. Landis was tough to follow as the man chosen to save baseball after the White Sox threw the 1919 World Series to Cincinnati. His solution was to set an example by barring the fixers for life, a tactic that seemed to work if one didn't dig too deeply.* Anyway, Landis was viewed as baseball's savior, and his rulings were obeyed without question for the next 25 years.

In his second year Chandler faced a crisis of major proportions. Jackie Robinson had just been brought up by Brooklyn and on their first trip west the St. Louis Cardinals, led by an outspoken Enos Slaughter, threatened to strike if they had to play against Robinson. NL President Frick, backed by Chandler, immediately announced that any player who carried out the threat would be suspended indefinitely. The game went on as scheduled.

There have been denials that any of this ever happened. Stan Musial, for one, said years later that there never was a meeting called by Slaughter and that a team strike was never considered. However, there is plenty of evidence to the contrary. The strike threat, revealed by some of our best sportswriters of the time, made headlines throughout the country and was written of by most of our most widely read columnists, led by Stanley Woodward of the *Herald-Tribune*.

What could Red Schoendienst have been thinking while denying that anything whatsoever had been happening among the Cardinals when such headlines were being read? "I was there," he said, "but I don't know anything about it. We went out and we played. There was no reason for the Cardinals to go out on strike. The media just looked for a good story."[9] Amazing.

Baseball's loss after Chandler has been for the most part a series of commissioners completely subservient to the owners, not to the interests of baseball. Bart Giametti died too soon in office and Fay Vincent was too independent to stay for long but the rest were either disgraceful or, like Peter Ueberroth, disinterested.

Ford Frick, General William Eckert, Bowie Kuhn and Allan (Bud) Selig, were the men who for years overlooked "greenies" and finally steroids, the latter having disgraced some of the game's biggest names and, I hope, will keep them out of the Baseball Hall of Fame. The sentiment for such action is increasing, with some talk of banning steroid users for life even on the first offense, a la Judge Landis. The latest spokesman for such action

---

*See page 23 on Cobb/Speaker.

has been David Wells, a roustabout for most of his career, even when he pitched a perfect game for the Yankees.

But Selig is the worst and holds a special niche in the history of the game. He is *an owner,* whether or not he has put his stock in some kind of trust or escrow doesn't matter. He has been an owner and he thinks like an owner. He need not be subservient to the owners; he *is* one.

The latest example of his ties to the owners — at the expense of the fans — is his approval of the Yankees and Mets outrageous 2009 ticket prices. The Yankees at season's start priced the seats behind home plate at an unbelievable $2,565 *for each game.* Not a peep out of Selig at the time. After the seats remained empty for most games, the Yanks lowered the price to $1,250 per game, with Selig announcing his approval. The Mets are somewhat lower, charging $565 for prime seats, outrageous enough. Again, not a word from Selig.

This would have been unbelievable in the days of my youth, but again, as I write this it is November 1, 2009, and the Yankees and Phillies are playing the second game of their World Series, take note, *in November.* The players can't complain because of the money they now make. But how about the fans, shivering in the stands?

As for Bill Veeck on that busy June 20, he was confident as he took over the Browns that he could challenge the Cardinals' popularity. He'd been successful in Cleveland and thought he could repeat in St. Louis. He apparently forgot or didn't realize that he had no competiton in Cleveland and that the St. Louis Browns were not the Cleveland Indians.

The Browns were, in fact, the most woeful franchise in major league history. The record books show that in their 52-year history, they were in last place 14 times, in seventh place 12 times, and finished in the first division, including their only World Series appearance, only seven times. Even their World Series, in which they lost to the Cardinals, was tainted — 1944 wartime ball in which a drunken brawler like Sigmund Jakucki was a starter for the Browns.

Jacucki was 0–3 with the Cardinals in 1935 and then disappeared to the minors until the Browns, desperate for pitching, called him up in 1944. Like many wartime ballplayers he was released after the 1945 season as the pre-war major leaguers were being discharged.

On that same June 20 the Giants came to life. Looking back it was an ominous day for the Dodgers, but of course no one could have realized it. The Dodgers had just gotten Andy Pafko from the Cubs, making the Brooklyn outfield one of the best in baseball history. The Giants had started the season with 11 straight losses and now almost into July had climbed over the .500 mark for the first time all season. The win was the eighth straight for Sal Maglie as he beat the Pirates, 8–2, at the Polo Grounds.

Dodgers fans like me paid no attention to what we considered a meaningless game. The Dodgers were unbeatable. They had just traded for Andy Pafko and thus had the finest major league outfield in many a year.

The next day Stengel, in Arthur Daley's "Sports of the Times" column saluting Braves manager Billy Southworth on his retirement, said unequivacably what many a lesser man like Charlie Dressen would never admit: the manager with the horses wins the race. He first told Daley that he wished "he could get just one more top-flight pitcher and then I'd be a smart manager again.

"I didn't start my career as manager of world champions. I'm the same guy who got nowhere as manager of the Dodgers and the Braves. The only difference now is that I have some real ballplayers to work with."[10] Casey was literate, outspoken, and honest but, as Red Barber used to say, only when he wanted to be.

CHAPTER SEVEN

July

On July 2 the suicide of Hugh Casey shocked the baseball world, especially in Brooklyn where he once been the Dodgers' most dependable reliever for years. The *Brooklyn Eagle* ran an eight-column banner on page one and then described how Casey, rifle in hand pointing at his head, was on the phone with his wife when he pulled the trigger. He was only 38 years old.

His last words to his wife Kathleen as she was begging him not to pull the trigger were, "I am innocent of those charges." She then heard the shotgun blast and knew he was dead. "I pleaded with him not to do it," she said. "I told him it was up to God and not him but he said he was ready to die, that this was his time."

Hugh had been speaking of a paternity charge brought against him by a Brooklyn woman who accused him of fathering her child, which he repeatedly denied. Hugh also had other troubles that were dogging him, mainly his separation from his wife, and financial problems that included unpaid back income taxes. He might have been saved by a close friend who, divining his purpose after talking to him on the phone, rushed to Casey's hotel but said he was some 30 feet from his room when he heard the fatal blast.[1]

Hugh was one of the most popular Dodgers ever, not only as a ballplayer but as the owner of Casey's Bar across from Ebbets Field. Casey's Bar was the place where Dodgers fans celebrated significant team victories inside, with Casey behind the bar, and outside, covering most of Bedford Avenue and Sullivan Place.

After a fine career Casey retired in 1949 at age 36, leaving an ERA of 3.34 with 75 wins and 42 losses, both great figures for a relief pitcher. But sadly enough he is best remembered by most baseball followers for the loss to the Yankees in the 1941 World Series, the game in which one of his spitballs got by catcher Mickey Owen.

CHAPTER SEVEN: JULY

The Dodgers, down 2–1 in the Series, were winning the fourth game 4–3 with two out in the ninth. Tommy Henrich struck out, but that third strike was a spitter that eluded Owen. By the time Mickey retrieved the ball at the backstop, Tommy was on first. Then disaster for Casey as DiMaggio singled, Charlie Keller hit a two-run double, Bill Dickey walked, and Joe Gordon hit another two-run double. Final score: 7–4, Yanks.

That spitter for years was called a passed ball as ruled by the scorer, making Owen the goat. Even though Reese and Coscarart called it a spitter, the writers apparently never heard them, or worse, ignored them. The issue was settled years later when Casey admitted to sportswriter Tommy Holmes of the *Brooklyn Eagle* and then the *Herald-Tribune* that the pitch was indeed a spitball that swooped downward under Owen's glove.[2]

Even today I read respected writers on how Owen "dropped the ball" or "let it get by him." Silly. If he had merely dropped the ball, he would have picked it up and thrown Henrich out by 30 feet. Even old and somewhat grainy newsreel clips show that the ball was uncatchable as it swooped downward under his glove and bounced all the way to the backstop. Passed balls didn't happen very often to Mickey Owen. He was probably the best defensive catcher of his time, in the big leagues for 13 years because of his glove, not his .255 average and 14 home runs.

On the Fourth of July, the traditional halfway mark in the season, the Yankees were one-half game behind the Cleveland Indians, and the Dodgers 4 1/2 in front of the Giants. The Dodgers had been leading all year and with their confidence growing saw no reason for a pennant that would wipe away some of the bitterness of 1950.

Though the Yankees were not in first place, they were as cocky as ever, knowing that their Big Three would come through as they did in '49 and '50. At this halfway point Raschi was 12–4, Lopat 10–4 and Reynolds, who started and relived, 10–4 — a combined 32–12.

They were the best three-man rotation in the history of the game and are barely remembered today; neither are the five straight Yankees World Series wins they made possible. This may be off the mark but of all the young people I've talked baseball to, including friends of the family, none remembered those great Yankees teams of the '50s or the Big Three who made possible the record five World Series in a row. And most of those I talked to were *Yankees* fans.

The five-year record of the three is almost unmatched in baseball history. Lopat was 81–36, Raschi 92–40 and Reynolds 83–41, for a total of 255–117 for the five championship years. Few three-man rotations have ever approached those figures other than Atlanta's Glavine, Maddux and

Another time-robbed great pitcher, Vic Raschi wasn't a full-time major leaguer until 1948 when he was 29. For the next six years he was Hall-of-Fame caliber, partners with Allie Reynolds and Eddie Lopat in that record World Series run. A burly 6'1", during those six years, he was 109–48 and then dealt away because he refused an undeserved paycut.

Smoltz during the years 1991 to 1995, and they weren't under the constant pennant pressure the Yankees' Big Three were.

Vic Raschi, big and burly at 6'1" and 205 pounds, was the leader of the Big Three at 92–40 for their five-year record-setting World Series run. Sportswriters nicknamed him "the Springfield Rifle," their tribute to him as one of the best fastball pitchers of his generation and to his hometown, West Springfield, Massachusetts. He also had a good slider, changeup, control and a level of concentration that was respected by all. Before and during a game it was wise to avoid Vic, to stay out of his way. When Yogi Berra would approach him on the mound during a crucial part of a game, he was told to get the hell back behind the plate.

In all justice Raschi, with a Yankees career winning percentage of .700, the result of a 120–50 record, should be the official all-time Yankees percentage leader. Instead their front office insists that Spud Chandler, at .717 based on his career record of 109–43, holds the Yankees record.

Their former public relations director, Rick Cerrone (no relation to the Yankees catcher), a superior type you would expect to represent the Yankees, wouldn't listen to my reasoning. Chander, I pointed out, pitched during the war and 38 of his 109 wins were against young kids and veterans brought out of retirement. I cited Joe Nuxhall, who pitched in a game for Cincinnati on June 10, 1944, at age 15; Tommy Brown, Brooklyn Dodgers shortstop at 16, also in 1944; and Babe Herman, one of many older men brought out of retirement, Babe in 1945.

On that June day Nuxhall became the youngest major leaguer in history, although he pitched only one-third of an inning. Cincinnati had been scouting young Joe as he pitched in junior high school, a 6'3", 195-pound "phenom." Young Joe was with Cincinnati during school vacation when manager Bill McKechnie, losing 13–0 in the ninth inning, decided to test his 15-year-old.

Joe later admitted he was scared to death, as any teenager would be, but willing. His stint was a nightmare — two-thirds of an inning, five runs on five walks, two singles and a wild pitch before McKechnie replaced him. He walked off with a 67.5 ERA. It all ended well, however. He was shipped down and came back at age 23 to become one of Cincinnati's better pitchers, retiring after 16 years at 135–117 and an ERA of 3.90.

Tommy Brown was a different story. He was never the star Brooklyn hoped he'd be but Rickey held on to him until 1950. During those six years he was inconsistent and not hitting well. Brown's moment of fame in Brooklyn was when he slugged a photographer smaller and much older than him for some kind of slight.

Babe Herman, once one of the most famous Brooklyn Dodgers, a .324 hitter over 13 seasons, was lured out of retirement by Brooklyn in 1945 at age 42 eight years after his last game, becoming one of many older men who were brought back. He played in 37 games and hit .265 before retiring again.

Chandler remains in the top Yankees spot but I still think I am morally, if not technically, right. In my opinion, no man who played wartime ball against such inferior competition should be in line for any record-setting recognition. Hal Newhouser in the Baseball Hall of Fame, for example, is a joke with 70 of his 207 wins against wartime competition, especially when you compare him to Bert Blyleven with 287 wins and Jim Kaat with 283, both with mostly second-division teams, and neither in the Hall.

Raschi's end with the Yankees came after the 1953 season, when he was 13–6 in that record-setting fifth of the World Series championship years. When George Weiss told him his pay would be cut, Vic refused to go along and was dealt to the Cardinals immediately. Such was his reward from General Manager Weiss for a great career and five of the most exciting years in baseball history.

Allie Reynolds was known as "Superchief" on the mound because of his commanding presence and his Native American

One of the Big Three in the Yankees' record five consecutive World Series wins, Allie Reynolds was a journeyman pitcher before Yankees coach Spud Chandler taught him to "think, not just throw." He then became one of the stars of the American League, a big, fastball-throwing Oklahoman, one-quarter Creek Native American. He retired in 1954 after six World Series with the Yankees and a 182–107 won-lost record.

ancestry and heritage. He was also a Yankees workhorse, starting and reliving during the five World Series wins, when he won 83 and lost 41.

A six-footer at 195 pounds, he was graduated from Oklahoma State University and later signed with the Cleveland Indians for a $1,000 bonus, paid as he reported to Springfield in the Class C Middle Atlantic League. Reynolds was 30 years old with a mediocre 51–47 record when the Yankees traded for him in October of 1946. Spud Chandler, in the last year of his career, gave Allie advice that made him a consistent winner.

"Don't just throw the ball," Chandler told him. "Think about what you're doing. Change speeds. Set the batter up. Think." As a result Reynolds became a pitcher, not just a thrower. In 1947, his first year as a Yankee, he went 19–8 and led the American League with a winning percentage of .704.

His record for his eight years as a Yankee was 131–60, a .680 winning percentage. During those years Allie pitched two no-hitters. The first was a 1–0 masterpiece on July 12 in Cleveland decided by a Gene Woodling homerun in the seventh inning.

The second was a storybook thriller at Yankee Stadium on September 28 that for the Yanks clinched a tie for the pennant. Allie said later he was aware of the no-hitter but knew he had to face Ted Williams for the final out. Reynolds threw two fastballs, Williams swung at the second and popped it up behind home plate. Berra waited under it and then dropped the ball.

Berra said Williams was angry and poured out his scorn on him, telling him he "blew the chance" and that he would bear down harder. But on Reynolds' next pitch, Williams popped up again. This time Berra held the ball.[3]

Lopat, the third of the Big Three, came to the Yankees from the White Sox, where for four seasons he won 50 and lost 49 for barely a .500 percentage with a second-division club. In his seven full seasons with the Yanks his percentage rose to .680 on his 109–51 record. In the record five World Series, he was 4–1.

Eddie was born in New York City, played stickball as a youth on the west side, and was graduated from De Witt Clinton High School. He broke into organized ball in 1937 and made the majors in 1944 with the Chicago White Sox. It was the beginning of a 12-year career during which his record was 166–112 for a .597 winning percentage.

Unlike Raschi and Reynolds, Eddie was not a big man with a blazing fastball. He was 5'10" and didn't have a fastball that he could throw consistently past hitters. He had excellent control and was a master at moving

Eddie Lopat was a journeyman who became a big winner in New York. He was known as "the Junkman" among American League hitters, a man without a fastball who depended on guile and location in winning 112 games in his Yankees career. With Vic Raschi and Allie Reynolds he helped the Yankees win five consecutive World Series.

the ball around, constantly keeping the hitters off balance by throwing "junk" as ballplayers described his pitching. Ted Williams, perhaps the greatest hitter the game has known, was so frustrated by Eddie's off-speed stuff that whenever Lopat's name came up, he'd say "that fucken Lopat."

"My main purpose was to make the hitter hit off-stride," Lopat said. "I couldn't overpower hitters so I had to work from a different angle." Instead of a "blazer" he used curveballs, sliders, a knuckler and screwballs — all delivered at various speeds from different angles.

Many batters, including Williams, complained that after facing Lopat their timing might be off for several games. In his final days as a Yankee Eddie had a bad start in 1955 and was 4–8 in July. Weiss traded him to the Baltimore Orioles where he was just 3–4 when he retired at season's end. He was 37 years old.

Again, those three, Raschi, Reynolds and Lopat, are the best threesome baseball has ever seen, but they were aided for all those years by one of the best catchers who ever lived. When he started in 1947 Yogi Berra was awkward and clumsy, far below Yankees standards. But thanks to Bill Dickey's coaching, by this year, 1951, he was among the best in the game.

Yogi was born in 1925 and as a youth played baseball against Pete Reiser and Joe Garagiola on the St. Louis sandlots and in American Legion ball. For some reason he quit school in the eighth grade. As we went to war he was drafted into the navy and served as a gunner's mate during the invasion of Normandy.

After the war the Yankees

At 23 Yogi Berra shaped up after a stinging lecture from Joe DiMaggio to become an eventual Baseball Hall of Fame catcher in 14 World Series, a record 75 games. A notorious bad ball hitter, he was .285 lifetime batter with 358 homers, but drove pitchers crazy trying to figure out how to pitch to him. The Robinson steal of home haunted him for years.

signed him for a $500 bonus, assigning him to the Triple-A Newark Bears as a catcher. He was brought up to the Yankees in 1947, a squat 5' 8" reserve catcher playing behind Aaron Robinson. When he became full-time at 23 he tended to dog it until DiMaggio put a stop to it, as related in Allen Barra's *Yogi*.

After a doubleheader with the Washington Senators in early 1948, Joe, then 34 with a lot of baseball mileage on him, came wearily off the field, wincing from the pain in his right heel. As he was peeling off his sweatshirt, he saw Berra, who had not played the second game, joking around in the clubhouse.

"What the hell's wrong with you," he said to Berra. "You're 23 years old and you can't catch a doubleheader. My ass." This was anger from on high, and Berra listened. Lopat said later that was the only time he ever heard DiMaggio lose his temper like that in the clubhouse. "Joe chewed him out for 20 minutes, and after that Yogi caught more games than any other catcher."[4]

There's always one play that stands out in a ballplayer's mind, be they sandlot or professional. For Yogi it was Robinson's steal of home in the 1955 World Series. Berra, whose reflexes were as fast as anyone's in baseball, was up for the play as Robinson was sliding home. From the replay on film it appears that Jackie was out, but there is some doubt. In any event that play has become one of Berra's crosses, but less so as the years have passed.

For example, my daughter Ann was having dinner at the Highland Pavilion, a pricey restaurant in the hills of West Orange, New Jersey, when she noticed that Berra and his family, who live in nearby Upper Montclair, were eating at the next table. She called me on her cell phone to tell me. "As you're leaving," I told her, "tell Mr. Berra that your father says Robinson was safe."

Yogi jumped up from his seat and repeated emphatically, "He was out, he was out," but without the bitterness of years past. "He was enjoying himself," Ann told me later. "Soon the whole place was laughing with him, everyone having a good time." Yogi in old age, finally smooth and content.

The '51 All-Star game, won by the Nationals, 8–3, stands out for several reasons, starting with the selection of DiMaggio. It was July 9, and Joe had missed 38 games with injuries and wasn't on the All-Star ballot. At the July 4 break he was hitting .261 with six home runs, yet Stengel chose to add him to the All-Star squad. Here the DiMaggio mystique comes into play again. Joe was having his worst season, injury plagued, arm gone, his once-superb baseball reflexes betraying him.

CHAPTER SEVEN: JULY   115

John Drebinger, sportswriter for the *Times*, describes DiMaggio's moods and demeanor during this midseason of his last year in baseball. Joe had given a "short and surly answer" to a writer who had asked him why he had dropped out of a game at Boston that day.

"What the scribe didn't realize was that had been DiMaggio's mood for a long time," Drebinger wrote. "In fact, he rarely talks to his teammates or manager, let alone anyone remotely related to the press. On a recent train ride following a night game in Philadelphia, DiMaggio, in the Yankees special diner, sat by himself at a table for four. It's a queer set-up but almost everyone traveling with the Bombers is leaving the Clipper severely alone."[5]

That Boston writer had ignored the unspoken rule in asking DiMaggio why he jogged in from center field in mid-game just after taking the field. Was he injured or, the unspoken question, was he removed on Stengel's orders? Casey said after the game that DiMaggio had free rein to play or not, depending on his condition, and that he chose to come out. A weird answer since Joe had left the dugout giving no indication that he wouldn't finish the game. The writers were reluctant, almost afraid, to question him later.

I once spent an evening with DiMaggio and others in 1968 at a restaurant opening in Newark and my impression of him was nothing like the above. Admittedly, he was there as a favor to the owner and was among friends in a safe area of Newark he was familiar with. But that aside, I found him friendly and open, an impeccably dressed man who seemed content with himself at age 54.

That afternoon I had received a call from a banker friend inviting me to meet DiMaggio at the restaurant's opening. When we arrived Joe was sitting at the head of a rectangular table flanked on each side by three elderly and obviously overawed Italian gentlemen. We sat opposite Joe and waited to hear the conversation. There was none. Being a nervy ex-reporter, I asked Joe how Dom was — anything to cut through the silence. There was a collective gasp from the overawed gentlemen. I was speaking to DiMaggio and *calling him Joe.*

"Dom's fine," DiMaggio replied. "He owns half of Boston."

"How about Vince?" I persisted, feeling the tension starting to evaporate. "Vince is doing great," was the answer. "I'm the only bum in the family, the only one without a job."

It broke up the room with laughter, and everybody relaxed and conversation started to flow. After an hour or so we left, but first I approached DiMaggio at the bar. "Mr. DiMaggio," I said, "I'm sorry I called you Joe in front of those gentlemen."

"That's all right, lots of people call me Joe. Besides I knew you were trying to break the ice and you did a good job." As we shook hands I asked him something I'd always wanted to ask a major leaguer of his caliber: who was the greatest of all ballplayers?

"Babe Ruth, no question," he said. "Cobb is number two, but most people forget that Ruth was a great pitcher before he switched to the outfield. I think he could have made the Hall of Fame as a pitcher." As I left I was glad that the great DiMaggio agreed with me, or vice versa.

It occurred to me later that Joe was completely at ease in those surroundings knowing that no one would ask him embarrassing questions about Marilyn Monroe or any other subject he was known to be touchy about. I have no doubt that some sportswriters had suffered DiMaggio's scorn at times, but his reported surly behavior was not seen that night — no doubt because there were no sportswriters around to pester or goad him. But surly or not I don't ever remember reading or hearing about him enjoying humiliating writers, old or young, in front of their peers as Mantle did for a good part of his career. He obviously never did or the world would have heard about it.

Joe kept his distance from most writers, and he was right most of the time. For example, years later he refused to allow Richard Ben Cramer to interview him for a supposed DiMaggio biography. The resultant book, without Joe's cooperation, was the most disgraceful on any sports personality that I have ever read, so unjust and distorted that I won't despoil this book by naming its title. And there is not one footnote, not one scintilla of proof for any of this writer's outrageous claims.

For the sake of space I'll give just one example. The following is what we are asked to believe, with no proof whatsoever.

During the San Francisco earthquake of 1989 Joe was the only person on his block allowed by police to check on his living quarters. He supposedly left his building with a bulging black plastic bag. In the bag, the author writes, was $60,000 or so in cash that Joe was given years before for safekeeping by Longy Zwillman, a big-time New Jersey gangster and allegedly a founding member of Murder Incorporated, the Brownsville murder-for-hire thugs led by Louis (Lepke) Buchalter, who was executed in Sing Sing in March of 1944. Zwillman was murdered by hanging in his West Orange, New Jersey, basement in February 1959, a murder that to this day is unsolved.

Why was Joe given the money? Did he even know Zwillman, and if he did why and when did they meet and where? And why many years ago would Zwillman give Joe a bag full of cash to take from New Jersey to San

Francisco at some unknown date? Not one word of explanation for this fairy tale.

Worse, Russell Baker, one of history's best newspaper columnists and a shining light of the *New York Times* for years, wrote a book on personalities that included Cramer's assassination of DiMaggio's character. Baker warned his readers that Cramer's book contained no footnotes or corroboration of any kind. Yet he ran the segment. Disgraceful.

This would have been no surprise to Joe in his playing days. He knew there were always sharks among the writers, those who always looked for the dirty side. He got the treatment early in his career when he first asked for a raise. Every Yankees writer took management's side. So even though he was wary of them and kept his distance, even without asking the writers were aware that in Joe's last season he and Stengel rarely spoke, and that they had never been close from the day Casey was hired by Yankees general manager George Weiss. One reason was Joe's uncharacteristic answer when he was asked for his reaction at the time Stengel became Yankees manager. "We hired a clown," he said, referring to Stengel's antics as manager of the Braves and Dodgers in the 1930s.

Example: When managing the Braves during one game, Stengel left the dugout to protest a decision at home plate. He approached the home plate umpire and tipped his hat as a bird flew off the top of his head. At another time in protest against wet conditions, he came onto the field with an open umbrella, closing it as he was thrown out of the game. Clownish, for sure, but Stengel was not a man to forget public disparagement, not even from Joe DiMaggio.

Why then did Stengel appoint him to the All-Star squad when he was having the most dismal season of his career? The answer to that question was given by Cleveland manager Lou Boudreau in a similar situation just before the 1949 All-Star game. Joe had been out for most of the year with a heel spur and therefore had not been on the ballot for the All-Star vote. When asked why he named Joe to the team in violation of the rules, Boudreau replied, "Joe DiMaggio is Joe DiMaggio." Obviously Casey Stengel felt the same way. Unlike Boudreau, however, Stengel, having paid respect to Joe's Hall-of-Fame stature, didn't play him. He publicly denied, however, that there was any kind of rift between him and Joe.

"Everyone who comes along asks me that question," Stengel told the press. "I ask them what's he doing here if we're not talking? Do you think Will Harridge (American League president) put him on the team?"

The naming of Ned Garver of the St. Louis Browns as the starter was another reason the game was memorable since he was the only pitcher from a last-place team to ever start an All-Star game. Ned was 11–4 at the time and proved to be the best pitcher of the day, giving up just one hit and one unearned run in his three innings.

The Nationals won, even though winning pitcher Sal Maglie had a bad outing, allowing three hits and two runs in the three middle innings. Loser Ed Lopat was pounded, giving up three runs on three hits in his one-inning appearance. Thus Garver, from a last-place team that only the hardiest of fans followed, was the pitching star of the day. At the time Garver was probably the best pitcher in baseball, and managers were very aware of the Browns' rotation, especially watchful that he pitch against their rivals.

In the heat of our 1951 American League pennant race, with four clubs in a virtual tie for first place, Red Sox manager Steve O'Neill heard a rumor that Garver would not pitch against the Yankees in an upcoming series. "If Garver doesn't start against the Yankees this weekend," he angrily told the press, "I'll never speak to Bill Veeck again." Strangely, since he was held in such high regard around the league, Garver never had a chance to play with a winner, or even with a first-division team.

Veeck dealt him to Detroit in 1952, a last-place team which, in turn, dealt him to Kansas City, a seventh-place team. As a result Garver never played with even a sixth-place team and, after 14 years, ended up with a 129–157 won-loss and .451 winning percentage. It's a wonder that such a great pitcher never went with a winner. Where were the Yankees, picking up guys like Stubby Overmire and Fred Sanford instead of Garver?

The third reason this '51 game stands out is because of the seven Dodgers named to the team — Preacher Roe, Don Newcombe, Gil Hodges, Jackie Robinson, Pee Wee Reese, Roy Campanella and Duke Snider. This was not a record, for up to that time nine Yankees of 1942 were on the All-Star roster. The Dodgers, however, were resented by the rest of the National League, mainly because of Jackie Robinson. To repeat what Clem Labine once said to me in a telephone interview, Robinson by 1950–1951 affected the whole team by his frequent flare-ups. Clem said the team was blamed for the animosity Jackie aroused. "We became the bad guys," he said. "And this continued throughout Jackie's career."

You really can't blame Robinson when you think of the abuse heaped on him by teams throughout the league during the 1947 and '48 seasons, especially by the Phillies and their mean-spirited and racist manager Ben Chapman. Shouts from the dugouts, especially in Philadelphia, included calling him "nigger" and telling him things like "go back to the cotton fields where you belong." Robinson wrote in his book *I Never Had It Made* that those early attacks "brought me nearer to cracking up than I have ever been."[6]

Imagine a man of Robinson's combative nature having to suffer such indignities and humiliations for two entire seasons because of the promise he made to Rickey that he would keep himself under iron control no matter the provocation from anyone or any publication.

After two years Rickey wanted the battering of Robinson to stop because he saw the effect of such sustained self-control under almost unbearable circumstances had on Robinson. Thus, after the 1949 season Rickey released Robinson from his vow of silence, telling him all controls were off and that he could respond to his tormentors. That is when Robinson, understandably, took offense easily and came back at his former tormentors at full heat when the occasions arose.

The racist remarks continued throughout Robinson's career, but they were now mostly sotto voice rather than shouted from the dugouts. His tormentors obviously realized that this was a man six-feet tall and 195 pounds who had been a four-sport standout athlete at the University of California in Los Angeles. He was, they knew, not a man to get involved with physically.

At All-Star time baseball fans with a feel for the history of the game were mourning the death of Harry Heilmann, dead of lung cancer at 56 in Detroit where he played during his Hall-of-Fame career. Harry was a .342 hitter over 17 seasons and, playing out in Detroit, was not nearly as well known by future fans as many lesser players in the country's more metropolitan areas.

In a way Heilmann's career marked the end of an era — years when .400 hitters were not that uncommon. Harry hit .403 in 1923 with huge figures, including 211 hits in 524 at-bats. Since Heilmann, only Ted Williams has hit the .400 mark, achieving the feat 18 years later in 1941 at .403.

It could very well be that the years of the .400 hitter ended with the coming of the slider, a pitch like the curveball of many years before that drove many a major league prospect back to the minors. According to Bob Feller, it was developed in the late 1920s by George Blaeholder of the St. Louis Browns.[7]

The slider is not a curve or a fastball, but a combination of both. The batter at first instant sees the fastball but as he swings the ball dips down and away. As the developer of a pitch that in some ways changed the game, Blaeholder should be famous, but his problem was that he pitched for the lowly St. Louis Browns. He also was gregarious and shared the pitch with anyone interested. As it was, he had a very decent career, mostly with the second-division St. Louis Browns, an overall 104–125 record and an ERA of 4.54 over 11 seasons.

In the strange ways of baseball, Mickey Mantle was demoted from the Yankees to Kansas City in mid-July to make way for pitcher Art Schallock, up from the Hollywood Stars. Schallock was a good Pacific Coast League pitcher but in four seasons, some part-time, he was just 4–1 in the Bronx. Schallock's short major league career brings up the importance of size on the mound. As an example, the Dodgers' Carl Erskine, fine pitcher that he became, was at first considered small at 5'10" and 165 pounds. That size, for the most part, is the usual minimum for a pitcher, though have been exceptions such as Bobby Shantz at 5'6" and 139 pounds. Schallock, however, at 5'9" and 160 pounds, was one of the many who proved just too small to survive in the majors.

It has been called the greatest home run ever hit, but since 2002 there have been doubts. Thomson, like all the Giants playing at home, knew what was coming, thus tarnishing the accomplishment.

After his decision Stengel made it clear that Mantle would be back. "He showed me he could do everything," Stengel said. "He could hit, run and throw, but his one weakness was that he strikes out too often. But he'll be back. He went down to Kansas City with front office orders that he play every day, no matter what, in centerfield." This was interpreted around the game as the Yankees brass being certain that Mickey would eventually replace Joe in center field.

As Mickey was heading to Kansas City, Leo Durocher optioned injured third baseman Hank Thompson to Ottawa for recall when recovered. Putting outfielder Bobby Thomson at third was a great move. Durocher knew Thomson had played third down in the miners Rocky Mount and nearby Jersey City, but he had no idea how. He soon learned he had a great new third baseman for the

Giants' run through August and September. A number of Thomson plays saved games that proved vital at season's end.

Bobby was born in Glasgow, Scotland, in 1923 but grew up on Staten Island after his family settled in New York in 1925. He was signed by the Giants in 1946 after serving in the air force during the war. Of course, he is known for the most dramatic home run in baseball history, but it bought him no loyalty. In 1954 the Giants traded him to Milwaukee in a multi-player deal. You would think the Giants would have kept him for his entire career, but there is no such thing as gratitude in sports. In 1953, just a year before the trade, he hit .288 with 26 home runs and 106 RBIs. Somebody in that Giants organization was not only ungrateful but crazy. Or perhaps they rationalized the trade by remembering the home run was tainted, as was the Giants' stretch run for the pennant.

I have friends who say the trade was justified because the Giants received Johnny Antonelli in the deal. True, Antonelli's 21–7 record certainly contributed heavily toward the Giants winning the pennant by five games over the Dodgers. Nevertheless, they might well have won without him. After that pennant-winning home run, not knowing what I know now, I would never have traded Bobby. But then I am not a businessman and baseball is certainly a business, not just a sport.

The following week Chuck Connors, the Seton Hall slugger and television's "Rifleman," surfaced in Chicago and hit his first of two major league homers to help the Cubs beat the Dodgers on July 19. We'll never know how good Connors might have been because he left the game before proving himself one way or the other.

Connors had one at-bat with Brooklyn in 1949 when the sold him to Chicago. After 66 games with the Cubs he saw other horizons. At 6'5" and very handsome, he was approached by a Hollywood scout and given a screen test. Soon Hollywood money drove all thoughts of baseball from his mind.

On July 23 the Dodgers sold pitcher Dan Bankhead to the Montreal Royals in a move that would draw little attention except that Dan was the first black pitcher in major league history. In two-plus years in Brooklyn, Dan didn't come close to living up to expectations, given his size and experience.

He was 6'1" and 185 pounds and a power pitcher in the Negro Leagues. He came to Brooklyn in 1947, the same year as Jackie Robinson, but from the start he didn't seem to have it. The Dodgers brought him back in 1950 for his best year at 9–5 but with a 5.50 ERA. They gave up on him the following year.

There are several possibilities for Dan's failure in the big leagues. First, he might have been too old. He was listed as 27 when he came up but might have been much older, faking his age as many others still do. Think of Sam Jethro—two very good years before fading out in 1954. Another possibility is that Bankhead's three years in the Marines in World War II took a lot of him, as it did many others, including DiMaggio and Johnny Beazley, a 21–6 Cardinals pitcher in 1942. Finally, there is also the possibility that he was simply overrated, as in the Ken Burns series on major league baseball. As noted, Burns' segment on the Negro leagues tended to imply that all black players had major league potential. Many of them did, and proved it when they got the chance, but certainly not all. Think of Pumpsie Green, among others. Even the muscle of the NAACP charging racism when the Red Sox demoted him couldn't keep him in the majors.

As Bankhead was leaving the Dodgers, Clem Labine arrived from St. Paul, an exchange of pitchers any team would welcome. Labine was only 24 when he first arrived and eventually became one of the great relievers of his time, with one of the best curveballs and sinkers baseball has ever seen. It helped that he served as a paratrooper in World War II, for nothing fazed him on the mound. If Charley Dressen had used him as he should have during the August/September Giants surge, the Dodgers would have faced the Yankees, not the Giants.

Clem was born in 1926 in Lincoln, Rhode Island, and was a major leaguer for 13 years, mostly with the Dodgers. He was the kind of relief pitcher we don't see anymore—he could start when needed. He threw two notable shutouts as a starter: his 10–0 win over the Giants in the 1951 playoff, and his 1–0 shutout of the Yankees in the 1956 World Series. This rookie year, he went 4–0 with an ERA of one when Dressen, in one of his stubborn fits, benched him for a mistake on the mound. Clem, then the hottest pitcher in the league, sat for 12 days, and there went the pennant.

On July 25, the Yankees, ever in the hunt, moved up to a tie for first place with the Red Sox on a 2–1 win over the Indians on a Johnny Mize double that gave Lopat the win. It was a win that warms a Yanks fan's heart as the Yankees, down 1–0 in the ninth inning, scored twice on Mize's hit to pull the victory out.

Mize is one of the Yankees trademarks, an aging veteran that no one else would take a chance on but who came through for New York time after time. John was 36 years old and seemed over the hill when the Yankees acquired him from the Giants in 1949. He had five productive years in the Bronx, mainly at first base. As a pinch-hitter during his five Yankees years, he was 43-for-154, an excellent .270 batting average in that difficult role. He was invaluable during three of the team's five World Series, 1951 to '53, before he retired at the end of the '53 season.

Johnny Hopp was another over-the-hill Yankees bargain. His stay lasted just over a season but part of it was crucial. The Yankees got him from Pittsburgh for the last 19 games of the 1950 season and, as with Mize, he helped them edge Detroit for their second of five consecutive pennants.

For those 19 games Johnny batted .333, with one homer and eight RBIs. As a young Dodgers fan I remember that .333 and some of those eight RBIs because of their importance during the last week of the season when the Yankees, tied for the lead with one week to go, clinched the pennant on September 29 by three games over Detroit.

For my last example there was Johnny Sain, who helped the Yankees win the 1952 and 1953 pennants with his 11–6 and 14–7 pitching that no doubt helped the Yanks beat Cleveland by three games in '52 and run away with the pennant by 8½ games in '53. Johnny had been a four-time 20-game winner with the Braves but after his 20–13 year in 1950 he fell to 5–13 in '51 when the Yankees obtained him.

He left the game with a 139–116 record and an ERA of 3.49. After he retired he became one of the best pitching coaches in the game's history. "No other coach succeeded with so many pitchers using different styles," his biographical account reads. "He coached a number of pitchers who never won 20 games until he joined their team and they never won 20 after he left." 8

There were others besides Mize, Hopp and Sain, but the point is that Dodgers fans like me, bitter over what we called "Yankee luck," was for the most part not luck at all. Without Hopp, for example, I doubt the Yankees would have edged Detroit. But was it luck that they bought him for the last 19 games? Not at all. That was front office brains and willingness to spend money. The Yankees have been doing such things for years that many people have attributed to luck.

Of course, Stengel had a hand in all of this, an underrated "clown" because of his years with hapless teams like the Braves and Dodgers of the 1930s. As a frustrated Dodgers fan during Stengel's Yankees years, I don't have to be reminded that he ruled the baseball world with a record five straight World Series wins (1949–1953) and that he did it by inventing the platoon system — substituting often to get the most out of journeymen Cliff Mapes, Johnny Lindell and the like. There aren't many managers who have added a new dimension to the game.

Red Barber in his book *Rhubarb in the Catbird Seat* gives a word portrait of Stengel that I'd never seen in any of the many interviews I'd read. I take Red's word since he's the best sports announcer of my lifetime and a very decent and intelligent man. Stengel in Red's words comes out as a human being, not the usual uncommunicative curmudgeon portrayed in the sports pages.

> When George Weiss hired him in 1949 you'd have thought he'd hired somebody out of the circus. I never found him to be a clown unless he wished to be. Casey was about the smartest man I ever met, but a deliberate and astute practitioner in the art of misdirection, a master of double-talk. He wanted you to *think* he was a clown. An example: there was a writer Casey didn't like, but knew it was bad practice to antagonize a member of the press. The writer started toward us and Casey said to me "Watch me take care of him." The fellow asked a question and Casey answered him in his double-talk, which sounded almost like an answer. The guy was hanging on every word, thinking he had it and then not having it. This went on for about fifteen minutes until the game was starting. The writer left, without a usable quote.

Red cited as a classic example Stengel's testimony before the Kefauver Committee hearings on baseball's reserve clause. He said Stengel didn't want to go to Washington since it spoiled a day off for him and therefore decided to double-talk the senators.

"He talked for an hour and the subcommittee was fascinated," Red wrote, "but they didn't know what he said. The only thing they understood was his story about a wooden ballpark of years past." It must have taken some kind of courage to double-talk a senate committee but he got away with it. I remember watching the hearing on television and I, too, was amazed at how he could talk on and on without saying anything tangible. I also recall Mickey Mantle following him to the witness chair, and when Kefauver asked him what he thought, he replied, "I agree with everything Casey said." It brought down the house.

In Barber's opinion Stengel never did that to people he liked or when he really wanted to tell somebody something. "I once asked him to go over his lineup for me the second day of spring training. He pulled out a roster and went down it man by man, giving me a detailed, analytical report on every last man on his roster. It was remarkable and all season long everything he told me about every man held up."[9]

And Red is not alone in his admiration for Stengel. Leonard Shecter, for years a sportswriter for the *New York Post*, wrote in his book *The Jocks* that "the only great man I ever knew was Casey Stengel." And Shecter was one of the few writers in the game who didn't suffer fools silently. Much reviled throughout the game for his part in writing Jim Bouton's *Ball Four*, he wrote of Stengel's retirement: "When he limped out of baseball he took with him, I suddenly realized, the last part of the sports business that had any meaning for me."[10]

Not that the old man was loved by everyone because he, like Shecter, couldn't abide fools or big mouths. At one point during the 1958 World Series when the Yankees trailed the Milwaukee Braves, sportscaster Howard Cosell asked Stengel if the Yankees were choking. "If there's any choking it'll be you when I shove this microphone down your throat," Stengel replied.[11] A man of many facets Mr. Stengel. It's a shame that the good side of him rarely, if ever, showed up in the sports sections.

Maybe it was the July heat or possibly someone put something in the coffee of Secretary Charles Iuggi of Local 802, American Federation of Musicians. He came out against the Dodgers Sym-Phony, a group of amateur musicians that had been entertaining Ebbets Field crowds since 1938. "They don't get peanuts for their work," Iuggi said in demanding that the group get paid at least $100 a week for their efforts.

That little band was Brooklyn, it was Ebbets Field, it was Uncle Robby and Babe Herman all rolled into one. Was it wrong for a group of guys to want to have fun strolling through the stands amusing thousands of fans? Their music certainly wasn't Tommy Dorsey but the crowd loved it for years. They didn't want to be paid and, with the rest of Brooklyn, resented some union clown sticking his nose in. They got free admission to the ballpark and they wanted nothing more.

The Sym-Phony members finally appealed to King's County Judge Samuel Liebowitz to step in and try to reason with the union leaders. Although the discussions were never revealed, it was obvious that the judge did the job. The boys kept on playing until that final last game, September 24, 1957, Dodgers 2 Pittsburgh 0, winning pitcher Danny McDevitt.

July closed out with the country reading about another congressional investigation into baseball, but this one for a change wasn't one of those boring hearings with politicians droning on for press and television coverage. Ty Cobb, the old "Georgia Peach" saw to that.

The House Judiciary subcommittee was inquiring into baseball practices that might have monopolistic tendencies. Representative Emanuel Cellar, subcommittee chairman, said the inquiry was to establish whether baseball's farm system might embody evils detrimental to the interests of ballplayers and the public.

Specifically, Cellar said, his subcommittee wanted to know whether the club owners used the farm system to unduly increase their profits, to keep worthy players from advancement, to stifle competition, and to manipulate pennant races. Most important of all and what took the greater part of the hearings was the reserve clause. Was it legal to bind a player to one team for his entire professional life?

As he took the stand Cobb recalled an experience he had involving the reserve clause when he held out for more money in 1913. He said he had won six batting titles in a row and was refused when he asked Detroit owner Frank Nevin for a raise from $9,000 to $15,000 a season. Cobb testified that he then asked to be traded to another team where he no doubt could negotiate for a better salary. Nevin again refused, telling Cobb that "he could play for the Tigers or not play at all in organized baseball."

That brought a sharp reaction from Senator Hoke Smith of Georgia. "This looks like peonage," the senator said. Cobb denied this, saying that he knew of no instances in which the reserve clause had worked to the disadvantage of players. This after telling the committee of his early Detroit experience.

"Baseball," he said, "has made it possible for hundreds of young men from small towns, like myself, to improve their lot in life and become useful members of their communities. I revere baseball. I'm loyal to it for what it has done for me. It has done similar things for hundreds of others."[12]

Ty Cobb was certainly a great ballplayer, the top vote-getter in the first Baseball Hall of Fame ballot in 1936. Cobb received 222 votes, followed by Babe Ruth's 215. But his memory seems flawed here. The game certainly improved the lives of thousands of young men through the years. Nevertheless, the reserve clause was, in essence, a form of slavery in that there have been hundreds of ballplayers in the past who would have changed teams had they been allowed to.

The hearings stalled after Cobb's testimony, but then on August 8 the case of first baseman Ferris Fain rekindled interest in the proceedings. It turned out to be one of the most flagrant abuses ever associated with the minor league draft.

Testifying was Damon Miller, business manager of the San Francisco Seals of the Pacific Coast league, on the major leagues' right to draft minor leaguers for a fixed price of $10,000 without the consent of the owners. This, he argued, prevented minor league clubs from maintaining strong rosters, forcing them to rebuild from year to year.

Fain, a future All-Star with the Philadelphia Athletics, was one of the players the Seals decided to hold onto, Fagan testified, thinking the major league representatives "would not have the gall" to draft them in the face of the owner's opposition. But the Athletics disregarded the Seals' position and drafted Fain for $10,000 — a player in Fagan's opinion who would have gone in an open market for at least $100,000. Fagan was certainly right. As the committee was sitting, Fain was on his way to a .344 average and a batting championship.

Even so, it was no surprise to many that Cobb would still take the side of the owners. The man was ornery, unpredictable and one of the nastiest ever to play the game. Many of his fellow players, even teammates, thought he was insane. He played the game without mercy and expected none, slashing second basemen with his sharpened spikes and even attacking a fan in the stands. The *Detroit Free Press* described his play as "daring to the point of dementia."

The most prevalent theory for his conduct was that he never recovered from the shock of his mother shooting his father when he was 19 years old. The official account of the shooting was that Ty's father came into his home one night through their bedroom window, ostensibly having forgotten his keys. Mrs. Cobb told the police that she thought he was a burglar and shot him. She was charged with murder but was acquitted on the grounds of self defense, never having to explain why she had a shotgun in her bedroom on that particular night.

The rumors, however, were that Mr. Cobb thought his wife was unfaithful and was coming through the bedroom window in hopes of catching her with a lover. The situation was never really resolved by her acquittal, and what drove Ty frantic were the rumors that persisted through the years.

Whether he was crazy or not, Cobb had his canny side. Coca-Cola was founded in 1888 but was still unknown when Ty, listening to his advisers for once, invested in the company in 1907. As a result, when he died in 1961 he was a multi-millionaire, owning 20,000 Coca-Cola shares and three bottling plants.

The hearings ended without any concrete action taken, as usual. The owners were happy with their reserve clause, content in their knowledge that Congress would remain silent on the matter as it had down through the years since 1922. That was when Supreme Court Justice Oliver Wendell Holmes, writing the majority in a suit involving the Federal League, ruled that baseball was a sport and not a business and was therefore not covered by any of the federal anti-trust laws.

Ty Cobb always denied it, but the intent behind the reserve clause was no less than slavery in its widest sense — once a player signed with a team he was bound to that team for life, unless he was traded. No matter what he did, he could not sign with another team without the consent of his "owners." Think of it: only in the pre–Civil War South could such a word be applied to a person.

In 1975 the clause was modified to one year as the result of a bombshell ruling that opened the way for today's free agency. Within a few years the issue faded away as television started killing many of the minor leagues, and finally when the Dodgers and Giants, led by Walter O'Malley, left New York for the riches awaiting them in California.

Free agency has been great for the ballplayers but maybe not so good for the fans. Sometimes it's hard to tell who is on what team and on what day. Just recently, during the week of February 15, retired Baltimore Oriole shortstop Cal Ripken, Jr., being interviewed on a sports show, was asked about his predictions for the upcoming 2010 major league season. He said there had been so many moves and free agent signings that he could no longer keep track of who is where. "For example," he said, "I no longer have any idea who's playing for the San Diego Padres." That's a Hall of Famer talking.

CHAPTER EIGHT

August

On August 1 the Yankees did some housecleaning for the stretch drive. They sold Cliff Mapes to the Browns, and promoted outfielder Bob Cerv and pitcher Bob Weisler from their Kansas City farm team, but showed once again that they didn't know what to do with Jackie Jensen.

Jensen had appeared in 56 games, producing eight home runs and a .298 batting average. What in the world was wrong with that? He was 24 years old and still adjusting to the life and competition in the major leagues. But for some reason general manager George Weiss ran out of patience with him and optioned him to his Kansas City Blues. Jackie came back, but not for long. He was sold to the Washington Senators, his next stop on his way to stardom with the Boston Red Sox.

At the same time the Dodgers' latest move was drawing gleeful comments among National League owners who were convinced, as quoted by Harold Burr of the *Brooklyn Eagle,* that Brooklyn had been sold damaged goods in the Andy Pafko trade.

The mid–June trade had made page one of the *New York Times.* When it was announced, executives throughout the league had raged at Chicago Cubs president Wid Matthews for sending Pafko to Brooklyn, thus giving the Dodgers one of the greatest outfields in baseball history. But in Andy's first few weeks with Brooklyn, it seemed that Matthews had taken a page from the Branch Rickey book on trading has-beens.

They forgot, Burr reminded his readers, that as he arrived in Brooklyn Pafko was suffering from several elbow injuries and had pulled a thigh muscle in his first week at Ebbets Field and was laid up a total of 16 days.[1] The feeling around the league was that, although only 30, Andy was getting brittle and injury-prone.

But on his first day back in the lineup, August 2 at Cincinnati, he hit two singles and a double, and from then on was at .285 for the rest of the season, quieting his wishful-thinking Dodgers haters. It was, however, a beginning to what for Dodgers fans was one of the strangest careers in the team's history, thanks to Walter O'Malley's erratic leadership.

As noted, Pafko was one of the premier outfielders in baseball and for a short time solved Brooklyn's long-standing left-field problem. He was traded away for practically nothing in a deal that O'Malley never explained, not a public word to anyone, including Pafko, who was as surprised as anyone about the trade. He wasn't with Brooklyn very long, but he'll never be forgotten as long as there's a Dodgers fan alive — the outfielder backed against the wall, looking up as Thomson's ball went over the wall, wiping out the Dodgers and carrying the Giants pennant with it.

Andy was as puzzled as anyone about the trade. "That January when they sent me to Milwaukee," he told Roger Kahn years later, "Walter O'Malley sent me a letter saying that he would explain why."[2] He never did. Andy was with the Braves for seven seasons, hitting .297 his first year. He retired in 1959 with a career average of .285 and 213 home runs. There were times, like the Pafko trade, that O'Malley the lawyer showed his lack of baseball brains.

It was about this time — mid–August or thereabouts — that Durocher's cheating scheme began as the powerful telescope was installed in the Giants clubhouse. No one has ever given an exact date for the start, but by subtracting the 44 days of the Giants' extraordinary closing streak, sometime between August 12 and August 15 seems to be about right.

The amazing thing about the scheme is that it was an open secret for so many years. As early as 1962 the Associated Press reported that a Polo Grounds clubhouse spy helped the Giants win the 1951 pennant. But little attention was paid since the sources were anonymous and the story vague. The only newsman of note to follow it up was Howard Cosell, who asked Branca to comment on the report. Ralph declined.[3]

There is no doubt, however, that all of the baseball world knew about it, but there was a conspiracy of silence as no one ever went public for almost half a century. It was even mentioned, but not extensively, in two baseball books: the 1991 edition of the late Ray Robinson's *The Home Run Heard 'Round the World* and by the *Times*' Pulitzer Prize winner Dave Anderson in his book *Pennant Races* in 1994. Neither caused much of a stir.

Finally, the telescope became national news on January 31, 2001, when the *Wall Street Journal* ran a long front-page article, with reporter Joshua

Prager outlining the entire scheme, naming names, dates and for the first time quoting ballplayers who were involved or knew about it.

In a *New York Times* interview Prager said that he first heard of the telescopic cheating when he bought some baseball memorabilia from the late Barry Halper, whose extensive collection was unmatched. Halper, he said, mentioned rumors that the Giants had stolen signs illegally during the latter half of the 1951 season and gave as some corroboration Robinson's book on the Thomson homer.

Prager said he then interviewed all surviving members of the 1951 Giants and none of them would talk about the sign stealing, the prevailing attitude being that they hadn't talked of it in 49 years and weren't about to in the year 2000. Even Branca, the victim of the cheating, wouldn't discuss the issue.

Finally Prager got to John "Spider" Jorgensen and hit paydirt. Jorgensen had played for the Giants in 1951, traded from Brooklyn because of arm trouble. He was a terrific third baseman when he came up to the Dodgers in 1947, a .274 hitter with a great arm that went bad during the following season. Brooklyn kept him on for three more years and then the Giants in '51, all hoping his arm would come back though it never did. Jorgensen said third baseman Henry Schenz, who had just come to the Giants from Pittsburgh, went to Durocher and coach Herman Franks with an idea for stealing signs with a powerful telescope he owned and had used to steal signs when he was with the Chicago Cubs.[4]

The Giants at the time were going nowhere, some 13 games behind Brooklyn. Durocher, knowing his club had little chance to catch the Dodgers otherwise, went for the idea immediately, even though most sign-stealing schemes in the past were almost immediately discovered.

They had been tried a number of times unsuccessfully through the years, going back to 1898 in Philadelphia in a game between the Phillies and the Cincinnati Reds. Cincinnati shortstop Tommy Corcoran got his spikes caught in the coaching box as he was trying to round third base. He started tugging at what he thought was a root but proved to be a telegraph wire that ran to the Phillies' clubhouse where a reserve catcher equipped with binoculars was stealing signs and buzzing them to the third-base coach.

In the modern era it had been tried by the Milwaukee Braves and Chicago White Sox, but both were soon discovered with not much damage done to the standings. In Detroit, however, there is strong evidence coming from none other than Hank Greenberg that stolen signals played a large part in the Tigers' pennant run in 1940 when they edged out the Cleveland Indians by a single game.

In the film *The Life and Times of Hank Greenberg*, Aviva Kempner's 1998 documentary, Hank said that he and Rudy York hit a slew of homers going down the stretch because the Tigers were stealing signs illegally and they therefore knew what type pitch to expect. Greenberg is quite frank about the scheme, saying that because of it Detroit was able to beat out Cleveland by one game for the 1940 pennant.

> We won the pennant by a freak thing that happened in the early days of September (1940). Tommy Bridges (a Tigers pitcher) purchased a rifle with a telescopic lens. Sitting in the upper deck in our stadium he was pointing the rifle looking through the telescopic lens.
> Sure enough he was able to see the catcher's signs and as result we brought in one of our minor league catchers to sit in the upper deck with a pair of binoculars. He could look right over the shoulder of the pitcher and see the signals. If he pulled his right hand off the binoculars it was a fastball but if he left his hand on, it was a curve. Well, you can imagine what that did for our ball club. Rudy York and I had a field day. Between the two of us we hit two home runs for 17 consecutive days during the month of September.

A sample of Hank's hitting during that month shows how effective the signaling system was for him and no doubt Rudy York:

AB	1B	2B	3B	HR	R	RBI	AVG
59	7	5	2	13	30	33	.458

With numbers like that, Hank, along with York, led the Tigers' charge to the pennant, but they couldn't carry their scheme through the World Series. In Greenberg's words: "We couldn't put our man out in centerfield in Cincinnati for fear somebody would pick up on what was going on and lynch him."[5] Cincinnati won the Series in seven games, 4 to 3. Greenberg hit 41 homers that year and York 33. The total would have been greater, Hank said, but the scheme, like all the others, could only be used at home.

The documentary also includes charges I've heard since I was a 13-year-old playing sandlot baseball in Newark: that Greenberg was the victim of an unspoken plot whereby American League pitchers would purposely walk him so that he would have no chance to break Babe Ruth's record of 60 homers. The supposedly underlying thought was that no Jew should be allowed to break such a hallowed record. That idea was, as I distinctly remember, generally believed by many people, including a number of prominent newspapermen, and even members of Greenberg's own team.

Billy Rogell, shortstop on that Detroit team, said in the documentary, "They walked that guy. Every time they got a chance they walked him. I don't think they wanted him to break Ruth's record because of the fact that he was a Jew."

Dick Schapp, prominent television sportscaster and reputed a baseball expert: "They weren't giving him good pitches. They wouldn't give him a chance to break Babe Ruth's record, just as many years later there were people who didn't want to see Henry Aaron, a black man, break Ruth's record. There were people back in 1940 who didn't want a Jew named Hank Greenberg to break Ruth's record."

They, and much of the country at large, could not have been more wrong, for the box scores tell a very different story. Greenberg was pitched to in every game right down to the last day of the season. There's an excuse for Rogell. He was an old man whose memory was probably fading and who would naturally feel that a beloved teammate was not given a fair chance.

But for Schapp, a highly paid television journalist, there is absolutely no excuse for his carelessness, or worse, bias, he being Jewish. There he was in 1998, almost 60 years after the fact, pontificating on events he knew absolutely nothing about and was too lazy to check on. He obviously never checked the box scores of September 1940 as he could have, as I have. The box scores show that Greenberg was pitched to during all of September, including that last week, the last day even, when his home run total was in the upper 50s. In my research I went back to September 16, but the final week, as follows, tells the true story.

- September 24 in a doubleheader against Cleveland: 4–7, including home runs number 55 and 56.
- September 26 against Cleveland: pitched to four times, 1–4.
- September 28 against the Browns: 3–5 including home runs 57 and 58.
- September 29 and 30 against the Browns: 1–7.
- October 2 against Cleveland: 0–4 facing Denny Galehouse.
- October 3 a doubleheader against Cleveland: a single, two strikeouts and a 430-foot out against Feller in the first game, during which Bob struck out 18, the record at that time. Then 3–3 against Al Smith.

How anyone can claim prejudice against Hank as a Jew when he hit homers 57 and 58, was pitched to 18 times during the last four games of the season, and wasn't walked a single time. The integrity of the game wasn't violated no matter how many people were screaming prejudice at the time.

The final word comes from Greenberg himself: "Some people still have it fixed in their minds that the reason I didn't break Ruth's record was because I was Jewish, that the ballplayers did everything they could to stop me. That's pure baloney. The fact is quite the opposite. So far as I could tell the players were mostly rooting for me, aside from the pitchers."[6]

Durocher certainly knew about the Tigers' binocular man, and he realized going in that, as with Detroit, he could use the telescope only at home. His edge was the size of the Polo Grounds. The telescope once placed in the clubhouse was about 30-feet high and some 500 feet from home plate, making it virtually invisible to the naked eye.

I recall, however, that some time during the Giants' September streak the Dodgers must have become suspicious. I was at the Polo Grounds with a ground-level seat and I saw a Dodger up on the dugout steps with a pair of binoculars trained on the Giants' clubhouse. I think it was Carl Furillo, but since I never got to see his number I'm not sure. But I am certain that I saw the plate umpire take the binoculars away from whoever had them.

I knew I was right when 50 years later, in 2001, I read Harvey Rosenfeld's fine book *The Great Chase* in which Dodgers coach Cookie Lavagetto confirmed the binocular incident, but without naming names. It was during the first two days of September when the Dodgers were beaten by the Giants by a combined score of 19–3 that foul play was suspected. "We took binoculars onto the bench to observe center field," he told Rosenfeld. "The umpire spotted us and ran over and took the binoculars away from us. There was nothing we could do. We told the ump we were just trying to observe center field. Whatever Durocher had out there he had a good system."

So it was apparent at the time that the Dodgers, and I would say the rest of the league, knew something fishy was going on. But they didn't know what and therefore could do nothing about it, even if they had wanted to, which most of them didn't. When the telescope was first installed, Durocher had no thoughts of winning the pennant, Giants pitcher Al Corwin recalled. During a team meeting Durocher reminded the players in his colorful way that although first place was beyond them, they had damn well better try for second.

The plan was fairly simple: a spotter in the clubhouse, a telescope trained on the opposing team's catcher, an electrical buzzer wire connected to the Giants bullpen, and someone there to flash the type of pitch to the batter. Simple, but with a telescope in a small clubhouse window some 500 feet from the opposing dugout, extremely effective.

CHAPTER EIGHT: AUGUST

The subject was first discussed at a team meeting on July 19, Monte Irvin recalled. Durocher explained the scheme and then asked each team member if he wanted to be in on it. About half the team declined, according to pitcher Al Corwin, or so they said. That is hard to believe, knowing Leo Durocher. Throughout his career, whether he was managing the Dodgers, the Giants or the Cubs, his men played the game the way he wanted it played or they went the way of Walker Cooper — out the door.

His players, no question, went his way. It could not have been said more succinctly and directly than by Allen Gettel, Giants pitcher and one of my old Newark Bear favorites. When the story broke in the *Wall Street Journal*, he told Josh Prager, "Every hitter knew what was coming. It made quite a difference." A refreshing admittance, right out there on page 1.

The man behind the telescope was usually Giants coach Herman Franks, who as a former major league catcher was adept at understanding signs. Herman was born in 1914 in Price, Utah, and had a six-year career interrupted by five years in the service during the war. He caught for St. Louis, Brooklyn, the Phillies and the Giants before retiring in 1949. According to Carl Furillo he was the Durocher type — win at all costs, dirty or not.

The man in the bullpen was, for most games, Sal Yvars, a second-string catcher who relayed Franks' signals to the batters: one buzzer for a fastball, two buzzers for an off-speed pitch. Sal, born in New York City in 1924, had an eight-year career, always a backup, seven with the Giants and his last year, 1954, with St. Louis. He was known as a tough battler, undefeated until he ran afoul of Walter Alston. Sal was open to discussing the telescope, but Franks would not discuss the matter with Prager or anyone else from the press, saying, "I haven't talked about it in 49 years and if I'm ever asked about it, I'm denying everything."[7]

He should have told Monte Irvin how he felt, for Monte spoke unequivocally about Herman's role. He told Prager that "Herman would sit in the clubhouse. He's sitting there with a telescope and he'd relay the signs to the hitter."

As soon as the *Wall Street Journal* ran Prager's story, I called Herman's partner in the scheme, Yvars, at his Westchester home. Sal, as usual, was frank and cooperative. I was then working on the 1951 portion of my second Dodgers book *The Last Years of the Brooklyn Dodgers*, so a cooperative Yvars was a Godsend to me. (I was pleasantly surprised during the call to find that he remembered me from a box seat we shared on July 16, 1999, the day the Newark Bears dedicated their new stadium on Broad Street in the heart of downtown Newark.)

"We had the buzzer system installed between Leo's (clubhouse) office and me in the bullpen," he told me during our telephone interview. "I would sit there and keep the ball in my hand if it was a fastball. If I tossed it in the air, it would mean a breaking ball. So our guys who wanted to know were tipped off on every pitch."

That was the hint for me that not every hitter on the Giants wanted to know, or pretended not to want to know, what pitch was coming. Monte Irvin, in Prager's account, recalled a team meeting during which each player was asked if he wanted to participate in knowing what pitch was coming. Irvin said he declined, but players like Yvars figured that at least 50 percent of the team was involved, probably more.

Monte Irvin was 30 years old when he came up, and later said words that many other late-coming black players would agree with: "I should have come up 10 years ago. I'm not half the ballplayer I was then." In his eight-year career he was a key player in two World Series and a leader in the Giants' 1951 pennant chase. Irvin was traded to Chicago in 1956, his last season. He was elected into the Baseball Hall of Fame in 1973.

Monte was from Orange, New Jersey, in the heart of *Newark Evening News* territory. He was a four-letter athlete at Orange High School, all-state in everything and a hitter who often broke windows in Orange High, about 400 feet from home plate. To hear my old friends on the *Newark News* sports staff, Monte was a Jack Armstrong, the All-American Boy.

He was a key man for the Giants from the time he came up from the Newark Eagles in 1949 along with third baseman Hank Thompson. Such was his arm that he could play the outfield or shortstop. During his seven years with the Giants, he was a .293 lifetime hitter

Chapter Eight: August

with 99 home runs. When Monte came up in 1949 at age 30, he spoke these sad words when he arrived: "This should have happened 10 years ago. I'm not half the ballplayer I was then." Joe Black and many others could have said the same thing. Late or not, Monte still had the skills to be voted into the Baseball Hall of Fame.

I had a personal encounter with Irvin 1954 and found him as nice as my sportswriter friends said he was.* As a reporter on the *Newark News* I was assigned to drive to La Guardia to meet the Giants plane on their homecoming from sweeping the Cleveland Indians in the World Series. Specifically, I was to ask Willie Mays if the rumor was true that he was going to buy a house in Orange, close to where Irvin lived.

Standing on the tarmac waiting for the plane was Monte Irvin, who was talking to Laraine Day, then married to Leo Durocher and just as beautiful as she appeared on the screen. I introduced myself, and until that plane arrived spent one of the most pleasant half hours of my life talking to two charming, good-looking and literate people. When the plane landed Willie Mays headed for Irvin, where I was able to question him about him buying in Orange. He wasn't sure at the time but obviously later decided against it.

Along with Mays, Hank Thompson joined our little group. Irvin, college-educated at Lincoln University in Pennsylvania, was no question the mentor of the two. The only thing Irvin and Thompson had in common was baseball. As a boy Thompson was constantly in trouble from shoplifting, muggings and other crimes that landed him in a reformatory at least once. As a ballplayer in the minor leagues he got into an argument with a man in a bar, took out a gun and killed him, but was acquitted on his plea of self defense, probably accepted because he was a star ballplayer in the town involved. Years later after he retired from baseball he was convicted of armed robbery and served time in a penitentiary. He died of a heart attack at his home in Fresno at age 43.[8]

Irvin never discussed Thompson's problems — or any other ballplayer's personal problems. But baseball was never off limits. In the matter of the telescope, for example, in later years he admitted its existence and how many of the Giants looked for Yvar's signals. But he would never refer to

---

*A later Irvin episode: I was sitting in my AT&T office at 195 Broadway one afternoon when a very attractive young lady stopped by and said that she understood I was on old-time Dodgers fan. I said yes and she asked if I could name the Dodgers/Giants 1951 lineup. I did and asked her the point. She said she wanted to meet a man who remembered those days and remembered her father. "My name is Pam Fields," she said, "and I'm Monte Irvin's daughter." A friendship was born.

Bobby Thomson's home run. As to Bobby himself, in all my research I have just once come across him answering yes to the question, "Was he in on the telescope plot, and did he know Branca was going to throw him a fastball?" And that yes had to be dragged out of him. He always, as the *Times* described it, "waffled" on the key question. I came across one emphatic answer, however, from an unlikely source, long-time American League umpire Ron Luciano's book *Remembrance of Swings Past*. In it he quotes Dodgers catcher Rube Walker as saying, "If Thomson knew what was coming he'd never have been in the batter's box. I signaled for a knockdown pitch." Could be, because the pitch was high and inside, but not high and inside enough to stop Thomson.[9]

Throughout the Giants' streak there was some hypocrisy in play. Wes Westrum in particular stands out. He was supposedly one of those who declined the signals but the statistics show otherwise. During his 11-year career he hit a total of 96 home runs. In 1951 he hit 20 with 59 runs batted in, with both figures representing the second-highest totals in his baseball life. Prager quotes him as saying, "Suppose he expects a curveball but gets a fastball. You could get ripped in two."

He was probably remembering how Dressen in his role as super sign stealer signaled curveball to Medwick when he was with the Dodgers and DiMaggio when he was a Yankees third-base coach. Both got fastballs, Joe being saved by his cat-like reflexes but Medwick beaned and never again the Triple Crown hitter he once was.

The late Ray Robinson, esteemed baseball writer and author of *The Home Run Heard 'Round the World*, was among the many who refused to believe in the cheating. He comes down on the side of honest baseball, saying at one point that "Whatever the truth, most of the Dodgers refused to blame purloined signals or Branca for their grievous defeat."[10] Of course they wouldn't. They knew to a man that Dressen's mistakes cost them the pennant.

Robinson is consistent in his denials, writing that Yvars said there was no sign stealing during that last playoff game or when Thomson hit his homer. I know this is not true from conversations I have had with Yvars and his appearance on the Westchester County television program *In the Game*. Yvars' position was emphatically that the sign stealing went on and Thomson knew what was coming. (See Appendix.)

"Have you seen the film of Thomson swinging at Branca's fastball?" he asked me. "It was up and in and Bobby leaned into that ball like he never did before. He practically leaped at the ball because he knew what was coming. The signs were the key to our winning that year. There was

Yvars, the signalman in the most spectacular cheating scheme in American sports, was unrepentant whenever interviewed, saying he was "just obeying orders" in relaying the signs to each Giants batter at the Polo Grounds. Without his signals, he says emphatically, the Dodgers would have won the pennant. Unlike other Giants, Sal was no hypocrite.

no way we could have won without them. I mean we were 13½ games behind a great team in August and we went on a streak that had never been seen before. Without those signs the Dodgers win."

I asked how Labine could have shut the Giants out in the Polo Grounds with the telescope at work. "Well, you have to remember he had one of best curveballs around," he answered, "and he was a very gutsy pitcher. With his curve mixed with his great fastball and sinker, you might know what was coming and still be unable to hit it."

How about the road trips where there was no telescope tipping off the hitters? "Those wins at home got us up," he said. "They built up our confidence, making us believe we could make that comeback. The home wins kept us rolling."

Then the big question: did Branca know about the telescope? "Not at the time but he was told later about it," Yvars replied. "He asked me once at a golf tournament why I hadn't told him and I said I felt sorry for him stretched out on those stairs. Bad enough he lost."

Branca told the *Times'* Dave Anderson that for years he knew he was the victim of cheating but he never mentioned it to Thomson. "It was a forbidden subject," he said. "Besides, Dressen lost the pennant for us, not that game. He wore our pitching staff out." Branca was absolutely right. Remember, as vindictive as he was, Dressen had to use Labine in the second playoff game because the other members of his pitching staff really needed a day's rest.[11]

Thomson, as noted, always had a terrible time handling the question regarding whether or not he knew. At the end of Prager's *Wall Street Journal* expose, he again asks Bobby if he knew what pitch was coming. He waffles again as he replies: "I'd have to say no more than yes. I don't like to think of something taking away from it. It would take a little away from me in my mind if I felt I got help on the pitch."

Prager kept at him until finally Bobby gave in, and when asked again if he knew what was coming, he said, "My answer is no. I was always proud of that swing. Stealing signs is nothing to be proud of."[12] To me that answer was bogus. He had to be badgered time and again to finally give it.

As noted earlier the Giants, in a spectacular moment of ingratitude, traded Bobby Thomson to the Braves for, in essence, Johnny Antonelli. And Hank Schenz received similar treatment, only worse. Schenz, remember, was the owner of the telescope and the man who suggested the cheating scheme to Durocher. He was sold by the Giants to Oakland of the Pacific Coast League on December 29, 1951, just 41 days before he would have

CHAPTER EIGHT: AUGUST   141

qualified for the major league's pension plan. He never played in the majors again. The Giants, meaning Leo Durocher, refused to keep the guy for the lousy 41 days that would have earned him a lifelong pension. Gratitude, big league, Leo Durocher style.

Just before the telescope came into play, the Dodgers hit their high-water mark for the year, going up by 13 games as they split a doubleheader with the Boston Braves. In winning the first game 6–1 behind Branca and Snider's two homers, the Brooks actually went up by 13½. Purists, however, say the lead that counts is the one at the end of the day, so it was 13 as they lost the second game, 8–4, to Max Surkont.

Common sense cuts in here to say that the telescope came into play on Sunday, August 12, as the Giants beat the Phillies in a doubleheader at the Polo Grounds. The were the first of 16 wins in a row for Durocher's men, strong evidence that Herman Franks was at his post in the Giants clubhouse using the telescope for the first time to steal the signs catcher Andy Seminick was flashing to his pitcher.

Going into that Sunday doubleheader at the Polo Grounds, the Giants were in second place, 13 games behind the Dodgers in what must have seemed like a hopeless case for even so upbeat a manager as Leo Durocher. No team in baseball history had ever overcome a 13-game lead in mid-August. But then again no team had ever had a catcher-savvy Herman Franks sitting 500 feet from home plate with a telescope trained on the opposing catcher.

The Giants' streak started with a three-game sweep of the Phillies at the Polo Grounds. The Sunday opener was no surprise as Maglie won his 16th against five losses with one of his masterful jobs — seven hits, one walk and two runs. He was helped in the first inning when with two out Russ Meyer, one of the better pitchers on the fifth-place Phillies, was spiked by Alvin Dark in a close play at first base and carried of the field on a stretcher.

The spiking was obviously an accident since that was not Dark's style of play. He came out of Comanche, Oklahoma, and was named Rookie of the Year in 1948 after he hit .322 and helped the team win the 1948 World Series. He was traded from the Braves to the Giants with Eddie Stanky in December of 1949. Dark was a good, steady shortstop and a .289 hitter in his 14-year career.

It was as a manager that he stirred up a storm, perhaps inadvertently. In July of 1964 while managing San Francisco, he was quoted by *Newsday* writer Stan Isaacs as having trouble with the team because of the number of Negro and Latino players who were "not able to perform up to the white players when it came to mental alertness" and didn't have the same pride in their team as white players. He singled out Orlando Cepeda as the worst example. Later Dark claimed he was misquoted, but he was fired anyway, ending his managerial career.

The second game of the sweep was different, a 2–1 win by Al Corwin, called Durocher's secret weapon by the New York writers. If ever there was a so-so pitcher, it was Al. In five years in the majors he was 18–10 but called up by the Giants in mid season, he had the major league touch — 5–1 and valuable in relief when George Spencer needed rest. Considering that the race went into a playoff, Corwin's five wins was one of the reasons the Giants won.

In Corwin's case the relief aspect was vital to the pitching staff because Durocher, a restless manager like Dressen, was apt to get a reliever up several times in what appeared to be crises before having to actually send him in. Spencer pitched 132 innings in real crisis situations, a lot of innings for that time. Those innings, combined with the up-and-down situations in the bullpen, eventually ruined his arm.

I looked up game appearances for relievers of Spencer's time, knowing there were no "middle relievers" or "closers" then. A relief pitcher went in and, well, *relieved*, not for a Mariano Rivera three or four outs, but for the rest of the game in most cases. Spencer's 132 innings was quite high for the time, and he said years later that Durocher's habit of "getting him ready" too often shortened his career. The next season George pitched in 35 games and then was just about through as a front-line pitcher.

That same Sunday as the Giants swept the Reds, the Yankees suffered a shameful loss at a crucial time for them, all because of a rule that never should have been on the books. In a tight race with Cleveland, the Yankees won the first game of a doubleheader against the Athletics but lost the second because of the Sunday curfew law then in effect.

The eighth inning started at 6:37 P.M. with the Yankees trailing, 7–4. They scored five runs to take the lead, 9–7 when the A's, knowing that play would be called at 6:59, used three relievers to eat up time while Casey Stengel paced the visitor's dugout fuming.

The Athletics' timing was perfect from their standpoint as the umpires called the game at 6:59, with the score reverting back to the seventh inning: A's 7, Yankees 4. With the five runs taken away, the Yanks fell out of first place, one-half game behind the Indians.

The next day was another disaster for the Bombers as they went down 16–8, again against the Athletics, who drove Vic Raschi from the mound in the second inning. Casey tried to get away with using second- or even third-line pitchers Stubby Overmire and Joe Ostrowski, making it an 18-hit day for the A's.

The Giants, meanwhile, took their third straight from the Phillies, with Jansen winning his 15th game, this one against Bubba Church. The winning runs were scored in the first inning on Whitey Lockman's homer with Alvin Dark and Monte Irvin on base. *Times* writer James Dawson wrote that the game put the Giants 4½ over the Phils for second place but didn't bother to mention the Dodgers-Giants margin. And no wonder.

That was the day Dodgers fans got even with the management of Local 802, American Federation of Musicians, which in late July tried have the Dodgers Sym-Phony either stop playing or get paid for their work. Like most unions, Local 802 had its wacky moments but should have known the Sym-Phony was sacrosanct. Finally it all blew over after Judge Samuel Liebowitz intervened and persuaded the union people to be reasonable, to recognize that the Sym-Phony was untouchable.

The instigator was Walter O'Malley, a man now powerful enough not only to challenge a labor union but to glory in his victory over it. In so doing Walter offered free admission to that night's Braves game to any and all who would bring a musical instrument to Ebbets Field to back up the night's Sym-Phony routine.

About 2,500 fans showed up with real and toy instruments that the *Times* described as "tootling, fiddling, banging. booming and squeaking." It all started at 5 in the afternoon as the "musicians" crowded into the two upper deck sections reserved for them. Mayor Vincent Impellitteri and other municipal officials attended. Milton Bracker of the *Times* wrote that a riotous night was had by all, with the "only loser of the night was music, which took an incalculable beating." There was no reaction the following day from anyone representing Local 802.

On August 14, George Spencer, like Labine an occasional starter, pitched a six-hitter in the opener against the Dodgers no less, winning, 4–2, with Lockman and Mueller homering. The Giants scored three off Erv Palica, who didn't last through the first inning. This once-fine pitcher, who the year before almost won the pennant with great clutch 7–1 pitching down the stretch, could stand for all that was wrong with egomaniacal Charlie Dressen, ruiner of pitchers. Criticizing a player before his teammates in the clubhouse, calling him "gutless," could destroy many a ballplayer. So it was with Palica, who might have been an All-Star under a reasonable manager. This is not just speculation. Labine once said Palica was as good a pitcher as anyone he ever saw.

The next day, Mays' outfield throw of the year, or almost any year, helped Jim Hearn beat the Dodgers, 3–1, at the Polo Grounds. The play came in the eighth inning to stop a Dodgers rally. With Cox on third, Branca on first, and the score 2–1 in favor of the Giants, Furillo hit one into the outfield that in most circumstances would have scored Cox. But Mays pivoted while on the run, caught the ball and threw it on a line to Westrum to get Cox and end the inning. The throw was so perfect a surprised Cox was tagged out by Westrum, who didn't even bother to take his mask off.

After a day off, Maglie's 17th win, a 2–1 four-hitter, was the Giants' sixth in a row, sweeping the Dodgers series. The Brooklyn lead was still a hefty 9½ games, but in the minds of some a tiny cloud of doubt appeared for the first time. Joe Sheehan of the *Times* felt that "maybe the National League is going to have a pennant race after all." It was no doubt due to the fact that the Giants were playing confident baseball behind incredible pitching, while the Dodgers were playing around the .500 mark or a little better.

The next day more of the same occurred as the Giants took their seventh straight in the opener against the Phils at Shibe Park. Although Corwin was knocked out for the first time, Spencer came on for the last six innings, finally giving up a meaningless homer to Bill "Swish" Nicholson in the ninth. With the Dodgers splitting a doubleheader in Boston, the lead went down to nine.

I figured the streak would end with the second game against the Phillies. Robin Roberts was pitching in his home park, going for his 17th win for the slumping Philadelphians. The final score was 2–0 Giants, Larry Jansen's shutout pitching just a bit better than the efforts of Roberts and Heinztleman. I was a bit shaken after that game, but still, how could my Dodgers blow a nine-game lead with only six weeks to go?

Jansen, along with Maglie, was one of the key elements in the Giants overtaking the Dodgers. It is true that the Giants hitters knew what was coming, but without Larry's 23 wins, the pennant would surely have hung over Ebbets Field, not the Polo Grounds.

Larry was an Oregonian born in 1920. He didn't have the longevity of many other great pitchers, having come to the majors at 28 in 1947. But he was a first-year star, going 21–5, with an .808 winning percentage that led the league. Larry didn't really belong on a team with a thug like Hank Thompson and the likes of Stanky and Durocher. But he pitched among them for nine years, compiling a 122–89 record with a 3.58 ERA.

He was known throughout the league as one of the "nice guys" on the Giants, a control pitcher who, from all accounts, never hit a batter

Larry Jansen was a latecomer to the majors but was a big winner in his first year, going 21–5 in 1947 with the fourth-place Giants. He was born in 1920 in Verboort, Oregon, and went on to win 122 games in his nine-year career. He led the league with 23 wins in the Giants' 1951 tainted pennant drive, his 23rd coming on the deciding playoff game.

deliberately in his career. His reputation was such that on the rare occasion he hit an opponent, there was never an outcry as there would be with "the Headhunter," Maglie.

On that same Sunday for me a bit of nostalgia blew through Sportsman's Park in St. Louis. There in the box score was the name Hank Borowy of Bloomfield, New Jersey, a suburb of my hometown Newark. He was an all-stater I saw pitch several times against my high school, Newark Central, and a number of times at Newark's Ruppert Stadium when the Bears were the best in the International League.

It was sad, I thought, that in a blow-out 20–9 Browns win over Borowy's Tigers, Hank had little left and was hammered in relief. Sad because I remembered my school days when Borowy was the best high school pitcher in our state. That Browns game was one of his last, as he was soon released and his career ended, his figures from 1942 to 1951 totaling 108 wins and 82 losses.

He was, however, a star wartime pitcher for the Yankees and Cubs, 67–32 against young kids going up the hill or older men who were over the hill. After the war he posted a mediocre 41–51 record, but this, except for one year, was all with second-division teams. All else aside, Borowy was important in his day because the deal that sent him from the Yankees to the Cubs caused such an uproar that the rules covering the reserve clause were changed.

It all started in 1945 when Larry MacPhail, then Yankees president, decided to sell Borowy. He didn't want his American League rivals such as the Red Sox to get him, so he would have to sneak him somehow to the National League. The Chicago Cubs were said by sportswriters to go as high as $100,000 for Hank since they were in the midst of a fight with the Cardinals for first place. Larry never gave a reason for wanting the trade, but it's my suspicion that he thought of Borowy as just a wartime winner.

In that day a club could put a player or an entire team on the waiver list any number of times and withdraw them at will. MacPhail did this several times knowing his rivals would never think he would let a star like Borowy go on waivers. No American League club bid, leaving the opening the Cubs were waiting for. They got Hank for $97,500, causing an uproar throughout American League front offices.

Clark Griffith of the Senators went on the attack, calling the move "detrimental to the welfare of the league." He added that he would fight to have the old reserve clause reinstated whereby an owner could put a player up for waivers once but the second time he goes. The old rule was finally put into effect for the years remaining until the arrival of Marvin Miller.

On Monday afternoon in Philadelphia the Giants won their ninth straight, thanks again to brilliant relief pitching by rookie Al Corwin. He held the Phils scoreless for the last two innings as the Giants rallied to win. I was lunching with old friends in Bensonhurst that day and felt there was some slight uneasiness spreading through Brooklyn after the Dodgers lost to the Cardinals. The doubt written by Joseph Sheehan in the *Times* two games before didn't seem so ridiculous that day.

August 19 was Eddie Gaedel's day in the sun, the first and only midget to take part in a major league baseball game. It was such a shock that the next day the *Herald-Tribune* ran a four-column picture of him on page one as he was at bat against Bob Cain of the Detroit Tigers. It was one of Bill Veeck's most spectacular stunts, and angered just about every baseball executive in America to the extent that years later when he tried to move the St. Louis Browns to Baltimore, he was refused permission. Vengeance day had arrived.

Veeck signed Eddie, 43" tall, to a one-day contract that was ruled valid by the umpires. With catcher Bob Swift playing on his knees, Gaedel walked on four pitches before Jim Delsing pinch-ran for him. His career ended there as the next day his contract was voided by league president Will Harridge. If that happened today the "little people," as many now prefer to be called, would be picketing the American League offices demanding equal rights in sports. Veeck, always needling the brass, called the decision unfair.

Wes Westrum hit another Polo Grounds homer as play resumed after a day off. The Giants won their tenth in a row, 7–4, over Cincinnati. This one was a homerfest, as Westrum was joined by Stanky and Lockman for the Giants and Bobby Adams, Connie Ryan and Johnny Pramesa for the Reds. Wes' 17th homer was a 450-footer into the distant left-field upper deck, very unfamiliar territory for him. But when you know what's coming.... In the stands that game there was a continuing and ominous trend at the Polo Grounds with only 6,315 fans in a park that seated more than 55,000. This continued, as we shall see, during the playoffs against the Dodgers, a team that Giants fans hated.

Win number 11 for the Giants was against one of the great pitchers the game has known, Ewell "the Whip" Blackwell of the Cincinnati Reds, a rail-like 6'6" right-hander with a murderous sidearm delivery. In 1951 he had recovered from arm trouble and was still good enough for a 16–15 record with a 3.45 ERA for the sixth-place Reds. His forte was his fastball delivered with a whip-like sidearm motion that to a right-handed hitter seemed like it was coming from third base, such was his height. Sportswriter Red Smith likened him to a "flyrod with ears."

In 1947 he won sixteen straight, including a no-hitter. In his next start, on June 22 against the Dodgers, he went 8⅔ innings into a second straight no-hitter when Eddie Stanky lined one through the box for a clean single. He would have tied Johnny Vander Meer as the only other pitcher with back-to-back no-hitters, but Blackwell didn't have Vander Meer's luck. He was pitching on a nice sunny afternoon, not under the comparatively dim, newly installed lights of Ebbets Field in 1938.

On this day, trying to stop the Giants' streak, he pitched a six-hitter while going for his fifth straight win, against Larry Jansen, but was beaten, 4–3 in the ninth inning when Whitey Lockman doubled to score Alvin Dark from second base. There was a pitiful crowd of 7,034 in the Polo Grounds stands to watch a team that, as Joe Sheehan wrote, "was restoring a measure of interest" to the pennant race.

Meanwhile, Brooklyn actually gained a half game in taking a doubleheader from the Braves, coming from behind in both games, 4–3 and 8–7. In the second game the Brooks won in the 10th inning on Jackie Robinson's fifth hit with Reese and Clyde King on base.

The next day as the Giants were trying for their 12th straight triumph, Bill Veeck was at it again by making the headlines with the latest of his stunts. This time he had approximately 1,100 fans in a special section behind home plate act as grandstand "managers" using placards to instruct Browns manager Zack Taylor what to do in certain situations. It may have worked since the wondrous Ned Garver won his 15th for the last-place Browns. Athletics manager Jimmy Dykes angrily told the umpires that he would call for a forfeit if such foolishness prolonged the game. Surprisingly, it took only 2 hours and 11 minutes, whereas today it probably would have taken five hours.

Back in New York the Giants, still on their homestand, won their 12th straight in their opener against the Cardinals. It took a two-run rally in the ninth to win it, 6–5, on a failed fielder's choice. Koslo and Spencer got knocked around but Sheldon Jones held the Cards in the ninth for his fourth win.

As the Giants won, the Dodgers were having trouble at Ebbets Field with the Cubs, whose pitcher, Bob Kelly, the Brooks should have handled easily. Bob had a four-year career with four teams and a 4.50 ERA but he was tough that day, aided a bit by the weather. He won, 5–1, in a rain-shortened eight-inning game, thereby helping the Giants by knocking the Dodgers lead down to seven.

However, the Dodgers seemed unfazed the next day as they sat for their team picture in anticipation of winning the pennant. But you can be sure they were starting to look over their shoulders since they were playing ordinary ball while the Giants were racing. The Giants' winning streak increased to 16 games in two days by winning doubleheaders against the Cubs on consecutive days at the Polo Grounds. Something had come alive around Coogan's Bluff, for the two-day attendance totaled almost 44,000.

In the first doubleheader Spencer got his 10th win in a thrilling victory in the ninth inning of the first game as Westrum hit his second homer of the contest with two and no one on. The score was 4–1 Giants starting the ninth inning when the Cubs scored three runs to tie it on a triple by Hank Sauer. With the Giants down to their last out, Wes stepped in against Walt Dubiel to win it. Thought of the game: when Mueller hits one and Westrum two, the telescope scheme was no doubt rolling along.

The second game was Jim Hearn's 12th win as he pitched a 5–1 six-hitter to bring the Dodgers lead down to six games. The Dodgers split a doubleheader with Pittsburgh at Ebbets Field. The second game was tied in the 10th inning when Robinson, for the second time in a week, homered, this time off Ted Wilks, for the win.

Jansen and Corwin were the winners the next day, 5–4 and 6–3, for a four-game sweep of the Cubs. It was Jansen's 17th win and Corwin's fifth. Jansen went 12 full innings and was down 4–3 in the top of the 12th after Frankie Baumholtz doubled and Ransom Jackson singled him home to put the Cubs one up. But, preserving the Giants' 16th victory in a row, Bill Rigney hit a long fly in the 12th inning with the bases loaded to score Irvin for the win. The Giants now had the longest winning streak since the Cubs won 21 in a row in 1935. The streak brought the Dodgers lead down to five games as August was winding down.

The Pirates ended it the next day with Howie Pollet reliving his great Cardinals days with a 2–0 six-hit shutout. Wildness by Sheldon Jones and errors by Stanky and Mueller did the Giants in, stopping them at 16 as but 8,803 watched in the cavernous Polo Grounds. The crowd was not only slim but, according to Joe King of *The Sporting News*, ungrateful. The Giants lost a 2–0 game because of errors, and in King's words at the end of the game "as the Giants came off the field they were booed."[13] After 16 straight wins.

On August 28 a future star was finally given a chance by Dressen. Clem Labine, up from Montreal, sat for three weeks as the Giants inched up on Brooklyn through much of August. As Clem finally took the mound at Ebbets Field against Cincinnati, the Dodgers knew that through Sep-

Wes Westrum was another hitter who had the Giants worried during their telescope run. With his .219 average, he started hitting drives over the roof and deep into the left-field stands, performances that aroused suspicions. He was, however, a great defensive catcher and handler of pitchers. Of baseball he once said: "It's like church. Many attend but few understand." He managed twice (250–366) but never in the first division.

tember they would be in a pennant race, unlike a few weeks before when they seemed to be runaway winners. As Clem threw his first pitch, the Dodgers lead had shrunk to 5½ games, 7½ games of their big lead gone in a matter of 15 days.

Clem threw a seven-hitter at Cincinnati and was tough in the clutch as he went all the way for a 3–1 win, using a sinker and curveball the likes of which hadn't been seen in the league for years. At 25 and a six-footer, he was also fast. The win, over Howie Fox, increased the Dodgers lead to six and was the second of a three-game sweep over the Reds. Snider, as usual grumpy and testy with the writers during a two-week slump, broke out of it with his 28th homer with Reese on first.

I remember being encouraged the next day as the Brooks actually gained a full game for the first time in two weeks. As Brooklyn won its third game against Cincinnati, the Pirates on Ralph Kiner's 39th home run in the ninth inning took a 10–9, 26-hit joke of a ballgame from the Giants. Murray Dickson won his 18th while in relief of Vernon Law. Murray, at 35 years old, ended the season at 20–16 for the seventh-place Pirates, putting him up there in class with the much-younger Ned Garver.

CHAPTER NINE

September

As September arrived the Giants, from manager Leo Durocher on down, were concerned about the recent outburst of long-ball hitting on the part of Wes Westrum and particularly Don Mueller. The week before Westrum had hit a 450-foot shot into the left-field upper deck of the Polo Grounds, and on the first day of September Mueller hit three home runs, one of which was described by the *Times* as "a towering wallop on to the right field roof," helping to beat the Dodgers, 8–1. The next day he hit two more home runs to help beat the Dodgers again, this time 11–2 — five home runs in two days by a man who lived by the line-drive single or double.

Not that Durocher had anything against the long ball. If Irvin or Mays hit one, no one was concerned. But Westrum was a .216 slap hitter as was Mueller, a much better hitter than Wes but never a home run threat. Singles through the infield were more his style. The Giants were fearful that with those two hitting homers, the league would start investigating and possibly discover the telescope in the Giants' clubhouse. It never happened, even though the Dodgers and other clubs were suspicious, yet could prove nothing.

Mueller, 24 at the time, was probably the hitter who benefited most from the telescope cheating. During the Dodgers series when he hit the five home runs, he joined the likes of Ty Cobb, Stan Musial, Ralph Kiner, Cap Anson and Tony Lazzeri in hitting five homers over a two-game span.

"Don was a very good hitter but he didn't have that kind of power," Yvars told me. "We had to tell Don to take it easy after those five homers or we'd surely get caught."[1] Sal was probably right. Mueller retired in 1959 with a .296 lifetime batting average, but with just 65 home runs, he was never feared as a power hitter. But he was a slugger during August and September when the telescope came into play. Don, as quoted by Ray

Robinson in his book *The Home Run Heard 'Round the World*, is being disingenuous if not downright hypocritical in saying that he was "as mystified as the next man" in trying to account for his slugging that September weekend.

"I guess it was something working internally," he said. "The whole thing was a traumatic experience for me. On Saturday when I hit those three homers I was thinking of my wife and our overdue baby back in St. Louis. It sounds funny, but maybe those home runs were premonitions."[2] If he had been honest, he would have said that he kept on eye on Yvars in the bullpen to see what type pitch was coming.

From his first months with the Giants everyone knew Don was a born hitter, as his .296 average over 12 seasons proved. He was a place hitter with little power. But with an eye on the bullpen, he bunched 16 home runs to help the Giants win their telescope pennant.

Following are the games of September as the Dodgers, thinking all they had to do was play .500 ball to win the pennant, could not match the Giants' closing pace, 20–5 from September 1 to October 1. This, of course, is part of the 37–7 pace from mid–August on, the best closing drive in the history of the game, telescopically speaking.

On September 1 Mueller's home-run barrage started during the opener of a two-game series with the Dodgers, at the Polo Grounds of course. In four at bats

Don Mueller led the Giants hypocrites by refusing to discuss Yvars' signals from the bullpen. He would only admit to having "premonitions" as to what was coming. A fine .286 hitter over 12 seasons, his five home runs in two days in 1951 alarmed the Giants, fearing an investigation. During their honest 1954 pennant drive, he hit .342.

Don hit three homers and drove in five runs before a crowd of 40,794, most of which had not been showing up for weeks. It was Maglie against Branca and as the game progressed the Dodgers must have been thinking the baseball gods had turned against them again, as they did the previous September when Richie Ashburn made the throw of his life to nail Abrams at the plate, giving Philadelphia the pennant.

This time it was the first triple play of the season as Brooklyn was rallying, behind 5–1. Abrams, batting for Branca, reached on an error, followed by a single by Furillo. Then it happened. Reese hit a liner that Dark caught while lunging to his left. He flipped the ball to Stanky, who stepped on the bag for the second out and then tagged Furillo coming into second. The final was 8–1 for Maglie's 18th win. The lead was again six.

Brooklyn was smarting enough from Mueller's three homers when he teed off against them the very next day with two more homers and another five RBIs, routing Newcombe. At this point I think someone should have done some investigating around the Polo Grounds. For Mueller to join such sluggers as Kiner and Musial was ridiculous. Again the game was a rout, 11–2, with Jim Hearn pitching a six-hitter for his 14th win as his Giants hit Newcome and Phil Haugstad seemingly at will, reducing the Dodgers league lead to five. My friends on Seventy-first Street in Brooklyn's Bensonhurst section finally realized that evening that the Giants were coming on. A bit older and having lived through Brooklyn's years of bad luck, starting in 1941 when I listened to Red Barber describing Casey's spitball to Owen, I was sure of it.

There was a heart-warming moment when Don hit his second homer. As he approached the plate, Monte Irvin ran up to tell him his wife had just delivered a six-pound baby boy. As he was rounding the bases he kept shouting, "It's a boy, it's a boy," with Durocher as third-base coach clapping as Don rounded for home. Phil Haugsted was in no mood for laughing and celebration after that second home run. He decked Thomson and then hit Mays, evoking a warning from umpire Al Barlick.

Many years later when the telescoped signals were revealed publicly in the *Wall Street Journal*, Mueller was asked about whether the sign stealing helped in his home barrage. He replied, "As for my home runs and the sign stealing, this has been much talked about and I'd prefer not to comment."[3]

The next day Brooklyn took two from Boston while the Giants were splitting a doubleheader with Philadelphia at the Polo Grounds. The Ebbets Field scores were a pair of 7–2 decisions, with Erskine and Labine going the full nine. When the Giants split, the pressure eased a bit on the

Dodgers as they moved six games ahead again with three weeks to go in the race.

Labine, after riding the bench for more than three weeks, was now 2–0, under the most intense pressure imaginable, especially for a rookie. Clem to me is the most startling example of Charley Dressen's most glaring weakness. For all his bragging about his knowledge of the game, he never understood pitchers but would never admit it. As noted, O'Malley hired Hall-of-Fame pitcher Ted Lyons, who later quit because Dressen would never talk to him about his pitchers or their problems. It was no accident that by the time the season was over, the Brooklyn staff was an exhausted one, slowly worn down by the whims of an egocentric manager.

On September 5 two of the game's best pitchers, Warren Spahn and Sal Maglie, were involved as the Giants won both games of a doubleheader at Braves Field. Spahn, was beaten, 3–2, by the erratic Sheldon Jones. In the second game the Giants' momentum continued even out of town as Maglie beat Jim Wilson, 9–1 for his 19th win.

Back in Brooklyn the Dodgers beat the Phillies, 5–2, the hit of the game being Gil Hodges' homer with the bases loaded in the fifth inning off Ken Johnson. For awhile Gil was second to Lou Gehrig in grand slams, holding the National League record at 14. Still, there have always been doubters as to his real slugging power since Ebbets Field was among the smallest parks in the major leagues.

Crazy talk. Gil could have hit the long ball in most of the parks of his time. He was a dead pull hitter, so think of Fenway, Crosley, Wrigley, the Stadium, Detroit: in fact, most of the parks then and now with left-field foul lines at 340 or less. Also think of parks built or altered for certain hitters, such as Greenberg Gardens and the Kiner's Corner in Pittsburgh. Or change the name from the House That Ruth Built with its 296-foot right field foul line to the House Built For Ruth.

September 7 was a standoff, the Dodgers lead staying at 5½ games with both teams winning, the Dodgers 11–6 for Roe's 19th win, and the Giants, led by Bobby Thomson's 5-for-5 performance, 7–3, over the Braves in Boston. Now in the first week of September it is certain, in my mind at least, that Sal Yvars' analysis of the Giants' play on the road, that they won because of the telescopic winning streak giving them confidence, was absolutely correct.

There is no other way to account for a team losing only seven games for the last five weeks of the season. Winning, as the saying goes, breeds confidence. The Giants were brimming with it, and not a guilty conscience among them, again telescopically speaking.

The Dodgers got the Giants away from the telescope and into Ebbets Field the next day where Newcombe threw a two-hitter, shutting them down 9–0, and boosting the lead to 6½ games. It seemed comfortable for Brooklyn at the time, they being eight games up in the loss column with games to play dwindling down 17 left for the Giants and 20 for the Dodgers.

But on September 10 Maglie took the mound at Ebbets Field. When the game was over, a play by Bobby Thomson at third base convinced me and probably thousands of other Dodgers fans that the pennant really could be lost. It was the fourth inning and Robinson had just tripled Snider home to make the score 2–1 Giants, with Maglie at his usual best against Brooklyn.

The next play was a smash to third by Pafko when, in the words of Roscoe McGowan of the *Times*, Thomson made "the killing play." Bobby backed up for Pafko's hard grounder, recovered and sprang forward off balance to tag Robinson who was trying to get back to third, and then still off balance rifled — the cliché is apt here — a throw to Lockman at first to complete the double play and end the inning. Describing the play doesn't nearly do justice to it. It was worthy of Billy Cox, the best of the best. It was so spectacular that here it is some 60 years later and I can still see it in my mind as I watched it on television.

After seeing that play, it left me thinking that what seemed impossible just a couple of weeks before was possible. Things were just going too well for Durocher and the rest of the Giants for any other conclusion. He puts a fine center fielder like Thomson at third to make room for Mays and Bobby starts playing like a combination of Cox and Brooks Robinson.

The loss was Branca's seventh and, given the circumstances, was one of the most bitter of his career, his only bad inning in the fourth when Irvin hit one with a man on first for both Giants runs. The lead had been going up and down for a week or so and now went back down to 5½. But the fear factor was evident after that Thomson play.

But not for Clement Walter Labine of Woonsocket, Rhode Island, who pitched a shutout against Cincinnati the next day, showing the skills under pressure that for the next decade made him one of the best relievers and spot starters in Brooklyn's history. It was his third straight outstanding game since Dressen brought him off the bench two weeks earlier. As the Dodgers won, the Giants split a doubleheader with the Cardinals, bringing the lead back to six, which suddenly seemed meaningless, it was fluctuating so.

On the following evening Lloyd Merriman, a five-year Cincinnati outfielder of no particular distinction, symbolized what was going wrong for the Dodgers and right for Leo's men during that dismal September for the people of Brooklyn. The Dodgers had gotten rid of one of their nemeses, Raffensberger, and were facing Blackwell, tied 3–3, when Merriman comes up in the eighth and hits a three-run triple for the game winner.

Consider: Merriman was a .242 career hitter and batted .083 against the Dodgers, and hits the triple off Erskine of all pitchers. The only bright spot of the game for baseball purists was the pitching of Blackwell, once the best in the game and now into his second year of arm recovery. The win was his fifteenth against 14 losses for the sixth-place Reds. He would finish at 16–15 with a 3.45 ERA, fine pitching in the second division.

It continued the next day, only worse. In the first inning Cincinnati batted around against Newcombe, scoring three runs on him before he left with what seemed to be a sore arm. During this hit parade Duke Snider fell down on a fly that was ruled a double by Ted Kluzewski. *Duke Snider fell down.* In all my years of seeing Snider at Ebbets Field and on television, even in that disgraceful, misshapen Coliseum in Los Angeles, I don't remember him even stumbling after a ball, let alone falling down. He had his faults, but he was a superlative outfielder, one of the best center fielders to ever play the game. That's the kind of night it was as the Reds went on to win, 6–3.

The league lead was still fluttering and settled at six again after the Cardinals routed Sal Maglie in the second inning at Sportsman's Park, winning 6–3 for pitcher Dick Bokelmann. He was brought up on August 3 and was 3–3 for what proved to be his only productive season. What was unusual was that this third win for Bokelmann seemed a serious blow to the Giants with the Dodgers idle. But it was only one of the seven losses Leo's men suffered during their historic run. Unconcerned, they came back for a 7–2 win the next day for Jim Hearn, aided by five Cubs errors.

During that afternoon Preacher Roe beat the Pirates, 3–1 for his 20th win, the only time in his career he topped 19. It was Pafko who won it with his 24th homer as Robinson scored ahead of him. Preacher had lost only two and was headed toward a record-breaking year if he could post two more wins. As I checked the box score I noticed that Hodges was batting seventh, behind Pafko. It took a great lineup to put Gil down to seventh considering that he was not in a slump but in the final weeks of a 40-homer, 103-RBI year.

That evening was the last time Brooklyn would lead the Giants by six games and the last time the lead would fluctuate very much. From that Roe win on, it would be a slow but inexorable downward path for Brooklyn. The diehards on the *Brooklyn Eagle* saw light from time to time, and they would have been right if Charlie Dressen in a fit of childish temper had not sat Labine down for almost two weeks.

As if mandated by heaven, the fatal slide started the next day, September 15, with a Brooklyn loss and a Giants win, cutting the lead by a full game to five. The Pirates tore into Branca, King and Schmitz, all of whom had nothing at a time the team desperately needed quality pitching. Three Pirates rookies — Frank Thomas, Jack Merson and Dick Smith — hit homers to lead the 11–4 win.

Thomas is the Frank we all remember with those sorry original Mets who lost 120 games in 1962, their first year. Like Richie Ashburn and a few others, he was once a name player, especially with the Pirates when he hit 35 home runs and drove in 109 in 1958. But there he was that miserable year, playing on the same team with Rod Kanelh and the immortal Elio Chacon.

Sheldon Jones showed up strong for the Giants the next day as he beat the Cubs, 5–2, backed by homers by Thomson and Mays. Jones was with the Giants for six seasons, always hovering around the .500 mark. But he was notorious in Brooklyn as the man seemingly responsible for, as previously noted, hitting Furillo in 1950 on Durocher's order with the pitch that put Carl in the hospital. He never forgot it, and his resentment festered over the months.

As noted, when it happened again in '53, he ran through the entire Giants team and throttled Durocher until Irvin and Hearn, seeing Leo's face turning blue, dragged Carl off. After he walked out of the dugout unmolested, his classic remark when asked why no Giant tried to stop his attack: "I wasn't afraid of any Giants attacking me. They all hate him too."

On September 16 Labine took the mound for his fourth start. It was another complete-game win, his fourth in a row, this time 6–1. Clem would have had a second straight shutout except for a walk to Randy Jackson, who was singled to third by Chuck Connors and scored on a fielder's choice grounder by Bob Ramazzotti. Again, this was the fourth complete-game victory by a rookie who gave up but four runs in the 36 innings. That is an earned run average of one, probably unmatched by any other pitcher just breaking in.

Harold Rosenthal of the *Herald-Tribune* questioned why Labine had been allowed to waste his time pitching in the American Association only six weeks before, adding that "with Newcombe and Branca faltering in the stretch Charlie Dressen can count his blessings every time this kid pitches." All true but in hindsight we know that if Dressen had really

Sal Maglie fled from the Mexican League at 32 and was a first-year star in 1950 at 18–4, and then in '51 was a vital part of the Giants' pennant run at 23–6. His feuds with the Dodgers went on for years, mainly with Jackie Robinson, but at times with the rest of the team, irate at times for being thrown at so often. Sal retired in 1958 at 119–62.

counted his blessing just a bit longer instead of being a petulant fool, the Dodgers would have won the pennant.

Even in the face of Labine's excellent pitching, the slide continued. While Brooklyn was winning the Labine game, the Giants took a doubleheader, bringing the league lead down to 4½ and just three in the loss column. The Giants faced seventh-place Pittsburgh, with Jansen going for his 19th and Maglie his 20th. Both won, 7–1 and 6–4. Maglie, that superb refugee from the Mexican League, had won his 20th for the only time in a great career that should have been greater had he arrived younger.

Sal was 32 when he came back from Mexico in 1950 and became an instant star, going 18–4 with a league-leading .818 winning percentage. He was born in Niagara Falls, New York, but lived in Riverdale for most of the 1950s. Looking back, the games he pitched against the Dodgers at both Ebbets Field and the Polo Grounds were charged with tension and excitement, mostly because of his skillful inside pitching, for which he was nicknamed "Sal the Barber" and aroused the ire of the whole Brooklyn team. The Maglie games were always stormy, particularly between him and Robinson and occasionally Furillo.

Sal pitched one no-hitter during his career, and I was there. He had been traded to the Dodgers in 1956 and went 13–5, helping the Brooks win the pennant. His no-hitter was at Ebbets Field on September 25, a rainy and foggy night. I was there on a *Newark News* press pass and had to sit in the open grandstand in the wet. I moved to a nearby reserved dry section where an usher asked me to move. There were 15,204 paid that night and the park was less than half full. The usher chased me anyway, reinforcing my impression that the park staff featured a bunch of mean bastards.

As I was leaving the reserved section a man in a reserved box called me over and urged me to sit with him and his family. I looked at him and the rest and they all looked like Don Newcombe. My host was Don's uncle, and I have seldom enjoyed a game more — a 5–0 no-hit shutout over the Phils among amiable, intelligent people who were Dodgers family. The usher never came near us.

The Newcombes at that time were a New Jersey family. Don was born on June 14, 1925, in Madison but grew up in Elizabeth. Always big for his age, Don was pitching semi-pro ball at age 13. He was with the Newark Eagles when Clyde Sukeforth, scouting at the time, approached him as he was pitching in an exhibition game at Ebbets Field and asked him to come to the Dodgers office to talk contract. He was promptly signed to pitch for the Dodgers farm team at Nashua, New Hampshire.

When he arrived in Brooklyn in 1949, he was an instant star, finishing the season at 17–8 and being named Rookie of the Year. Further laurels were to come in 1956 when he became the first pitcher to win Most Valuable Player and the Cy Young Award recognition of his best season, with a record of 27–7.

Don had one acknowledged weakness: his attention span. Sometimes during a game, even one as important as the playoff against the Giants, for instance, his mind would wander. Jackie Robinson could tell when it was happening and became his spur. Jackie would approach the mound and confront Don saying, "Don't give me that bullshit. Stop dogging it. Get in there and pitch." Strangely, although Don for years was with the team now known as Roger Kahn's "Boys of Summer," he is not included in the book, although Joe Black, with the team just about two years, is. To my knowledge no one has ever asked Kahn why.

As Maglie was pitching his no-hitter, he was only a short-term Dodger, with Brooklyn from May 5, 1956, to September 1, 1957. In going to the Yankees for $37,500, he became one of the few men to play for all three New York teams, an obvious impossibility today. Strange that such a great pitcher was not a great pitching coach. After he left the Seattle Mariners, he was castigated for constantly second-guessing his pitchers and often second-guessing himself and then blaming it on the pitchers. But there are others, Jim Lonborg and Don Drysdale, for examples, who credit him with making them better by teaching them to pitch inside, his specialty.

September 18 was not just a bad day for the Dodgers, it was a very bad day. They lost to the Cubs, 5–3, with Campanella beaned in the second inning by a pitch that got away from Omar Lown, a rookie soon to be a good, solid reliever known as "Turk." The Dodgers clubhouse was almost funereal after the game. Bad enough to be beaten by a rookie at such a crucial time, but then the word came down that Campy would be out indefinitely. Plus, the lead was down to four.

Roy was hit on the left ear where the helmets of that day provided no protection. Even though he was carried off the field on a stretcher, the injury proved to be not as serious as first thought. The X-rays showed no fracture so Roy left the hospital the next day but was not allowed to play until five days later, during which time the team was 2–3.

In the Newark of my youth it would be said that Joe King put "the horns" on the Dodgers in his *The Sporting News* think piece on September 19. He wrote the Dodgers "just about sewed up the flag" and were "heading west in a wonderful position to tune up their pitching and rest their ailing."[4]

King couldn't have been more wrong. The Brooks opened in St. Louis where rookie Tom Poholsky beat them, 7–1, on an eight-hitter. Branca gave up two runs in the second inning and then five in the sixth, when he was relieved by Johnny Schmitz and then Phil Haugsted. The Dodgers played so poorly, even allowing a steal of home by Stan Musial, that the *Times'* Roscoe McGowan called the game "a humiliation" of the team, especially on defense.

At the same time the Giants were in Cincinnati ,where Dave Koslo and George Spencer pitched them to a 6–5 win, slicing the Dodgers' lead to three games. The Reds got three runs in the ninth but were unable to score the tying run off Spencer.

George, 25, was from Columbus, Ohio, and a workhorse which, under Durocher, was his undoing. He was 10–4, pitching under the great pressure of trying to catch the Dodgers. He worked in 57 games, sometimes as long as five or six innings in that era before relievers were one- and two-inning prima donnas. With Durocher being one of those nervous managers whose relievers are up and down during a game, it was too much even for the 6'1" and 215-pound Spencer.

He was never the same after the playoffs, drifting from team to team for managers who hoped he might come back before they finally gave up. He was 16–10 overall, worn out by a manager who, like Vince Lombardi, never worried about overworking his players. But even with his telescope, Durocher never would have overtaken Brooklyn without George Ewell Spencer.

Mantle was back the next day as the Yankees were playing musical chairs, bringing Mickey up from Kansas City when they sent Bob Cerv back just weeks after they promoted him. Cerv never got the chance he should have that first year because DiMaggio was immovable. In New York it was unthinkable to replace Joe even though he was having his most miserable season. Cerv, when given the chance, had a 12-year career with a .276 lifetime average and 105 homers, most coming when he became a regular.

The next Brooklyn game was Preacher Roe Night, the kind of promotion I could never understand. Some 1,000 of his Arkansas friends gathered in a group near the infield to participate in giving Roe an automobile. Preacher was making about five times as much as most of the gathering and they give an expensive gift that most of them couldn't afford.

Roe responded well, beating Max Lanier by shutting out the Cardinals on five hits for his 21st win against but two losses, bringing him one win shy of setting the National League won-loss percentage record. With the

Giants idle, for once the Dodgers lead increased, if only by a half game, to 3½.

The time of the game was 2 hours and 13 minutes, a little below normal for that time but not out of line. Once in a while in that era a game would be played in less than two hours. Today games typically approach three hours. The reason for that, I believe, is the rules aren't being enforced. Batters constantly get out of the batter's box to adjust their batting gloves after almost every pitch. Pitchers often take more than the legal 20 seconds between pitches. Managers slavishly follow the lefty versus righty matchup to the point of craziness. And not to be overlooked, in almost every game there's a setup man and a closer involved, taking up a lot of time near game's end.

How different was it only yesterday? Mike Hargrove was a first baseman brought up by Texas in 1974, dividing his 11-year career between the Rangers and Cleveland. Hargrove was a fusspot at bat, getting out of the box to adjust his hat, gloves, pants, or whatever. He didn't take the time most of today's hitters do, but it seemed so at the time. His nickname: Rain Delay. Today we have too many Rain Delays.

On Friday, September 20, the owners elected Ford Frick as baseball's third commissioner, succeeding Happy Chandler, who was three votes short of re-election. He had handled himself well, as did Frick, when Robinson came up to Brooklyn in 1946. His suspension of Durocher, the man who blackjacked a disabled veteran into the hospital and constantly consorted with known gangster and gamblers, was thoroughly justified and should have been done sooner by Landis. Happy was treated unfairly by the owners and the press, but that wasn't Frick's fault.

Chandler did not go happily, and not many people could blame him. As a former governor and senator he was trained to keep his feelings to himself. But this time the bitterness spilled over and he went after the owners as well as his successor Ford Frick.

"When the clubs pushed me out they had a vacancy and decided to keep it," he said, "so they named Ford Frick."[5] The matter died right there; Frick did not comment. In fairness to Frick, when he was National League president he was instrumental in the founding and development of the Baseball Hall of Fame. In one of the few times he was challenged, he faced up to it at a very difficult time — the arrival of Jackie Robinson and the hatred he faced throughout much of the National League, especially when the Cardinals threatened to strike if Robinson was allowed to play against them.

Frick ended that by threatening to suspend any player doing so. There must have been some resentment carried over among the owners, for Frick's election was a tough one. It took eleven hours through sixteen ballots before the backers of Warren Giles gave in and made it unanimous.

I thought Frick's most controversial ruling as commissioner, on placing an asterisk beside the listing of Maris' 61st home run, was absolutely right. Numbers do not lie: 162 games is not 154 games. Maris hit number 61 on October 1, the last game of the 1961 season. He therefore got at least 32 more at-bats than he would have had the season before. Besides, 1961 was an expansion year, and Maris faced a number of pitchers who were in Double-A or Triple-A the year before. His 61st victim, Tracey Stallard, was not exactly Robin Roberts.

As September 16 dawned the Yankees started their move toward their third consecutive pennant, aided as usual by their opponents not rising to the occasion. The day before Cleveland was up by one while Johnny Sain had the worst game of his 11-year career, giving up four home runs as Detroit beat the Yanks, 7–4, in the final game of the season at the Stadium.

During the following week they took over first place, aided by Cleveland's fold and the kind of wonderful baseball we rarely, if ever, see anymore — a game-winning squeeze play done to perfection by DiMaggio and Rizzuto.

Bases loaded, one out in the ninth inning and a 1–1 score. Rizzuto, possibly the best bunter the game has ever seen, laid one down as DiMaggio, with perfect timing, came in from third with the winning run. One felt sorry for Bob Lemon as he stood there holding the ball helplessly as DiMaggio crossed the plate to give the Indian pitcher his 13th loss of the season against 17 wins.

On September 19 Bobby Shantz, all 5'6" and 139 pounds of him, won his 17th of the year, beating Detroit, 8–1, at Shibe Park. Bobby, among the smallest pitchers in baseball history, was one of the pitching phenoms of the 1950s. He posted 18 wins in 1951, his 18th against the Yankees as the season was ending on the 28th, and 24 in 1952. Small as he was, he lasted 16 years, ending up at 119–99 while pitching mostly for woeful teams.

Those two paragraphs bring to mind the fact that the bunt and the small pitcher are now relics of baseball's past. Today everything is power — power pitching and power hitting — no matter the consequences. Six-foot-three on the mound is becoming the norm, even going up to 6'10" in the case of Randy Johnson. This lust for size and power knows almost no bounds, even though those users through the recent steroid years knew of

Lyle Alzado and the risks involved. Roger Clemens is a good example. Six-foot-four and 205 pounds wasn't enough for him. He wanted more size and more power, and some day he may have to pay the price.

Someone always seems to step up for the Yankees and this pennant race was no exception. On September 20 they were down, 4–2, in the bottom of the ninth against the Sox at the Stadium, just barely clinging to the league lead. The game had started badly for New York with Johnny Sain knocked out in the first inning. But Joe Collins, playing to give Johnny Mize a rest, came up in that ninth and hit a three-run homer off Saul Rogovin to preserve the Yankees' half-game lead over Cleveland.

On this high note they went up to Boston and took two out of three while Cleveland lost three straight to Detroit, putting the Yanks 2½ games up, a lead they held to the end. And the end was classy indeed. They took a doubleheader from the Red Sox on September 30 in clinching the pennant at Yankee Stadium.

A fiction writer would blush writing this, but this was how they did it. Allie Reynolds took the mound in the first game and pitched a *no-hitter* to assure a tie, his second no-hitter of the year. This was the game noted earlier where Berra dropped Williams' pop-up in the ninth and Reynolds got him to pop-up again on the next pitch.

With the pennant race tied, Raschi went out for the second game, winning his 21st decision, 11–3, aided greatly by a DiMaggio three-run homer in the seventh. The Sox had thrown their best—Parnell, Scarborough, Masterson and Stobbs—but it was the Yankees' 18th pennant, including three in a row.

As the season ended in Yankees celebrations, Ned Garver of the St. Louis Browns became the only pitcher in baseball history to win 20 games for a team that lost more than 100. He finished the season at 20–12 as his St. Louis Browns would win but 52 and lose 102 in closing the season in last place, as was their custom.

Garver thus joined an exclusive club, the seven pitchers who won 20 for last place clubs in the twentieth century: Frank Hahn, 22–19 for Cincinnati in 1901; Scott Perry, 21–19 for Cincinnati in 1918; Howard Ehmke, 20–17 for the 1923 Boston Red Sox; Hollis Thurston, 20–14 for the Chicago White Sox in 1924; Steve Carlton, 27–10 with the 1972 Philadelphia Phillies; and Nolan Ryan, 22–16 with the 1974 California Angels.

Ned stands alone in this club in that in his 14-year career, he never played with a first-division team. In his years with the Browns, the Detroit Tigers, the Kansas City Athletics and the California Angels, he was often in the second division, sometimes in last place. As a consequence this great pitcher finished at 129–157, although with a respectable 3.73 ERA.

Over in the National League the Dodgers had a three-game lead over the Giants on the 21st, but earlier that day their manager made a decision that lowered his team into the 1951 playoff and eventually cost them the pennant. The telescope would have made the race a close one but it didn't decide who would go to the World Series. A childish and petulant Charlie Dressen took care of that by benching Clem Labine, the hottest pitcher in the league at the time.

Labine started that day against the Phillies at Ebbets Field, beginning the game 4–0 with an ERA of 1.00 after allowing four runs in 36 innings. Things did not go well for Brooklyn, starting in the first inning. Rookie second baseman Dick Young started it with a grounder that took a high hop over the head of Rocky Bridges. Then Ashburn with his speed beat out a bunt. The next batter hit a pop-up that was dropped. With the two runners on, Rube Walker threw the ball into center field while trying to pick Young off second base. Dressen then ordered Bill Nicholson walked to set up a double play. With the count 2–1, Willie Jones hit a pitch into the left-field stands.

Dressen was furious when he took Clem out of the game. You could see him on television gesticulating at and obviously berating his young pitcher. I couldn't figure out why. Clem had some bad breaks, and a home run into the Ebbets Field stands was not exactly a rarity, even with the bases loaded. Podbielan came on in relief but also ran into trouble, the Phillies winning, 9–6.

Here I give Labine's full side of the succeeding controversy because Dressen's stubborness was almost psychotic. To lose one's temper is one thing, but to let it eat at you for almost two weeks is another. Clem told writer Peter Golenbock:

> After going 4 and 0 I didn't pitch the last three weeks [sic] of the season. I went on Charley's list. You see, Charley was a very vindictive type person and his vindictiveness cost us the pennant in 1951. Not because Clem Labine was going to pitch one game and win it, but because Clem Labine could have pitched and given the other fellas, who were tired, a rest. But no, he didn't even let me go to the bullpen. He sat me on the damn bench. And now I'll tell you why.
>
> We had traveled all night and all day because we had trouble with the train. That's a tough thing and I was pitching. I got the first two men out but I was having trouble getting my curve ball over, so I walked two men and somebody hit a popup, but the ball was dropped. I had the bases loaded and I went into a stretch and Charlie came out and

told me not to go into a stretch. I told him I couldn't get my curve ball over, that I could get it back much better in a stretch. Again he told me not to. I told him that I knew better what I could do.

I was stubborn in those days and I took a stretch, and Jones hit a grand slam home run. Charlie came out and got the ball. He never talked to me. Not one day, two days, three days. Never talked to me, not one lousy word. He bit off his nose to spite his face. Because most assuredly we had a staff that was so overworked it wasn't funny. All he needed was someone to spell it. That's all, and he might have gotten another win out of it because, hell, I was pitching well, and it might have been different.[6]

If the pop up hadn't been dropped Clem could have been out of the inning.

Nevertheless, twelve days went by as Clem sat with the Dodgers lead dwindling and the pitching staff tiring. Finally, needing a rested starter badly, Dressen pitched him in the second playoff game with brilliant shutout results. It has always been Branca's contention that Dressen lost the pennant by wearing out the pitching staff. There is no doubt in my mind that he is right, and that by depriving Labine of at least three, maybe four starts, Dressen gave the Giants the flag.

His attitude toward Labine may have been because of some mysterious quick in his mind about him. Roger Kahn tells Golenbock about a day Dressen was evaluating ballplayers for him. "The trouble with Labine," Dressen said, "is that as a starting pitcher he was an incubator baby, and no incubator baby could go nine innings."[7] How did a man with a mind like that ever get to be a major league manager? My answer: Baseball is a simple game where the word genius is much overused. It doesn't take a high IQ to manage. It's the personnel that requires managing, not the game. The best managers are great only when they have the horses and the ability to control them — Stengel, McCarthy, McGraw, etc.

September 22 was another disasterous day for Brooklyn. The Phillies beat them again at Ebbets Field, handing Newcombe his ninth loss, 7–3, while the Giants reduced the Dodgers lead to three behind Larry Jansen's 20th win, 4–1, over the Braves. The pitching was great, as was Herman Franks out in the clubhouse signaling Warren Spahn's every pitch.

In winning the final game of the Phillies series Preacher Roe set a National League record of 22–2 with a 6–2 complete game, breaking the previous record of 16–2 set by Fred Fitzsimmons of Brooklyn in 1940. After the game Dressen announced he would protect the record and the .917 winning percentage by pitching Roe only in safe situations just to keep him sharp for the World Series. It was not to be. It would have been, however, if Labine had been allowed off the bench.

The Giants won, too, 4–1 over the Braves at the Polo Grounds. Notable was Maglie's 22nd win, the best of any Giant since Carl Hubbell in 1937 when the Giants had that great pennant-winning staff that included Cliff Melton and Hal Schumacher. They were no match in that Series, however, for Lefty Gomez, Monte Pearson and Red Ruffing.

The lead was down to 2½ the next day as the Giants swept the Boston series, winning the game, 4–3, on Eddie Stanky's ninth-inning single that drove in the winning run. It was the last game of the season at the Polo Grounds, played before just over 6,000 paid, an incredibly low attendance at any time, but especially with the Giants putting on the drive of a lifetime. I can imagine what Horace Stoneham was thinking — 6,000 in a stadium that seated 55,000. Of course, there were other factors than the pennant race. The Polo Grounds was hopelessly run down and in an area of Upper Manhattan that was becoming so dangerous that white fans were becoming increasingly fearful of going there. Stoneham, through the alcoholic fog he was usually in, had been talking to Minnesota representatives but no one paid attention until it was too late.

September 24 left Brooklyn and Dodgers fans throughout the metropolitan area stunned. There was no other word for it. The lead over the Giants was down to one game after being at 13 just a few weeks before. And worse for the Dodger faithful, they realized the Giants had momentum while the Dodgers were struggling.

The Giants were playing a night game in Philadelphia and knew when they took the field that Brooklyn had lost the first game of a twi-night doubleheader in Boston, reducing the lead to 1½. It proved to be the most disastrous doubleheader in Brooklyn Dodgers history.

I hate to apply the word choke to a team I was so fond of, but for that doubleheader there seems no other honest term. The *Herald-Tribune*'s Harold Rosenthal wrote, "The Dodgers had to be seen to have been believed in this dreadful demonstration," during which starters Branca and Erskine were routed early, Branca in the first inning and Erskine in the second.

Except for the pitching of Branca, the first game at 6–3 was semi-respectable since there is no shame in losing to Warren Spahn. But the second at 14–2 was a nightmare. Six runs scored in the first inning on two wild throws by Erskine, one by Furillo, and an easy grounder that went right through Reese. In all my years of watching that team at Ebbets Field and on television, I had never seen anything so dreadful from a team with such skills at every position.

I particularly remember Branca walking off the mound in that first game, shoulders slumped in defeat, as I wondered at Dressen's continuing faith in a pitcher who seldom came up big under real pressure. Even back in '47, his 20-win year, he pitched four good innings against the Yankees in the World Series opener and then fell apart. In 8⅓ innings in that Series, his ERA was 8.64. His record of 88–68 over a 12-year career shows he was never anything close to a "big game" pitcher. To leave Labine on the bench and pitch Branca in that situation showed the pettiness of Dressen, his vindictiveness as Labine called it. His faith in Branca continued during the playoffs with disastrous results.

Cutting the lead to one was the work of Hearn and Maglie as they combined for a 5–1 win over the Phillies in Shibe Park. Hearn pitched well until the seventh inning when Durocher, true to his motto of win today and then worry about tomorrow, brought in Maglie, who had pitched a complete game just two days before. Sal gave up one hit in the last 2⅔ innings. As Durocher walked into the clubhouse jubilant at the Dodgers first-game loss, Louis Effrat of the *Times* quoted him as saying, "It couldn't happen to a nicer bunch of guys."

With the citizens of the borough fearing disaster for the second year in a row, the *Brooklyn Eagle* saw the bright side, as it always did with the Dodgers. The newspaper noted the lead was down to one game, but added, "We're still two up in the loss column," before quoting Captain Reese as saying, "All I know is that we're still in first place." It's sad to look back now and remember that within six years of that day both the Dodgers and the *Eagle* would be gone, the ballclub because of Walter O'Malley's greed and the paper killed by the stubbornness of the New York City Newspaper Guild.

On the 26th the lead not only dipped to one-half game, but Preacher Roe lost his chance at setting a National League won-lost record. Dressen, who had promised to keep Roe's 22–2 record safe, used him out of desperation, the staff being so tired, all except Labine, still confined to the bench.

Roe's loss was bad enough, 4–3 at Braves Field, but the game and the pennant might well have hung on a tempertantrum plate umpire Frank Dascoli went through in the last of the eighth inning with Roy Campanella and then with the entire Brooklyn team.

Outfielders Bob Addis and Sam Jethroe had singled, bringing the Brooklyn infield in for a play at the plate. Addis was rounding third as Earl Torgeson grounded to Robinson, who threw to the plate where the sliding Addis was called safe, bringing Campanella up screaming.

Rosenthal of the *Herald-Tribune* wrote that after the call, Campanella jumped up, threw his glove to the ground and was immediately thrown out of the game by Dascoli. There was an immediate uproar on the Dodgers' bench. When angry remarks about Dascoli's lack of self control came from the Dodgers' dugout, he cleared the Brooklyn bench of everybody except Dressen, coach Jake Pitler and batboy Stan Strull. The Brooklyn players swarmed Dascoli, shouting at him to the effect that a player of Campanella's importance should not be ejected from a game with his team just one game in front in a torrid pennant race.

There was some justification. Dascoli, in his third year in the league, was noted for his fiery temper and quick thumb. I thought then and still do that whatever the provocation, Dascoli should have used better judgment at that crucial time in the race. And to most of the Dodgers, clearing the bench smacked of hysteria, for which Dascoli should have been reprimanded by the commissioner. Even some Boston writers came down on the umpire, saying that in vew of Campanella's importance in such a close race, "Dascoli acted hastily and that a bit more tolerance with an excited player would have been commendable."

The Associated Press quoted Dascoli as saying that throwing his glove to the ground and sailing his mask into the air [*sic*] "called for an automatic ejection." Contrary to some reports, Campanella denied calling Dascoli any names. "I never called an umpire names in my life," he said later. "I just asked him how he could call Addis safe when I had the plate blocked — and he just threw me out of the game."

The controversy continued after the contest, with the Dodgers now just one-half game ahead of the Giants. The Brooklyn players were increasingly bitter, feeling that Campanella would have been the batter in the ninth inning after Reese doubled with one out. Batting in his place was Wayne Terwiliger, a good utility man but no Campanella. Twig grounded to third for the second out, Reese holding, followed by a Pafko strikeout that ended the game. The feeling throughout Brooklyn was, of course, that if Dascoli had been able to control himself, the race would not have ended in a tie and subsequent playoff. "Dascoli is just incompetent," Dressen said. "We've had five (other) incidents with him this year."

Tempers were still running so high among the Dodgers after the game that the Boston Police Department stepped in. One of the Dodgers, first thought to be Robinson but later known to be Roe, kicked and splintered the door to the umpires' dressing room. As the Dodgers were milling about the door shouting, six policemen showed up to move them along and calm everyone down.

Nothing changed the next day as the Dodgers, one day too late, lashed back at the Braves with a 14-hit, 15–5 win for Newcombe's 19th victory. The Giants routed the Phils, 10–1, as Larry Jansen won his 21st decision easily at Shibe Park, thus sweeping the three-game series at Philadelphia. As the Giants were leaving, the Dodgers were arriving to face the Phillies for what would have been their last series of the year.

That night the incredible finally happened as the Dodgers lost to Philadelphia, 4–3, dropping them into a tie with the Giants, who had the day off. In what had become a pattern, the Dodgers behind Erskine were ahead, 3–1, for most of the game until Andy Seminick tied it up in the eighth with a homer with a man on base. As if preordained, Andy's homer was his first in a month and a half. Brooklyn lost it in the ninth on Willie Jones' single, driving Ashburn in from second with the fourth and winning Phillies run.

As the sun rose the next morning, September 29, the Dodgers and Giants had each won 94 and lost 56, with both teams having two left to play — the Dodgers at Philadelphia and the Giants at Boston. This meant that the pennant would not be decided until the last day of the season, making the race the tightest in baseball history while the Giants had come back from so far in such a short time.

For years afterwards this Giants team was known as miracle workers until word of the telescope finally surfaced. My vote still goes to the 1914 truly Miracle Braves led by manager George Stallings. They came from last place, 11½ games back of John McGraw's Giants on July 15, to win the pennant by 10½ games. They won the World Series in four straight against the Philadelphia Athletics, and they did it honestly, with no Herman Franks cheating with his telescope out in center field.

On the next-to-last day of the season the tie held as both teams won, the Giants' Maglie 3–0 over the Braves for his 23rd win and Newcombe 5–0 over the Phillies for his 20th. This was Newcombe's second win for the week and the start of one of the most courageous stretches of pitching under the most intense pressure in baseball history. Yet during the playoff when he reached the point where he couldn't throw another pitch, he was called a choke by people who should have known better or were blinded by the color of his skin.

Hollywood could not have scripted the last day better. Both teams won, setting up the second playoff in National League history, with both involving the Dodgers. The Giants won, 3–2, in Boston behind Larry Jansen, but the Dodgers had to go 14 innings in Philadelphia, winning 9–8 as Robinson's spectacular play kept the game tied in the 12th inning. He then won it in the 14th with his 18th home run.

At Braves Field Jansen was superb in the clutch, winning the most important game of his career by tossing a five-hitter against the combined pitching of Jim Wilson, Max Surkont and Vern Bickford. The Braves threw three of their best against the Giants, not only to avoid any possible taint of favoritism but also to try to be a factor in the pennant race. It wasn't always that way years before.

Boston scored once in the first inning, the Giants going ahead in the second on Bobby Thomson's 30th home run with a man on. The third and winning run came in the fifth after Dark singled, stole second and scored on Monte Irvin's line single. The Braves scored a run in the ninth on Bob Addis' second double, followed by scratch singles by Jethroe and Cooper. Jansen was carried off the field by teammates after he retired Willard Marshall for the third out with the tying run on third. The Giants' celebration intensified in the clubhouse with toasts all around when the news that Brooklyn was trailing Philadelphia, 6–1. Philadelphia had scored four runs in knocking out Preacher Roe in the second inning and scored two more off Branca in the third.

But the Giants' jubilation was short-lived, for the Dodgers scored three in the fifth off starter Karl Drews, the big hits being Robinson's triple with Snider aboard and Pafko's single that sent Jackie home. At that time, 3:35 P.M., a roar went up throughout Shibe Park as the scoreboard showed the Giants had beaten the Braves, 3–1. It was a dramatic moment as, starting with Robinson, every one of the Dodgers turned to the scoreboard knowing that it was all over if Philadelphia won. It was win this one, or else.

In the eighth inning Carl Furillo got the most important hit of his life. With Furillo on deck, Walker hit a long double to left, driving in Hodges and Cox, who had singled ahead of him. At this point, with Furillo approaching the plate, Phillies manager Eddie Sawyer replaced Drews with one of baseball's best pitchers, Robin Roberts.

In the bygone days of Cobb and Wagner, a starter of Roberts' stature would probably not have been brought in. In such situations favoritism was often the rule. But by 1951 all that kind of thing, teams favoring one team over another, was gone. In our modern era those out of contention play the spoiler role when possible. Thus Sawyer brought in his best in trying to win.

The move didn't help. Furillo lined a one-and-one pitch into left-center for the single that tied the game as Don Thompson, running for Walker, crossed the plate. At this point in his *Times* story of the game, Roscoe McGowan wrote that perhaps Furillo rather than Robinson should be the gilt-edged "hero" of the contest rather than Robinson. Reading this account today I am reminded of how overlooked Furillo was during his entire career and has been ever since. After the game was over, it was all Robinson and rightly so, for he played one of the best games of any second baseman in history. All but forgotten, even by such a staunch Dodgers and Furillo fan as I, was that without Furillo's hit there would have been no extra innings for Jackie's unprecedented clutch play.

This game in my opinion was a microcosm of Furillo's career. One of the best right fielders in baseball annals, a .299 lifetime hitter, 1953 batting champion, and with what was the best outfield arm of his era — or maybe any era — he has been totally ignored while much lesser outfielders (Harry Hooper for one) are in the Baseball Hall of Fame. I guess some of this was because of Carl's retiring nature. He was seldom heard from, unlike his fellow outfielder, headline hunter Duke Snider.

After Furillo's hit, things settled down until the twelfth inning. With two out Newcombe, with one on, walked two to load the bases. Eddie Waitkus then lined what in any other circumstance would have been a one-hop single to center. But somehow Robinson, edging toward first on the left-handed–hitting Waitkus, reversed ground and made an almost impossible diving catch just before the ball hit the ground. It was one of the most dramatic putouts ever seen, particularly since it was the third out, keeping the Dodgers alive.

Robby had hurt his shoulder as he fell hard to make the catch, and he lay on the ground for several minutes before he rose groggily and was helped to the dugout. It was a wonder that he came back to play, for even though he was just 32 years old, he was an old 32 from his tough years in the Negro leagues, the abuse he took as the first black major leaguer, and the years of pounding he eceived as a college and pro football player.

If ever there was a baseball Frank Merriwell, it was Jackie Robinson in that game. After that game-saving catch in the twelfth inning, Jackie came up in the fourteenth and hit a home run that sailed high into the upper left-field stands of Shibe Park. He was overwhelmed by the entire Brooklyn team as he entered the dugout.

But the tension wasn't over. Bud Podbelian came in to pitch the bottom of the inning. Bud was just 1-2 for the year but Dressen had to use him, the pitching staff down so that even Labine the exile pitched in the middle innings. There was a tense moment or two. First man up, Richie Ashburn, lined a single to center and was sacrificed to second, bringing up Del Ennis, who on a full count lifted an easy pop to Hodges.

Waitkus hit a routine fly to Pafko for the third out, triggering a wild scene at the Dodgers dugout as all realized they had survived to face the Giants in a playoff. If you asked 1,000 fans today who won that game, I'd bet that not one would say Bud Podbielan. In later years Mrs. Podbielan, when the occasion called for it, would remind listeners that her husband Bud won that game. (That often reminds me of Mrs. Oscar Hammerstein telling listeners that Jerome Kern did not write "Ol' Man River." "Mr. Kern wrote bum bum ba ba," she would say, "but my husband wrote 'Ol' Man River.'") Bud was traded to Cincinnati in 1952, a nine-year reliever with a 25–42 record.

It was getting late in the season in that era, so there was no time off. The playoff started the next day, October 2. There were no playoff or World Series games played in 40-degree weather in those days. Today's November bone-chilling Series are the result of the continuing stupidity and greed of, as Dick Young always called them, the Lords of Baseball.

Chapter Ten

October

Dressen for some unknown reason chose to have the playoff open at Ebbets Field, giving the Giants two games at the Polo Grounds, if necessary. As we know it was necessary and proved fatal to Brooklyn. But nobody could talk to Charlie, he being baseball's ranking genius.

It was Branca versus Jim Hearn in the opener, a fairly dull pitcher's battle as compared to the excitement of the previous week. New York won, 3–1, on two homers off Branca. Dressen's faith in Ralph is beyond understanding when one remembers his mediocre pitching in big games over the years. It was a decent enough game, but Branca always seemed to find a way to lose the important ones.

The winning runs came in the fourth inning on a home run by Bobby Thomson — who else — with Monte Irvin on base. In the eighth Monte hit one for the insurance run that gave Jim Hearn a two-run cushion as he finished up in the ninth. Thomson said later in the clubhouse that it was a fastball he hit for the two runs. Dressen never learned that Thomson feasted on Branca fastballs.

Jim Hearn was never a big name but he was a big pitcher coming down the stretch during the Giants' telescope pennant drive. In light of Thomson's homer, Jim, one of Durocher's big three, is mostly forgotten as the man who won the first playoff game, 3–1, limiting the Dodgers to just five hits. He was bought from St. Louis in July of 1950, just one season before his 17–9 pitching helped the Giants win their only questionable pennant.

Hearn was one of those big, hard-throwing right-handers, 6' 3" and 205 pounds, a Southerner born in Atlanta in April of 1920. He was with the Giants for seven seasons, traded in October of 1956 to the Phillies for Stu Miller, the pitcher later famous for being blown off the mound in the constantly windswept Candlestick Park.

"Jumbo" Jim Hearn was 17–9 during the Giants telescope run to the pennant in 1951. But even with the cheating, without Hearn, Maglie and Jansen, Leo Durocher's men would have finished second. Jim spent almost seven seasons in New York, and during his 13 years in the majors, after three years in the service, he was 109–89.

Chapter Ten: October

Dressen finally gave in and started Labine in the Polo Grounds opener. He really had no choice, the staff being so worn down. Clem made a fool of his manager by pitching a shutout as the Dodgers stomped the Giants, 10–0, to even the playoff at a game each.

Labine, the 25-year-old rookie, was unflappable. The day was misty and rainy on and off, not a great day for pitchers, but young Labine let nothing bother him. He sat out a rain delay of 41 minutes in mid-game, an interruption most pitchers can't survive. When the tarps were removed Clem took the mound and came out to finish his shutout.

As Red Barber would say, the Dodgers had their hitting shoes on as they pounded three Giants pitchers — Sheldon Jones, George Spencer and Al Corwin. In all the Brooks scored their 10 runs on 13 hits and four homers, starting with a Robinson two-run drive in the first inning. Then Hodges hit his 40th, Pafko his 30th, and Al Walker his fourth since coming from Chicago in the June 15 Hermanski-Schmitz trade.

Al "Rube" Walker was one of the most underrated of all Dodgers. He rode the bench most of the time but when he played he always seemed to come up with a key hit, as was his double to help put Brooklyn into the playoff. Coming off the bench as he did most of his career is not easy, but Rube had no choice. With the Cubs he was second to Mickey Owen, and with the Dodgers he played only when Campanella, one of all-time great catchers, was injured.

After he retired he became one of the game's best pitching coaches, first for Gil Hodges when he managed the Washington Senators and then when he followed Gil to the New York Mets. He is a footnote in baseball history as the catcher for Branca when Thomson hit his pennant-winning playoff home run.

After the game Labine told the writers that he used his curveball, fastball and sinker throughout the game, the three pitches he used most of the time. The curve he threw to strike out Thomson in the third inning with the bases loaded and two out would have been ball four if Bobby hadn't swung. Bobby later agreed.[1] The Giants didn't come that close to scoring for the rest of the game.

Dressen as usual ducked the important question of where Labine had been for the past two weeks. The questioners, of course, knew the answer but were baiting Chuck to see if he had the guts to own up to his stubbornness in keeping Clem on the bench. He didn't, answering the question with meaningless generalities.

The next day was the saddest in the long history of the Brooklyn Dodgers. A game and pennant they had in their grasp was thrown away in the ninth inning by Dressen's move that a high school coach would not have made. But to add to the sadness, even today so many years later, is the thought of who won and how they did it.

What should be remembered as probably the most thrilling game in baseball history, with the pennant decided on one swing of Bobby Thomson's bat, is now known to be the culmination of some 45 days of cheating by the New York Giants. That center-field telescope was used to the very end, to the point where Bobby Thomson knew for certain that final pitch from Branca was to be a fastball.

Worse even is to think of the people who benefited from all that cheating. For example, Leo Durocher was one of the nastiest and most dishonest men who ever played the game. A man, remember, who when managing Brooklyn had a heckler brought under the stands where he blackjacked him so badly that the victim, a medically discharged veteran, had to be hospitalized.

Eddie Stanky wasn't nicknamed "The Brat" for nothing. He was known thoughout the game as a nasty little man who was constantly causing trouble. Enos Slaughter as he left the Cardinals said, "The Cards were all fine people, except one. That was Eddie Stanky." And Slaughter was known to be easy to get along with. Phil Rizzuto, who had trouble with Stanky in World Series play, said, "He plays a snarling dog-eat-dog kind of baseball." For a while during one season Stanky would stand by second base waving his arms to distract the batter until National League president Ford Frick forbid it.

Eddie was born in Philadelphia but was a Southerner at heart, settling in Daphne, Alabama. His career began in 1943 when he was draft exempt because of the loss of hearing in his left ear as the result of three beanings. In all my years of following baseball I've never read or heard a good word about him. The following, however, may be accepted as half and half. Stanky was one of the Dodgers willing to sign the petition protesting Robinson's joining the Dodgers in 1947. Then when he got to know Jackie during the years when players throughout the league were taunting and sometimes physically abusive, as Slaughter did when he deliberately spiked him at first base, Stanky was on his side.

I once passed him outside Ebbets Field and was surprised at how short he was. It was June 20, 1946, and I was out of the navy just four days when I went over to see Joe Hatten in action. Going up the subway stairs to the main entrance I saw this little, somewhat-bowlegged man in front of me. I passed him and it was Eddie, either ignored or not recognized by the crowd. He's always listed at 5' 8". I was that size then and was looking down at him, at probably 5' 5" or 5' 6".

The rest of the Giants overall were not of the Durocher/Stanky school but they tolerated the cheating, and when it was exposed most of them denied it. Don Mueller, for example, told author Ray Robinson that "he was as mystified as the next man" in trying to figure out his five-homer spree in two days. It pains me to think that such hypocrisy — on the part other Giants as well — was rewarded with a pennant and World Series share.

It came down to the final game, the 5–4 win that ended what was at the time thought to be the greatest pennant drive in baseball history. The following account is from the *New York Times*, my second book *The Last Years of the Brooklyn Dodgers*, and my personal experiences during the closing days of the race as well as the playoff.

The weather had cleared overnight and was perfect for baseball as Maglie warmed up for the Giants and Newcombe for Brooklyn. At the time Maglie was going through one of the best three-year stretches the game had ever known. He came back from Mexico in early 1950 and the next three seasons was 59–18, a seldom-reached .766 winning percentage.

Newcombe was 20–9 and at 6' 4" and 220 pounds was a workhorse. As he took the mound he had gone 14⅔ innings during the previous two days, nine in shutting out Philadelphia on September 30 and 5⅔ in relief the next day to beat the Phillies again in that 14-inning Robinson game.

For most of the game there was little scoring. The Dodgers struck in the first inning when after Maglie walked Reese and Snider, Robinson singled to center to drive Reese home. Newcombe shut out the Giants until the seventh when Irvin doubled and scored on two sacrifice flies, the second by Thomson.

The Dodgers scored three in the eighth and appeared to have it wrapped up. Reese and Snider singled, Reese scoring on a wild pitch from an obviously tiring Maglie, who then walked Robinson and gave up singles to Pafko and Cox for two more runs.

As he took the mound for the last half of the eighth, Newcombe told Dressen he was too tired to go on. In the stands and on television it was obvious that Robinson started getting on him as he often did. Later Jackie said he kept telling the big pitcher: "Don't give us that tired bullshit. Don't start dogging it. Get the hell in there and pitch." As ordered, Don pitched a strong eighth and needed just three more outs for the pennant.

But he like Maglie was obviously very tired; exhausted would not be too strong a word. The Giants ninth began with a single by Dark, at which point Dressen made the worst decision of his long career, costing Brooklyn the game and the pennant. There were none out and a man on first when, with his team ahead by three runs, Dressen ordered Hodges to hold Dark on first, leaving a gaping hole between first and second base. This was against all managerial strategy, Dark being a meaningless run with the Brooks ahead by three.

Ray Robinson exonerates Dressen in *The Home Run Heard 'Round the World*, his book on the Thomson's home run. "With Dark edging warily off first, *Hodges for some inexplicable reason* played close to the bag," he wrote. "There was no chance that Dark would try to steal — the Giants needed more base runners right now [*sic*]. Some in the press box scratched their heads *at Hodges strategy*— or was it Dressen's — and wondered what the man was doing."[2]

That's crazy writing. Infielders, especially first basemen, don't decide on strategy. In any event a first baseman of Hodges judgment would never hold the runner in that situation. Of course it was Dressen's idea. And as for writers noticing Hodges holding first, I can't find one report of the game that mentions Dressen's unforgivable carelessness.

Don Mueller up, and he grounded one into the hole, Dark taking second as the ball hopped into the outfield literally inches from Hodges' outstretched glove. Given that Hodges was the best fielding first baseman in the game, that grounder would have been a sure double play if Gil had been in position off the bag and Dressen not ordered him to hold Dark on. What could Dressen have been thinking, if anything?

Speculation or not, one thing is sure: were it not for Dressen's incompetence, that double play would have been made, resulting in nobody on and two out, a far cry from two on and nobody out. Irvin's pop-up to Hodges off a Newcombe fastball would then have ended the game, giving Brooklyn the pennant. These are the hard facts that the sportswriters, amazingly, ignored.

There was a sigh of relief among Dodgers fans seeing such a dangerous hitter as Irvin pop up with no damage done. But then Lockman doubled, scoring Dark and sending Mueller to third where he injured his ankle sliding in. Clint Hartung, the much-ballyhood rookie of some years before, ran for Mueller. Dressen, seeing that Newcombe had nothing left, called for Branca, who was warming up alongside Erskine. Carl had thrown a curve in the dirt while Branca's ball seemed alive, so bullpen coach Clyde Sukeforth recommended that Ralph go in. That decision was to cost him his job.

It's a baseball truism that no pitcher really wants to go into a game that is that vitally important. In later years whenever he was asked what his best pitch was, he would say, "The curveball I bounced in the dirt in the Polo Grounds bullpen."[3]

Chapter Ten: October

Dressen called the bullpen. "I asked Sukey who was pitching better and he said Branca," Dressen said in explaining his choice to *The Sporting News*. "He told me Branca. That's our usual system and that's how it was." A reminder: Sukeforth was a catcher, not a pitching coach.

As Newcombe was leaving the mound, he had pitched 22⅔ of great baseball under the most intense pressure within memory. Yet there were those who called him a choke, some even in the press box. Nothing I've heard in a lifetime of watching baseball was more unfair.

As Branca took the mound Bobby Thomson stepped in, with one eye on Sal Yvars in the bullpen. He took the first pitch for a fastball down the middle. The next pitch was one that Branca intended to be a high and inside waste pitch. It was inside and high but not enough of either. Thomson swung, and we saw on television Pafko back against the left-field wall, looking up and watching the ball fly into the stands. There was pandemonium throughout the Polo Grounds as Giants announcer Russ Hodges kept shouting, "The Giants win the pennant, the Giants win the pennant" over and over again. And there is the enduring picture of Stanky joyfully tackling Durocher on the third-base line. As the rest of the players were heading to their clubhouses, the Giants mobbed by jubilant crowds, Jackie Robinson, ever the competitor, stood watching Thomson round the bases, making sure he touched every one.

There's no question the ball was hit well, and on television it seemed to have just enough rise to clear the 315-foot mark as it went into the left-field stands. Branca said it was a waste pitch, up and in. Thomson agreed, telling James Dawson of the *Times*, "If I was a good hitter I'd have taken that pitch. It wasn't a good pitch. It was high and inside, the kind they've been getting me out on all season."[4] Yes, Bobby, but you knew what was coming.

As the Giants celebrated, there is that famous picture of Branca stretched full length on a stairway, a sweatshirt covering his number 13, a number he changed the following season. Coach Cookie Lavagetto is sitting next to him smoking a cigarette with a stunned look on his face. When he recovered enough to start dressing, Ralph told Roscoe McGowen, the *Times* Dodgers beat man, "I guess we weren't meant to win it. The ball was high and inside, not a good pitch and it only cleared the wall by that much." He made a motion indicating inches.

I remember watching the ending on television. As a Dodgers fan what hurt me almost as much as losing was seeing Stanky and Durocher in joyous celebration, two of the most rotten and undeserving people in all of baseball. As they were celebrating, Branca provided one more clue that the Dodgers knew all along that somehow their signs were being stolen.

As he was heading for his car in the Polo Grounds parking lot, he said to a photographer, "Why are you taking my picture. You should take pictures of those guys over there, the ones who were stealing our signals all year [*sic*]."[5] So the Dodgers knew but they could not pinpoint where and how the stealing was going on. They tried, as noted, but the umpire "took the binoculars away from us," Cookie Lavagetto told the *Times*.

That evening Ralph and his fiancee, Dodgers heiress Ann Mulvey, went to Ann's cousin, Father Patrick Crowley, for guidance. When Ralph kept asking "why me, why me," the priest told him that God knew he was strong enough to bear the burden of such a crushing loss. In any event Ralph was never the same again. He drifted from Brooklyn in 1952 to Detroit, to the Yankees and then back to Brooklyn in 1956 but never got it back. He was released after one game in Brooklyn and then retired.

It's a tossup with Ralph. It was either psychological from the playoff loss, problems with his back, or arm problems at age 30 because he was always on his own as far as pitching was concerned. The Dodgers, as noted, had no pitching coach to guide the staff and correct errors in form. I think Branca with his physique — 6'3" and 220 pounds — would have pitched much longer if Dressen had such a coach instead of catchers running the staff. Although he never came back as a ballplayer, Branca eventually got over the trauma of that fatal pitch. He and Thomson soon became friends to the extent that for a number of years they did a vaudeville-like routine for benefits and appeared on a number of television shows.

As Giants fans were celebrating throughout the city, a vast crowd of Dodgers fans were mulling around Brooklyn's Borough Hall, calling Dressen all kinds of names. Based on the tone of it all as well as a number of signs, the main problem was Dressden's treatment of Labine. The *Brooklyn Eagle* received many letters on the same subject, Where was Labine? Why was he on the bench when with three starts he would have won the pennant for us? None mentioned Dressen's mistake in ordering Hodges to hold Dark on first base. It would have taken a discerning fan to notice what all the newspapers ignored.

As Dodgers fans suffered through their second heart-breaking year in a row, none of their questions were answered. After the loss to Philadelphia Dressen said he would "never have a doghouse" on his team, a transparent shot at his predecessor, Burt Shotton, whose attitude toward Eddie Miksis cost him the 1950 pennant. Yet Charlie went the same way. His banishment of Labine was a major factor in this 1951 loss, worse since it went all the way through a playoff.

Nobody was held accountable except poor Clyde Sukeforth, fired because he was just a catcher, not an unwanted pitching coach who might have chosen someone other than Branca — even Labine possibly. Dressen received his undeserved reward: a contract for 1952 after guiding the most mismanaged pennant race in Brooklyn history.

Charlie's managing was bad enough, but after he was signed he disgracefully blamed his players for the 1951 loss, taking not one bit of responsibility for his terrible decisions late in the season. In an article in the *Saturday Evening Post* before the 1952 season began, he said his 1951 ball club was "overrated" and that "they weren't good enough to be out in front by 13½ games in August. The defeat wasn't my fault." What a disgraceful little man.

Charlie was lucky to be working for an owner who knew little and cared less for the game. O'Malley was a successful lawyer who never should have gained control of such a valuable and historic franchise as Brooklyn. His eye was always on the money and not the game. If he noticed the treatment of Labine or Hodges holding Dark on first in that fatal ninth inning, he never mentioned it. Signing Dressen, however, said it all.

Before starting on the Series, a look at the ticket prices of the day is almost painful. As the Yankee Stadium gates were opened for the first game, reserved seats were selling for $6, box seats at $8, and seats in the bleachers $1. Standing room, while space lasted, was $4. These were baseball prices before free agency, fan friendly prices before George Steinbrenner and his ilk.

Today such ticket costs are in the hundreds and often thousands of dollars. How else to pay a ballplayer $25 million *a year*, or as the Yankees did in the fall of 2009, pay $483.5 million for three players — almost half a billion dollars? As Major Bowes used to say, "Where it stops nobody knows." Certainly have-not teams like Kansas City and Pittsburgh can't pay those salaries.

Before the opener started there was a flurry of excitement in the box seats behind home plate. A police escort accompanied New Jersey deputy attorney general Nelson Stamler to his car after informing him that Willie Moretti, a high-ranking Mafia underboss, had been murdered in a Cliffside Park, New Jersey, tavern. It was later revealed in the *Times* that Moretti, suffering from advanced syphilis, had been slain gangland style because he was talking too much to the wrong people.

For all the good it did them, the Giants were given Dodgers chief scout Andy High's reports on the Yankees before the Series started. The reports included his evaluation of DiMaggio, that Joe was unable to throw, run or pull the ball any longer. However, Joe hit about as well as any

Yankee during the Series, batting .261 with two doubles, a homer and five RBIs.

Unlike today, the World Series started the day after the playoff, on October 4th in Yankee Stadium. With his star pitchers Maglie, Jansen and Hearn needing rest, Durocher started journeyman Dave Koslo, a 10–9 pitcher during the season. The Durocher luck held as Koslo pitched a seven-hit complete game in beating the Yankees, 5–1.

Backing Koslo's great pitching, Monte Irvin not only had four hits but stole home — a clean steal, unlike the 1955 Robinson move that Berra has been disputing ever since. Reynolds, usually up for such key games, took the loss, giving up eight hits in six innings.

The Yankees were shocked, thinking that Dave would be easy meat, a surprise starter who had always been a journeyman lost against the brilliance of Jansen, Maglie and Hearn. Born Joseph Koslowski in Menasha, Wisconsin, Dave had a 12-year career, compiling a 92–107 record, and was with New York 10 years before being traded to Baltimore in 1954.

Irvin remained hot the next day with three more hits, but otherwise Lopat was almost untouchable, going all the way for a 3–1 win. The only Giants run was scored in the seventh on a fly ball with the bases loaded by pinch-hitter Bill Rigney. Loser Jansen said later he made only one bad pitch all day, a curveball that hung for Collins to hit into the right-field bleachers.

At the start of the game it was announced that Mantle would be out for the rest of the Series because of a strained muscle inside his right knee. It's a wonder those fragile knees held up for an amazing 18 years under major league pressure. I recall that Mantle missed most the 1955 World Series, an important factor in the Dodgers winning their first World Series.

The Giants, at home in the Polo Grounds for Game 3, went one up as Jim Hearn went all the way, backed by a three-run homer by Whitey Lockman. The game was atypical of the Yankees. They made two errors in the fifth inning as the Giants scored five times, and Raschi was knocked out in mid-game after Lockman's homer.

The key play came in that fifth inning. With Stanky on first, Berra called for a pitchout and had Eddie nailed at second as he tried to steal. But as Rizzuto was waiting to make the tag, Eddie kicked the ball out of his glove and into the outfield, giving him time to take third and then score on a hit through the infield by Dark. This was the kind of play Durocher loved. He delightedly told the press, "That's the way he plays the game."

Phil protested vigorously that Stanky should have been called out for interference. The call held, however, mainly because there was no precedent for such a play. Not even Ty Cobb ever attempted such a minor league stunt. Phil never talked to Stanky again, having nothing but contempt for such a "bush" tactic.

That play and that inning were the high-water marks for the Giants. The Yankees swept the next three games, including a 13–1 embarrassment back at the Stadium. They were down two games to one when Reynolds took the mound for Game 4. As usual, Allie had it.

John Drebinger started his *Times* story thusly: "As Joe DiMaggio goes, so go the Yankees." He was reaching back a few years but it was pardonable since Joe hit a Maglie pitch deep into the upper-left-field stands with Berra on in the fourth inning to give Reynolds a three-run lead on his way to a 6–2 win. It was a breakout game for DiMaggio, who went 2-for-5 with a home run and two RBIs. Maglie's lament: "I couldn't get loose." One of the best curve ball pitchers in the game told the press that Joe had hit one of his curves "but not one of my best."

Although Maglie didn't have it, his offense suffered because the youthful Willie Mays had one of the worst games of his career. Al Dark had three successive doubles and Monte Irvin stoked another two hits, but they were stranded each time as Willie hit into three double plays.

Rizzuto must have been gloating as he passed Stanky between innings of the Yankees' 13–1 rout of the Giants' Larry Jansen and those who followed him. The game got out of control in the fifth inning when five runs crossed the plate, four of them on Gil McDougald's homer with the bases loaded. With Lopat at his best, Leo's boys had no chance. DiMaggio was having a great swan song Series, as he again had a great game going 3-for-5 with three RBIs.

It was the worst Series defeat since 1936 when Joe McCarthy's Yankees took Bill Terry's Giants, four games to two, including scores of 18–4 and 13–5. Terry, sitting in a field-level box, said later that "for a moment I thought it was the same nightmare." It was during that Series that Tony Lazzeri hit a grand slam into those same Polo Grounds seats.

Stengel's Yanks had the Giants by the throat, and the Stengel teams of that era never let go. It was over the next day. Raschi, Sain and Kuzava outpitched Koslo and the Giants' bullpen, winning 4–3, to give the Yankees their third World Series in a row and 18th overall.

It was tight until the sixth inning when Hank Bauer, up with the bases loaded, hit a triple to score all three. He said later that it was "a fastball right down the middle." The Giants scored two in the ninth before Kuzava shut them down, aided by a great Bauer catch of an Yvars liner to right-center. It was a fitting year's end for Bauer, a .296 hitter during 1951. Mapes was gone but Hank still chafed under Stengel's platoon system. But, as noted, you can't argue with success.

So 1951 ended with the wrong team sharing Series glory and money with the Yankees. The great Joe DiMaggio would not be back and neither would Durocher's telescope. For the next two years without the benefit of cheating the Giants would finish 4½ games behind Brooklyn in '52 before falling into the second division, 35 games behind the Dodgers, in 1953. Leo would win it in 1954 when Johnny Antonelli won 21 games.

Years later *Times* sportswriter Dave Anderson wrote a column in which Ralph Branca admitted he had known since 1954 that the Giants had cheated, that they had used a high-powered telescope to alert their batters to every opposing pitch.

Ralph, as many others, had suspicions of foul play. Yet it wasn't until that year that a fellow pitcher took him aside and told him what others had been avoiding, that the Giants had been cheating and that Thomson knew what pitch was coming.

"A guy on the Tigers (Ted Gray) who had a friend on the Giants told me about the sign stealing," Branca told Anderson. "I've known it since 1954 but I never said anything. I didn't want to cry over spilled milk. I became friendly with Bobby and I didn't want to demean his home run. I didn't want to cheapen a legendary moment in baseball."[6]

No, Ralph, no. You wouldn't have demeaned a legendary moment in baseball. Bobby Thomson and the rest of the Giants demeaned that moment with their cheating.

It was a disgrace then and still is, a seven-week period in 1951 that all of baseball should be ashamed of, including all of the Giants, as well as all of the players on the various teams that knew or suspected what was going on. Baseball players as a whole have never been the most intelligent people in the world or, in the heat of the game, the most honest.

But there are limits. To view Bobby Thomson and his home run with awe in light of what we know today are beyond them.

Appendix: The Telescope Scheme

The following are the highlights of two telephone interviews with Sal Yvars, the former New York Giants catcher who was the main signalman during the Giants' 37–7 run in August and September of 1951. Yvars, sitting on the Giants bench, would get the sign from the telescope man and then pass it along to the batter, thus alerting him as to what type pitch to expect. In the eyes of many the Giants thereby stole the pennant. Sal had an eight-year career in the National League, including six-plus with the Giants.

Rudy Marzano: How did the telescope scheme come about?

Sal Yvars: Someone, I think it was a young guy we got from the Cubs, told Leo about a powerful telescope he used in the Navy and suggested we use something like it to steal signals. My recollection is that we started using it on August 12 or sometime around there, the 12th to the 15th. We started winning right away. With our hitters knowing the pitches, we couldn't lose — at home that is.

How did it work?

We had a buzzer installed in the clubhouse. I was in the bullpen holding a baseball waiting for the signals. A buzz meant breaking ball, no buzz a fastball. I would hold the ball in my hand for fastball and throw it in the air and catch it for a breaking ball. So our hitters knew what was coming.

With the telescope being that successful for you, why didn't you continue you use it the next year and beyond?

The word had gotten around, especially all over the National League, about the telescope. You know, all during the last half of '51 everyone was suspicious, especially the Dodgers, that something was going on but they couldn't figure out what. The Dodgers used binoculars once at the Polo Grounds and were aiming them at our clubhouse, trying to figure out what was going on, when the umpires confiscated them. I think it was Lavagetto, but I'm not sure. But anyway Brooklyn knew something was up. They just couldn't figure out what. And neither could anyone else.

Sal, did you ever feel guilty about what went on?

No, because Durocher was my manager and I did what I was told. It was just like when I was in the air force during the war. I obeyed orders. Plus, winning ballgames didn't hurt. Winning eased a lot of doubts. Any doubters knew that we played it Durocher's way or we were gone. And Leo loved that telescope.

How about around the league? Didn't anyone question all that slugging by the likes of Westrum and Mueller and all those wins at home?

Oh, lots of people suspected things but they couldn't pin anything down. And I'll tell you, most of them didn't care as long as it was the Dodgers being hurt. I don't want to go into it, but the Dodgers were disliked throughout most of the league.

I know there were a couple of books in the nineties that mentioned the scheme but nobody paid attention. But even before that, how could it have stayed a secret from the public for almost 50 years?

Well, I didn't want to talk about it and I was right in the middle of things. I guess a lot of the ballplayers figured let sleeping dogs lie. A factor on the Giants was that we didn't want to cheapen both our stretch run and Bobby's home run. As far as I know, none of us were even asked about it until the *Wall Street Journal* article.

I've read that you and Branca became good friends.

Yes. We met at affairs and both live in Westchester County.

Did you ever tell him about the telescope?

No. Why rub it in? I knew he'd find out eventually. I didn't want it coming from me. I remember seeing that picture of him stretched out on the stairs after that game and I felt sorry for him. I said to myself, "Let somebody else do the dirty work, somebody not involved." I know Bobby Thomson never told him, but I'll get to Thomson later.

As in past such schemes I assume you couldn't use the scope all the time.

Yes, only home games. We didn't dare try the telescope on the road. At the Polo Grounds we'd use the scope until we were five runs ahead.

Then we'd shut it down and only go back to it if the other team started catching up.

Would you explain further how you worked it?

Coach Herman Franks and I became a team with the signals. He would relay the signs to me and I'd relay them to the hitter. The Polo Grounds bullpen was in right center field and I stood at the corner so that the batter could see whatever I was doing. I would have a ball in my hand, and if there was no sound from the buzzer it was a fastball and I did nothing. The buzzer meant a breaking ball, so I'd throw the ball in the air, like I'm foolin' around out there. A change of pace we treated as a curveball. If Herman thought it was a knockdown pitch, I stood up. So we even knew when we were going to be knocked down. Believe me, we knew every pitch that was coming, and I relayed every pitch to every batter. If the batter didn't want the signal that was his business, but I relayed everything just the same.

Now for Bobby Thomson. He was in a slump until we started. But from the time we started signaling until he hit the home run, he gained about 60 points. But later he told the press and TV guys, "I was taking the signs until I hit the home run." Then he would say whether he knew what Branca would throw: "I could say yes or I could say no, but I'd rather say no." What sense did that make? He should have said that he knew Branca was a fastball pitcher and he was looking for a fastball. If he had said that it would have been over. Anyway, he took a fastball right down the middle. The next pitch was a little high and inside, and he smacks it out of the ballpark.

What about the World Series?

We didn't use the scope during the World Series because there was too much activity, too many guys floating around poking into everything. Plus, we couldn't use it at the Stadium anyway.

I've read where Durocher was worried that you guys were hitting too well.

Right. We had Don Mueller, who was a bloop hitter but hit five home runs in two days. Guys were telling him to bloop the ball again or we'd arouse suspicions and get caught. We'd tell him he'd just tied Musial in hitting five home runs in two days. We also tried to slow Wes Westrum down. He was hitting them into the upper deck. But we had the signals and the guys used them. We never would have won the pennant without them. We once won 16 in a row at home and 37 and 7 overall with the signals.

Did they ease off on the long ball?

Some, but not entirely. They listened to us but you've got to understand. These are major league hitters. When they know what pitch is coming, their baseball instincts take over. There are some things you just can't stop.

I can't recall Branca ever discussing that home run publicly. Do you have any idea how he feels now—resentment, acceptance, or whatever?

I think he's resigned to it. I don't think any pitcher who ever lived wouldn't be regretful to be the loser in one of the most important games ever played. And the thing, is Branca has known about it since 1954 when he was traded to the Tigers. Ted Gray, a Tiger pitcher friendly with Ralph, told him the whole story. But he has learned to live with it, especially since that *Wall Street Journal* article told the world the real story of how he was cheated. Ralph is a great guy, one of the most charitable people you'd ever want to meet, he and his wife.

Sal, it had been my contention that there was no hatred between the Dodgers and Giants as teams. It seems to me that the hatred centered around Durocher, Robinson and Furillo, with Maglie not, personally involved but following Durocher's orders. Am I right?

I would say you're mostly right.

I remember in '53 with Furillo at bat, Durocher yelled to Reuben Gomez to "stick it in his ear." Gomez then hit him, and after Carl took first, he charged the Giants dugout and ran through the entire Giants team to get at Durocher.

That's right. I was with St. Louis by then but we all knew what happened. Nobody stopped it until it got dangerous. Carl was choking Durocher, who was turning red. Then I think it was Hearn and Irvin who pulled Carl off. He then walked out of the dugout with nobody stopping him.

I remember his classic remark that he wasn't afraid of the Giants because all of his players hated him.

That's a little strong but mainly true. Leo's dead now. God rest his soul, but he wasn't very well liked. Great baseball brain but too devious. He was a thief at heart.

I've always thought it was disgraceful for a lot of Brooklyn fans and some in the press who say Newcombe choked in that final game. What did you ballplayers think?

We thought it was one of the best stretches of pitching we ever saw. He was totally exhausted in that last game. I think he pitched something like 25 innings in four or five days — and the pressure. The pennant was riding on every pitch. I can't explain that choking business. Maybe it was racial.

Sal, one more thing: you truly believe Thomson knew what pitch was coming?

Have you seen the newsreels of Thomson swinging? Bobby leaned into that ball like he never did before. He practically leaped at it because he knew what was coming.

Chapter Notes

Chapter One: January

1. Rickey/Hornsby fight: Polner, *Branch Rickey*, p. 89.
2. Damaged feelings under Shotton: *Brooklyn Eagle*, 4/16/51, p. 15.
3. The big "I": Robinson, *The Home Run Heard 'Round the World*, p. 57.
4. Bowman/Durocher elevator remarks: *Herald-Tribune*, 6/20/40, p. 27.
5. DiMaggio says "No more signals": Kahn, *Memories of Summer*, pp. 74–75.
6. Medwick beaning: *The Sporting News*, 6/20/40.
7. Speaker defends Chapman: Lieb, *Baseball as I Have Known It*, p. 134.
8. Condition of the ball: Ritter, *The Glory of Their Times*, p. 55.
9. We were young: Clem Labine interview.
10. Importance of batting helmet: Bobby Bragan interview.
11. Reiser beaning: *New York Times*, 5/1/41, p. 28.
12. Reese on Robinson, petition: Golenbock, *Bums*, pp. 147–148.
13. Robinson on Reese: Robinson, *I Never Had It Made*, pp. 64–65.
14. Reese will never make it: Durocher, *Nice Guys Finish Last*, p. 133.
15. One of the most dramatic putouts in history: *New York Times*, 6/5/47, p. 33.
16. Hermanski differs: Gene Hermanski interview.
17. Pete should have rested: Heinz, *The Rocky Road of Pistol Pete*, p. 237.
18. Reiser, who could have been the best: *Biographical Encyclopedia of Baseball*, p. 284.
19. O'Malley's phony baseball career: Kahn, *The Era*, p. 264.
20. O'Malley and Rickey cursing: Barber, *The Broadcasters*, p. 170.
21. Dodgers profits in the 1950s: *The Sporting News*, 7/3/57.
22. Woodward on baseball writers: Kahn, *Beyond the Boys of Summer*, p. 120.
23. Can't risk dead body: Parrott, *The Lords of Baseball*, pp. 24–25.
24. Snider only one to say he was glad Rickey gone: *The Sporting News*, 1/10/51.
25. McGraw: Nobody touches Mel Ott: Hynd, *The Giants of the Polo Grounds*, p. 266.

Chapter Two: February

1. The ball is juiced: Kahn, *Head Game*.
2. The Cobb, Speaker, Leonard, Wood conspiracy: *New York Times*, 12/22/26, p. 1.
3. Jackie a strict pain: Clem Labine interview.
4. His mother's tough life: Robinson, *I Never Had It Made*, p. 6.
5. Refuses back of the bus: *Ibid.*, pp. 18–19.
6. Robinson's Rickey interview: *Ibid.*, pp. 31–34.
7. Campanella's Rickey interview: Frommer, *Rickey & Robinson*, pp. 109–110.
8. Furillo's limited education: Clem Labine interview.

9. The true Dodger-Giant relationship: Kahn, *The Era*, p. 314.
10. Get a shoebox: *Biographical Encyclopedia of Baseball*, p. 948.
11. Rizzuto retirement, Yankee style: *Ibid.*, p. 948.
12. Dressen's no doghouses: *New York Times*, 2/21/51, p. 28.
13. Shotton a dumb SOB: *Eddie Miksis interview*.

Chapter Three: March

1. Stadium cost DiMaggio at least 200 homers: Smith, *Voices of Summer*.
2. Joe D. announces retirement: *New York Times*, 3/2/51.
3. Scouting report on DiMaggio: *Life*, 10/22/51, p. 134.
4. DiMaggio in Pacific Coast League: *Biographical Encyclopedia of Baseball*, p. 220.
5. Life in the Pacific Coast League: *Pete Coscarart interview*.
6. "Many attend but few understand" quote: *Biographical Encyclopedia of Baseball*, p. 1212.
7. Lockman the hypocrite: Thomson, *The Giants Win the Pennant*, p. 270.
8. Roe tips off his spitter: Kahn, *Boys of Summer*, p. 306.
9. Luxurious life in Mexican League: *Life*, 6/24/46, pp. 119–120.
10. Mickey Owen leaves Mexico: *The Sporting News*, 8/14/46.
11. Gardella bribed for $300,000: *New York Times*, 6/15/50, p. 32.
12. Owners vote against Robinson to majors: Werber, *Memories of a Ball-player*, p. 228.
13. For Chandler, not one cent more: *Herald-Tribune*, 6/21/51, pg. 19.
14. Erskine hid shoulder injury: *National Pastime*, 5/05, pp. 68–69.
15. Shuba gets the runaround: Kahn, *Boys of Summer*, p. 225.
16. Vander Meer a moocher: Werber, *Memories of a Ballplayer*, pp. 184–185.
17. Dimmer lights favored Vander Meer: *Pete Coscarart interview*.

Chapter Four: April

1. Kirby sticks to his beliefs: Higbe, *The High Hard One*, p. 107.
2. Best pitch a bounced curveball: Erskine, *Tales from the Dodger Dugout*, p. 87.
3. No pitching coach Branca's problem: Westcott, *Splendor on the Diamond*, p. 188.
4. Dumping on Branca: *The Sporting News*, 11/26/47, p. 9.
5. Erskine gutted it out: *National Pastime*, 5/05, pp. 68–69.
6. The ruination of Erv Palica: *Clem Labine interview*.
7. Allie Reynolds dumps on Dressen: Gittleman, *Reynolds, Raschi and Lopat*, p. 216.
8. The press avoiding Ebbets Field: Kahn, *The Era*, p. 112.
9. Making fun of the Dodgers: Kahn, *Memories of Summer*, p. 206.
10. Three men on base: Ritter, *The Glory of Their Times*, p. 216.
11. Mays never said "say hey": Kahn, *Memories of Summer*, p. 255.
12. DiMaggio says Gionfriddo's catch better: Kahn, *The Era*, p. 128.
13. Many resent Robinson being spokesman: Frommer, *Rickey & Robinson*, pp. 113, 178.
14. Robinson often a team liability: *Clem Labine interview*.
15. Dodgers accept Robinson or else: Durocher, *Nice Guys Finish Last*, p. 205.
16. Robinson says he was after Maglie: *The Sporting News*, 2/1/56, p. 10.

Chapter Five: May

1. Dressen in his Captain Queeg mood: Snider, *The Duke of Flatbush*, pp. 42–43.
2. Snider's ravings against Dodger fans: *New York Times*, 8/27/55, p. 10.
3. Tragic result of Robinson/Maglie feud: *Brooklyn Eagle*, 5/1/51, p. 14.
4. Brooklyn diocese Durocher ultimatum: *Herald-Tribune*, 3/1/47, p. 15.
5. No one could control Durocher: Lowenfish, *Branch Rickey: Baseball's Ferocious Gentleman*, p. 228.

6. Hearing a Labine fastball: Kahn, *Boys of Summer*, p. 55.
7. Veeck first to consider moving a franchise: *New York Times*, 5/10/51, p. 35.
8. A midget comes to bat: *Herald-Tribune*, 8/19/51. p. 1.
9. Humor breaks tension: *Gene Hermanski interview*.
10. Durocher calms Mays: Durocher, *Nice Guys Finish Last*, pp. 309–310.
11. Meyer and Robinson tangle: *Brooklyn Eagle*, 6/1/51, p. 18.

Chapter Six: June

1. MacPhail develops batting helmet: *New York Times*, 3/8/40, S 1.
2. Eddie Gaedel banished after one at-bat: *Herald-Tribune*, 8/19/51, p. 1.
3. Casey makes the mistake of being 70: *Biographical Encyclopedia of Baseball*, pp. 1080, 1082.
4. Robinson: *I Never Had It Made*, pp. 99–100.
5. Pafko comes to Brooklyn: *New York Times*, 6/16/51, p. 1.
6. Tommy Byrne with a return address: *Brooklyn Eagle*, 9/9/54, p. 17.
7. Pafko trade angers league: *New York Times*, 6/19/51, p. 35.
8. The most senseless sale in baseball history: *Ibid.*, 1/18/53, p. 1.
9. Schoendienst denies Cardinal strike threat: Frommer, *Rickey & Robinson*, p. 138.
10. Stengel on managerial success: *New York Times*, 6/21/51, p. 34.

Chapter Seven: July

1. Casey was almost saved: *Brooklyn Eagle*, 7/2/51, p. 1.
2. The pitch under Owen's glove was a spitball: Holmes, *The Dodgers*, p. 89.
3. Berra drops no-hitter popup: Berra, *Yogi*, p. 154.
4. Berra dogged it once too often: *Ibid.*, p. 68.
5. DiMaggio left severely alone: *New York Times*, 7/9/51, p. 20.
6. Robinson close to cracking up: Robinson, *I Never Had It Made*, p. 59.
7. Little-known George Blaeholder invented the slider: Einstein, *The Baseball Reader*, p. 114.
8. Johnny Sain, one of the great pitching coaches: *Biographical Encyclopedia of Baseball*, p. 994.
9. Red Barber on Casey Stengel: Barber, *Rhubarb in the Catbird Seat*, pp. 97–98.
10. Leonard Shecter on Casey Stengel: Shecter, *The Jocks*, p. 169.
11. Stengel puts Cosell in his place: Berra, *Yogi*, p. 254.
12. All that baseball has done for Ty Cobb: *Herald-Tribune*, 7/31/53.

Chapter Eight: August

1. Pafko's injuries temporary: *Brooklyn Eagle*, 8/3/51, p. 12.
2. O'Malley never explained Pafko trade: Kahn, *Boys of Summer*, p. 268.
3. Spy story virtually ignored: *Wall Street Journal*, 1/31/01.
4. Reserve from the Cubs gave Leo the telescope idea: *New York Times*, 2/12/01, p. C 9.
5. Tigers couldn't cheat on the road: Greenberg, *The Story of My Life*, p. 139.
6. Players were rooting for Hank: *Ibid.*, p. 121.
7. Franks isn't talking: *Wall Street Journal*, 1/31/01.
8. Hank Thompson's rap sheet: *New York Times*, 10/2/69, p. 47.
9. Home run pitch should have been a knockdown: Luciano, *Remembrance of Swings Past*, p. 183.
10. Dodgers refused to blame Branca or stolen signs: Robinson, *The Home Run Heard 'Round the World*, p. 235.
11. Thomson homer a forbidden subject: *Dave Anderson interview*.
12. Bobby finally says no: *Wall Street Journal*, 1/31/01.
13. Giants booed after 16 straight wins: *The Sporting News*, 9/5/51, p. 1.

Chapter Nine: September

1. Mueller's slugging had the Giants worried: *Sal Yvars interview*.

2. The innocent Don Mueller's premonitions: Robinson, *The Home Run Heard 'Round the World*, p. 1.
3. Don Mueller prefers not to comment: *Sal Yvars interview*.
4. Dodgers have just about sewed up the flag: *The Sporting News*, 9/19/51.
5. Chandler lashes out at Frick: *Time*, 3/12/51, p. 58.
6. Labine into Dressen limbo: Golenbock, *Bums*, p. 278.
7. Dressen says Labine an incubator baby: *Ibid.*, p. 305.

2. Claims Hodges decided to hold the bag: Robinson, *The Home Run Heard 'Round the World*, p. 221.
3. Erskine says best pitch bounced in dirt: *National Pastime*, 5/05, p. 87.
4. Thomson hit bad pitch: *New York Times*, 10/4/52, p. 42.
5. Branca tells photographer to take picture of Giants stealing signs: *Brooklyn Eagle*, 10/4/51.
6. Ralph wouldn't cry over spilled milk: Anderson, *New York Times*, 2/1/01, p. D1.

Chapter 10: October

1. Bobby strikes out on bad pitch: *New York Times*, 10/3/51, p. 42.

Bibliography

Books

Anderson, Dave. *Pennant Races: Baseball at Its Best.* New York: Doubleday, 1994.

Barber, Red. *The Broadcasters.* New York: Dial Press, 1993.

_____. *Rhubarb in the Catbird Seat.* Garden City, NY: Doubleday, 1968; rpt. Lincoln: University of Nebraska Press, 1997.

Berkow, Ira. *The Corporal Was a Pitcher: The Courage of Lou Brissie.* Chicago: Triumph, 2009.

Berra, Allen. *Yogi Berra: Eternal Yankee.* New York: W.W. Norton, 2009.

Cramer, Richard. *Joe DiMaggio: The Hero's Life.* New York: Simon & Schuster, 2000.

Durocher, Leo. *Nice Guys Finish Last.* New York: Simon & Schuster, 1975.

Durso, Joseph. *Joe DiMaggio: The Last American Knight.* Boston: Little, Brown, 1995.

Einstein, Charles. *The Baseball Reader: Favorites from the Fireside Books of Baseball.* New York: Bonanza, 1989.

Erskine, Carl. *Tales From the Dodger Dugout.* Champaign, IL: Sports Publishing, 2000.

Frommer, Harvey. *Rickey & Robinson: The Men Who Broke Baseball's Color Barrier.* New York: Collier-Macmillan, 1985.

Gittleman, Sol. *Reynolds, Raschi and Lopat: New York's Big Three and the Great Yankee Dynasty of 1949–1953.* Jefferson, NC: McFarland, 2007.

Golenbock, Peter. *Bums: An Oral History of the Brooklyn Dodgers.* New York: Putnam, 1984.

Greenberg, Hank, and Ira Berkow. *Hank Greenberg: The Story of My Life.* Chicago: Triumph, 2001.

Heinz, W.C. "The Rocky Road of Pistol Pete." *True* (March 1958): 20–28.

Higbe, Kirby, with Martin Quigley. *The High Hard One.* New York: Viking, 1967; rpt. Lincoln: University of Nebraska Press, 1998.

Holmes, Tommy. *Baseball's Greatest Teams: The Dodgers.* New York: Macmillan, 1975.

Holmes, Tot. *Brooklyn's Babe: The Story of Babe Herman.* Gothenburg, NE: Holmes, 1990.

Hynd, Noel. *The Giants of the Polo Grounds: The Glorious Times of Baseball's New York Giants.* New York: Doubleday, 1988.

Kahn, Roger. *Beyond the Boys of Summer.* New York: McGraw-Hill, 2005.

_____. *Boys of Summer.* New York: Harper & Row, 1971.

_____. *The Era, 1947–1957: When the Yankees, the Giants and the Dodgers Ruled the World.* New York: Tichenor & Fields, 1993.

_____. *Head Game: Baseball Seen from the Pitcher's Mound.* New York: Harcourt, 2001.

_____. *Memories of Summer: When Baseball Was an Art and Writing About It a Game.* New York: Hyperion, 1997.

Lieb, Fred. *Baseball As I Have Known It.* New York: Coward, McCann and Geoghegan, 1977.

Lowenfish, Lee. *Branch Rickey: Baseball's Ferocious Gentleman.* Lincoln: University of Nebraska Press, 2008.

Luciano, Ron, and David Fisher. *Remembrance of Swings Past.* New York: Bantam Dell, 1998.
Parrott, Harold. *The Lords of Baseball.* New York: Praeger, 1976.
Pietrusza, David, Matthew Silverman, and Michael Gershman, eds. *Baseball: The Biographical Encyclopedia of Baseball.* Kingston, NY: Total Sports/Sports Illustrated, 2000.
Polner, Murray. *Branch Rickey: A Biography.* New York: Atheneum, 1982; revised ed. Jefferson, NC: McFarland, 2007.
Prager, Joshua. *The Echoing Green: The Untold Story of Bobby Thomson, Ralph Branca and the Shot Heard Round the World.* New York: Pantheon, 2006.
Ritter, Lawrence. *The Glory of Their Times.* New York: Morrow, 1984.
Robinson, Jackie, with Alfred Duckett. *I Never Had It Made: An Autobiography.* Hopewell, NJ: Ecco, 1995.
Robinson, Ray. *The Home Run Heard 'Round the World.* New York: HarperCollins, 1991.
Rosenfeld, Harvey. *The Great Chase: The Giants-Dodgers Pennant Race of 1951.* Jefferson, NC: McFarland, 1992; rpt. Provo, UT: Boomerang, 2001.
Shecter, Leonard. *The Jocks.* New York: Warner, 1970.
Smith, Curt. *Voices of Summer: Ranking Baseball's 101 All-Time Best Announcers.* Cambridge, MA: Da Capo, 2005.
Snider, Duke, with Bill Gilbert. *The Duke of Flatbush.* New York: Zebra, 1998.
Thomson, Bobby, with Lee Heiman and Bill Gutman: *The Giants Win the Pennant! The Giants Win the Pennant!* New York: Kensington, 1991.
Veeck, William, with Ed Linn. *Veeck—As In Wreck.* New York: Putnam, 1962.
Werber, Bill, and C. Paul Rogers. *Memories of a Ballplayer.* Cleveland, OH: Society for American Baseball Research, 2001.
Westcott, Rich. *Splendor on the Diamond: Interviews with 35 Stars of Baseball's Past.* Gainesville: University of Florida Press, 2000.

Newspapers

Brooklyn Eagle
New York Herald-Tribune
New York Post
New York Times
Newark Evening News
Newark Star-Ledger
St. Louis Post-Dispatch
The Sporting News
Wall Street Journal

Interviews

Dave Anderson
Bobby Bragan
Pete Coscarart
Gene Hermanski
Clem Labine
Eddie Miksis
Sal Yvars

Magazines

Life
Saturday Evening Post
The National Pastime (Society for American Baseball Research)
Time

Wire Services

Associated Press
United Press International

Index

Aaron, Hank 92, 133
Abrams, Cal 100, 154
Alexander, Grover C. 21, 22
Alston, Walter 98, 135
Alzado, Lyle 21
Amoros, Sandy 100
Ashburn, Richie 154, 158, 166, 171, 173

Bankhead, Dan 84, 87, 121, 122
Barber, Red 97, 123, 124, 177
Bauer, Hank 40, 41, 42, 78, 185, 186
Baumgartner, Stan 65
Berra, Yogi 111, 113, 114, 165, 184, 185
Black, Joe 137
Blackwell, Ewell 147, 148, 157
Blaeholder, George 119
Blass, Steve 75, 76
Borowy, Hank 146
Bowman, Bob 7
Bragan, Bobby 10, 63
Branca, Ralph 2, 63, 64, 65, 88, 130, 131, 138, 140, 141, 154, 156, 167, 169, 175, 177, 181, 183, 186, 189, 190
Bresnahan, Roger 9
Bright, Harry 86, 87
Brissie, Lou 80
Brown, bobby 77, 95
Buchalter, Lepke 116

Cain, Bob 89, 95
Campanella, Roy 31, 32, 34, 71, 102, 118, 161, 169, 170
Carleton, Steve 75
Casey, Hugh 106, 154
Cellar, Rep. Emanuel 181
Cepeda, Orlando 102, 142
Cerv, Bob 42, 77, 129, 162

Chandler, Albert B. 3, 55, 56, 59, 85, 102, 103, 163
Chandler, Spud 109, 110, 111
Chapman, Ben 92
Chapmen, Ray 8, 9, 94
Clarke, Fred 23
Cobb, Ty 20, 22, 23, 24, 97, 126, 127, 152, 172, 185
Cochrane, Mickey 24
Collins, Eddie 24
Collins, Joe 77, 88, 165, 184
Connors, Chuck 121
Cooper, Walker 47, 135
Corwin, Al 134, 135, 142, 144, 147, 149, 177
Coscarart, Pete 46, 47, 60, 107
Cox, Billy 48, 49, 50, 75, 144, 156, 172, 179
Crawford, Sam 9

Dark, Alvin 141, 142, 143, 148, 154, 172, 179, 180, 182, 183, 184, 185
Dascoli, Frank 169, 170
Day, Laraine 85, 86, 137
Dickson, Murray 151
DiMaggio, Joe 2, 7, 28, 40, 41, 42, 44, 45, 70, 77, 78, 95, 114, 115, 116, 117, 138, 164, 183, 185, 186
DiMaggio family 45, 46
Doby, Larry 43, 53
Dressen, Charley 2, 5, 14, 32, 38, 63, 64, 65, 66, 67, 71, 76, 82, 88, 93, 105, 121, 138, 140, 155, 167, 170, 173, 175, 177, 178, 179, 180, 181, 182, 183
Drews, Karl 172
Drysdale, Don 33, 161
Durocher, Leo 1, 6, 7, 10, 12, 14, 34, 47, 65, 72, 76, 84, 85, 86, 92, 131, 134,

199

135, 137, 141, 152, 154, 169, 178, 179, 181, 184, 186, 187, 188, 190
Dykes, Jimmy 76

Erskine, Carl 60, 63, 64, 66, 71, 120, 168, 180

Fain, Ferris 126, 127
Feller, Bob 119
Fewster, Chuck 68, 69
Foxx, Jimmie 17, 18, 24
Franks, Herman 48, 131, 135, 141, 167, 189
Frick, Ford 59, 71, 72, 103, 163, 164
Furillo, Carl 28, 34, 35, 49, 134, 135, 144, 154, 168, 172, 173, 190

Gaedel, Eddie 89, 95, 147
Gardella, Danny 56, 58, 59
Garver, Ned 117, 118, 151, 165
Gettel, Allen 135
Gibson, Bob 75
Gibson, Josh 52, 53
Gionfriddo, Al 70
Goldberg, Hy 43, 79, 80
Goliat, Mike 70
Gomez, Lefty 35
Gomez, Reuben 190
Grant, Charles 52
Gray, Ted 186, 190
Greenberg, Hank 131, 132, 133, 134
Grim, Charley 90

Hargrove, Mike 163
Hartung, Clint 180
Hatton, Joe 64, 178
Hearn, Jim 34, 84, 144, 149, 154, 169, 175, 176, 184, 190
Heilmann, Harry 119
Henrich, Tommy 2, 77, 107
Herman, Babe 68, 69
Hermanski, Gene 13, 37, 38, 84, 91, 98
Higbe, Kirby 62
Hodges, Gil 28, 32, 33, 48, 93, 98, 101, 102, 155, 157, 172, 173, 177, 180, 182, 183
Holmes, Oliver W. 56, 57, 58
Hornsby, Rogers 6, 25
Houk, Ralph 95
Howard, Elston 43, 44
Hubbell, Carl 22, 25

Irvin, Monte 34, 47, 53, 72, 136, 137, 143, 154, 175, 179, 180, 184, 185, 190

Jackson, Ransom 149
Jacucki, Sig 104
Jansen, Larry 41, 71, 84, 144, 145, 148, 149, 171, 172, 184, 194, 195
Jensen, Jackie 2, 42, 43, 44, 77, 88, 129
Jethroe, Sam 169
Jones, Sheldon 148, 149, 158, 177

Kahn, Roger 9, 17, 60, 68
Kaline, Al 13, 68
Kampouris, Alex 53
Kellogg, Junius 20
King, Clyde 71, 148, 158
Kluzewski, Ted 157
Konstanty, Jim 71
Koslo, Dave 148, 162, 184, 185
Kuzava, Bob 98, 185

Labine, Clem 2, 9, 34, 66, 72, 73, 84, 118, 121, 143, 149, 151, 155, 156, 160, 165, 167, 169, 173, 177, 182, 183
Landis, Kenesaw M. 23, 52, 53, 103
Lanier, Max 57, 162
Lavagetto, Cookie 63, 134, 181
Leonard, Dutch 23
Lockman, Whitey 47, 48, 143, 147, 148, 180, 184
Lodigiani, Dario 46
Logan, Johnny 33
Lopat, Eddie 1, 2, 41, 76, 77, 95, 107, 111, 112, 113, 118, 122, 185
Lopez, Al 89
Lyons, Ted 63

Mack, Connie 76
MacPhail, Larry 7, 8, 9, 12, 15, 59, 60, 69, 94, 146
Maglie, Sal 47, 71, 72, 73, 76, 8, 85, 106, 141, 144, 146, 155, 156, 157, 159, 161, 169, 171, 179, 184, 185, 190
Mantle, Mickey 2, 41, 42, 43, 44, 78, 79, 88, 120, 162, 184
Mapes, Cliff 42, 129, 186
Martin, Billy 79
Mathews, Eddie 33
Mathewson, Christy 69
Mays, Carl 8, 9
Mays, Willie 3, 14, 47, 70, 92, 137, 154, 156, 185
Mazzone, Lee 22
McCarthy, Joe 185
McDougald, Gil 77, 185
McGraw, John 52, 167, 171

INDEX

Medwick, Joe 7, 8, 10, 137
Melchiorre, Gene 20
Meuller, Don 47, 48, 143, 149, 152, 153, 154, 179, 180, 189
Meyer, Russ 93, 141
Miksis, Eddie 39, 71, 98, 182
Miller, Marvin 58, 147
Minoso, Minnie 80
Mize, John 122, 123, 165
Molinas, Jack 20
Moretti, Willi 183
Morland, Mantan 92
Moses, Robert 17
Mulvey, Ann 182
Mungo, Van Lingle 68
Musial, Stan 92, 103, 152, 154, 162, 189

Neun, Johnny 54
Newcombe, Don 64, 70, 71, 84, 115, 154, 156, 160, 161, 167, 171, 173, 179, 180, 181, 190
Nichols, Kid 26
Nuxhall, Joe 109

O'Malley, Walter 3, 5, 14, 15, 16, 17, 18, 55, 90, 97, 100, 128, 130, 143, 155, 169
Ott, Mel 19, 47
Owen, Mickey 56, 57, 106, 107, 154, 177

Pafko, Andy 98, 99, 104, 129, 130, 156, 157, 170, 172, 177, 179, 181
Page, Joe 41
Palica, Erv 66, 88
Pasqual, Bernardo 56
Pasqual, Jorge 56
Podbielan, Bud 173, 174
Podres, Johnny 100
Pollet, Howie 149
Potter, Nelson 37
Prager, Joshua 1, 131, 135, 140

Raffensberger, Kenny 91, 100, 157
Raft, George 85
Raschi, Vic 1, 2, 41, 76, 77, 88, 107, 108, 109, 142, 165, 184, 185
Reese, Pee Wee 10, 11, 12, 34, 37, 48, 51, 107, 148, 151, 154, 168, 169, 170, 179
Reiser, Pete 10, 11, 13, 14, 57, 84, 100
Reynolds, Allie 1, 2, 41, 67, 76, 107, 110, 111, 165, 184, 185
Rhodes, Dusty 70
Rickey, Branch 6, 7, 13, 14, 15, 16, 18, 30, 32, 48, 53, 56, 59, 62, 67, 71, 72, 73, 84, 85, 91, 92, 93, 97, 103, 114, 118, 119, 148, 149, 156, 157, 169, 171, 172, 173, 177, 179, 190
Robinson, Wilbert 67
Roe, Preacher 48, 49, 84, 118, 155, 157, 162, 167, 169, 170, 172
Ruppert, Jake 45
Ruth, Babe 9, 13, 22, 58, 85, 92, 132, 133, 134

Sain, Johnny 37, 123, 164, 185
Sauer, Hank 149
Schenz, Henry 131, 140
Schmitz, Johnny 98, 100, 162
Schoendienst, Red 103
Schultz, Howie 16
Selig, Bud 103, 104
Seminick, Andy 141, 171
Shotton, Burt 5, 6, 39, 87, 182
Shuba, George 59
Silvera, Charlie 67
Sisler, George 26
Slaughter, Enos 103, 178
Snider, Duke 18, 34, 67, 70, 82, 83, 84, 118, 141, 151, 157, 173, 179
Spahn, Warren 75, 92, 155, 167, 168
Speaker, Tris 20, 22, 23
Spencer, George 71, 142, 143, 144, 148, 149, 162, 177
Stallings, George 171
Stamler, Nelson 183
Stanky, Eddie 34, 147, 148, 149, 168, 178, 179, 181, 184, 185
Steinbrenner, George 35, 37, 183
Stengel, Casey 44, 49, 77, 88, 95, 96, 105, 117, 120, 124, 125, 142, 167, 185, 186
Stephens, Vern 57
Stoneham, Horace 168
Sukeforth, Clyde 3, 30, 63, 64, 180, 181, 182

Telescope 1, 2, 3, 39, 48, 76, 130, 131, 134, 135, 137, 140, 141, 149, 151, 152, 154, 156, 162, 166, 171, 175, 178, 187, 188, 189
Terry, Bill 185
Terwiliger, Wayne 170
Thompson, Hank 136, 137
Thomson, Bobby 5, 47, 48, 64, 100, 120, 121, 138, 140, 154, 155, 156, 172, 175, 177, 178, 179, 181, 186, 188, 189, 191
Traynor, Pie 27

Vance, Dazzy 68, 69
Van Cuyk, Chris 64
Vander Meer, Johnny 60, 61, 148
Veeck, Bill 89, 90, 104, 118, 147, 148

Waitkus, Eddie 28, 42, 173
Walker, Dixie 12, 48, 63, 69
Walker, Rube 63, 98, 138, 166, 172, 177
Walsh, Ed 27
Weiss, George 45, 117
Westrum, Wes 47, 138, 147, 149, 150, 152, 189
Williams, Davey 73, 84, 85
Williams, Ted 28, 38, 111, 113, 165
Wilson, Hack 68

Wood, Smokey Joe 23
Woodling, Gene 40, 78
Woodward, Stanley 17, 103
Wyatt, Whitlow 62

Yawkey, Tom 13
Young, Cy 27, 28
Young, Dick 16, 69, 174
Yvars, Sal 48, 135, 138, 139, 140, 181, 185, 187, 188, 189, 190, 191

Zeckendorf, William 16
Zimmer, Don 11, 94
Zwillman, Longy 51

www.ingramcontent.com/pod-product-compliance
Lightning Source LLC
Chambersburg PA
CBHW051050230426
43666CB00012B/2643